HOW YOUR
MIND
CAN HEAL YOUR
BODY

HOW YOUR
MIND
CAN HEAL YOUR
BODY

David R. Hamilton, Ph.D.

HAY HOUSE, INC.
Carlsbad, California • New York City
London • Sydney • Johannesburg
Vancouver • Hong Kong • New Delhi

Published and distributed in the United States by: Hay House, Inc.: www.hayhouse
.com • *Published and distributed in Australia by:* Hay House Australia Pty. Ltd.: www
.hayhouse.com.au • *Published and distributed in the United Kingdom by:* Hay House
UK, Ltd.: www.hayhouse.co.uk • *Published and distributed in the Republic of South
Africa by:* Hay House SA (Pty), Ltd.: www.hayhouse.co.za • *Distributed in Canada by:*
Raincoast Books: www.raincoast.com • *Published in India by:* Hay House Publishers
India: www.hayhouse.co.in

Design: Nick C. Welch

Library of Congress Cataloging-in-Publication Data

Hamilton, David R.
  How your mind can heal your body / David R. Hamilton.
    p. cm.
  Includes bibliographical references.
  ISBN 978-1-4019-2148-4 (tradepaper : alk. paper) 1. Mind and body. 2. Thought and
thinking--Religious aspects. 3. Mental healing. I. Title.
  BF161.H22 2010
  615.8'51--dc22
                                        2009015132

ISBN: 978-1-4019-2148-4

12 11 10 9 8 7 6 5 4 3
1st edition, February 2010

Printed in the United States of America

To Ryan, Jake, and Ellie.
You have brought huge
amounts of joy to our family.

CONTENTS

Introduction.. ix

PART I: The Mind Can Heal the Body

Chapter 1:   The Power of Positive Thinking.............................3
Chapter 2:   The Power of Believing..17
Chapter 3:   Drugs Work Because We Believe in Them..........27
Chapter 4:   The Power of Plasticity.......................................37
Chapter 5:   The Science Behind Mind-Body Healing............43
Chapter 6:   The Power of Visualization.................................53
Chapter 7:   To Stress or Not to Stress...................................69
Chapter 8:   How to Visualize..77
Chapter 9:   The Power of Affirmations.................................91

Part II: True Stories

Introduction.. 99

Chapter 10:   Cancer.. 101
Chapter 11:   Heart Issues.. 119
Chapter 12:   Regeneration... 127
Chapter 13:   Pain and Chronic Fatigue................................. 133
Chapter 14:   Viruses, Allergies,
                 and Autoimmune Conditions........................... 139
Chapter 15:   You Can Do It.. 153

Part III: In Closing

Chapter 16:   The Power of Love 157

Appendix I: Quantum Field Healing (QFH) 169
Appendix II: Visualizations 181
Appendix III: DNA Visualizations 239
References 243
Acknowledgments 261
About the Author 263

"Nothing splendid has ever been achieved except by those who dared believe that something inside them was superior to circumstances."
— **Bruce Barton**

INTRODUCTION

This is a book about using the mind to heal the body. After I wrote my first book, *It's the Thought That Counts,* which describes the mind-body connection (and the mind-world connection), people began to ask me how to use it to heal themselves. At talks I found myself explaining how our minds have the power to heal our bodies, and at workshops I found myself teaching it. At one of my seminars, a lady asked if I was planning to write about it. I started what you have in your hands the following day.

In these pages, you'll find practical tools that you can use to heal a whole variety of medical conditions. About ten years ago, it would have been true to say that there was little medical evidence that the mind could heal the body, although there was plenty of proof pointing toward it. But now research that's published every other week is building a considerably strong case that our previous assumptions and beliefs—that the mind could not heal the body— are just plain wrong.

Since 2006, visualization has shown positive results in stroke and spinal-injury rehabilitation, as well as improving the movement of Parkinson's-disease patients. Patients use their minds to just imagine moving normally, and the moment they do so, the arm or leg that they envision in motion is stimulated at a microscopic level, and the brain area that governs each limb is also triggered. The result is that over time their movements improve. In stroke cases, some damaged brain areas even begin to regenerate.

The placebo effect has shown us for years that the power of belief can influence the course of an entire range of medical conditions, including asthma, hay fever, infections, pain, Parkinson's disease, depression, congestive heart failure, angina, high cholesterol levels, high blood pressure, arthritis, chronic fatigue syndrome, stomach ulcers, and insomnia—and even alter immunity and growth-hormone levels. And recent research has shown that when people take a placebo and believe it to be real medicine, chemical shifts occur in the brain based on this assumption. Now we know for certain that thoughts, emotions, and beliefs aren't just subjective ideas in the mind, but that they cause real chemical and physical changes in the brain and throughout the body.

I've made some sizable leaps in this book in suggesting that almost any illness can be healed using the mind, or at least that improvements can be made. I'm aware that this is a big claim to make, but I feel that when our health is at stake—and indeed our lives—we can't always wait for science to catch up and publish research to show that what many believe to be reality is actually true. Those of us who are in need don't always have that long.

It would be more of a mistake for me to write that the mind *can't* heal the body, at least until the day science discovers that it can. We're barely scratching the surface in our understanding of real human potential. Einstein said, "We still do not know one-thousandth of one percent of what nature has revealed to us." I believe we need to entertain the real possibility that much of what we haven't yet proven includes the ability of the mind to heal the body of almost anything.

Some might say that I'm giving people false hope, but I think that's a rather negative stance to take. As the old saying goes: "You can please all of the people some of the time and some of the people all of the time, but you cannot please all of the people all of the time." I'd rather give some people hope and see them turn that into wellness, than refrain from trying just because others might not get the results.

I remember that when I was a scientist in the pharmaceutical industry, I enjoyed looking at the plants in the office I shared with about 20 others. There must have been about 30 different plants, which helped to create a nice atmosphere. Many of them were small and sat on a windowsill, which meant that they were the first things I saw when I arrived in the morning.

One day, after I'd been in that office for over a year, a co-worker carelessly knocked one of the plants down and it almost landed on his foot. It didn't, but it was classified as a "near miss." The next day a memo came around the whole department saying that from that day forward, no plants were to be allowed on that ledge in case they fell and injured someone . . . and that ledge remained bare for the remainder of my time there.

There was no need to ban small plants from the windowsill—a note to remind everyone to be more careful would have sufficed. I think that we can focus too much on the negatives at times and, especially with goals, we often don't shoot for the stars just in case we fall short.

With this book, I've aimed for the stars. I believe that the majority of readers will find something helpful in it, but I know that I can't please everyone. If you don't get results, please understand that my sincere motivation here is to help, and I really do believe that we all have reservoirs of untapped potential within us.

I've always been a motivational type of person. When I was growing up, I'd always be helping people shoot for their goals and believe in themselves. In my 20s I became a track-and-field coach, and most of the time I'd get good—and often great—results. But occasionally people (observers) would criticize me, saying that I was giving these young athletes false hope, and that it was best just to tell them to aim lower or to be "realistic." But what is realistic? It's someone's opinion, not fact.

I've always understood where the faultfinders were coming from, even though I didn't agree with them. I felt pain when I saw how sad a young triple jumper was when he didn't jump as far as he wanted to in the 1999 U.K. National Junior League Athletics Finals—especially when I'd instilled the mind-set in him that he could win the gold medal. But I think that without that faith, the chances of a gold medal were almost zero. *With* the belief, he really was capable of winning it.

Actually, he would have won the gold medal by over a foot had one of his jumps not been judged a foul because the tip of his toe went barely over the line. I felt so sad for him because I could see that he was sorely disappointed that he hadn't performed as well as he'd wanted to. But without the belief that he could in fact win, I'm certain that he would never even have made the final, let alone been anywhere near the kind of jumper he was.

And so it is with using the mind to heal our bodies. I believe that when we aim high—even shoot for the stars with the hope that we can heal ourselves completely—great things are possible. If we don't try, then we'll never know what was attainable.

Of course, using the mind to heal isn't new. People have been using their minds to cure themselves for thousands of years. Vedic teachings that are more than 3,000 years old, for instance, refer to the use of the mind for healing through meditation.

So, from the space of my belief that the mind can impact almost any condition, I've included an A–Z list of medical conditions, illnesses, and diseases at the end of this book and have suggested one or more visualizations that could be used to heal or positively affect each one.

My research into the power of the mind over the past 26 years (I read my first book on the topic, *The Magic Power of Your Mind* by Walter M. Germain, when I was 12) has shown me that human beings intuitively know how to heal themselves. We know that we need to become calm, rid ourselves of stress, and develop positive attitudes; but we also need to know the appropriate visualization principles.

As confirmation of this, I've collected several stories from people all around the world who have healed themselves of serious illnesses such as cancer or diabetes, and not-so-serious conditions like hay fever or shoulder pain. As I read through them, I was astonished to notice a striking similarity: the people all used the same principles—which they just seemed to intuitively know—and these were the ones that I had also been teaching and was somehow innately aware of.

This book is organized into three parts, the first of which outlines research in the rapidly emerging field of mind-body science. I've included evidence for the power of positive thinking and the placebo effect, the most up-to-date research into how our thoughts and emotions cause microchanges in the brain, and cutting-edge studies into using the mind to heal the body.

Part II of the book contains actual stories of healing. Some individuals were kind enough to share how they used their minds to heal themselves of various diseases, as well as to describe the images they used and how often they visualized them. The hope is that their personal journeys may inspire others to believe that they can be healed, too, as well as to provide readers with some practical information on how to go about it.

Part III of the book is the shortest section—but in many ways the most powerful—and it talks about the power of love, because I've always been a believer of the idea that love heals.

The book also has three appendices. The first is a healing technique that I call Quantum Field Healing (QFH), the second is a list of medical conditions and visualizations for their healing, and the third contains two DNA visualizations.

Throughout the book I recommend that if you decide to use visualizations, you should continue any treatment that you are currently receiving. What I'm saying is that visualization should be used *as well*. My premise for this is that when you're receiving medication, you must think. This book provides direction for those thoughts and suggests what you could think *about* to aid your recovery.

I hope you enjoy the book and that you can take something positive from it.

Warm wishes,
David Hamilton

֍֍֍֍

PART I

THE MIND CAN HEAL THE BODY

CHAPTER 1

THE POWER OF
POSITIVE THINKING

*"A pessimist sees the difficulty in every opportunity;
an optimist sees the opportunity in every difficulty."*
— **Winston Churchill**

Optimists live longer than pessimists do! That's the conclusion of a 30-year study involving 447 people that was conducted by scientists at the Mayo Clinic. They found that those with a more positive outlook had around a 50 percent lower risk of early death than negative thinkers and wrote that "mind and body are linked and attitude has an impact on the final outcome, death." This is a startling statistic! Optimists also had fewer physical and emotional health problems; had less pain and increased energy; and were generally more peaceful, happy, and calm than pessimists.

A 2004 study published in the journal *Archives of General Psychiatry* found something similar: it concluded that there's a "protective relationship between . . . optimism and all-cause mortality in old age"—that optimism protects you from illness.

The scientists studied the responses given by 999 Dutch men and women between the ages of 65 and 85 to a range of statements that included the following:

- "I often feel that life is full of promise."
- "I still have positive expectations concerning my future."
- "There are many moments of happiness in my life."
- "I do not make any more future plans."
- "Happy laughter often occurs."
- "I still have many goals to strive for."
- "Most of the time I am in good spirits."

The results were startling. Those who showed high levels of optimism, who would perhaps respond affirmatively to the first statement, had a 45 percent lower risk of death from any cause, and a 77 percent lower risk of death from heart disease in particular, than people who reported high levels of pessimism.

Another study examined the autobiographies of 180 Catholic nuns that were written when the nuns first entered a convent. Scientists examined what they had written 60 years later and discovered that the nuns whose stories were more positive lived much longer than their colleagues who had been more negative.

One of the reasons why a positive attitude is so important is because it boosts our immune systems and therefore our ability to fight illness. In a 2006 study conducted at Carnegie Mellon University, scientists analyzed the effects of common cold and influenza viruses on people with different attitudes. One hundred and ninety-three healthy volunteers were interviewed to determine the levels of positive or negative feelings that they felt in their lives. They were then exposed to either of the viruses using nasal drops, and it turned out that the subjects with a brighter disposition were much more resistant to the sickness than those who had a bleaker outlook.

As we go through our lives, our attitudes affect how we react to viruses, bacteria, and other pathogens. A positive, optimistic perspective is ultimately best for our overall health and longevity.

We also deal with situations differently depending upon our attitude to them. A positive approach helps us cope with challenges and even see them as opportunities, which ultimately benefits our health.

A University of Chicago study examined the attitude and health of 200 telecommunications executives who had been affected by corporate downsizing. It found that the employees who saw the cutbacks as an opportunity for growth were healthier than those who saw it as a threat. Of those with the positive attitude, less than one-third developed an illness during or shortly after the downsizing. But of those with a negative attitude, more than 90 percent became ill. In other words, looking at the same event as positive or negative has a hugely different effect upon health.

Some of the best-studied effects of attitude show that it power-fully affects the heart. One such study, involving 586 people that was conducted by scientists at Johns Hopkins University, found that a positive attitude was the best prevention against heart disease.

In 2003, scientists at the Duke University Medical Center, upon examining 866 heart patients, discovered that the subjects who routinely felt more positive emotions (happiness, joy, and opti-mism) had about a 20 percent greater chance of being alive 11 years later than those who experienced more negative sentiments.

And in a 2007 study, Harvard scientists studied the effects of "emotional vitality," which was defined as "a sense of energy and positive well-being in addition to being able to regulate emotions effectively." The study involved 6,025 volunteers and found that those who had high levels of emotional vitality were 19 percent less likely to develop coronary heart disease than those with lower levels.

Hard Marriage, Hard Heart

The above subhead is taken from a scientific review paper that discussed a 2006 study by scientists at the University of Utah, which found that the attitudes of married couples profoundly impacted their hearts.

The scientists videotaped 150 married couples discussing mari-tal topics and categorized them according to how they related to each other. They found that the couples who were most supportive of each other had healthier hearts, and the couples who were most hostile toward each other had more hardening of their arteries. Hard marriage, hard heart! As you can see, being supportive of another person is much better for health than holding anger and bitterness and constantly criticizing him or her.

In some research, hostility is defined as evading a question, irritation, or direct or indirect challenges to a person asking a ques-tion. Other research labels it as an attitude of cynical beliefs and lack of trust in other people, and it's also been described as being aggressive and challenging. In one 25-year study that used these types of definitions as a criterion to determine hostility levels, the people who were most hostile had five times more incidents of coronary heart disease than those who were least hostile and more trusting, accepting, and gentle.

The connection between attitude and the heart is so reliable that a 30-year study published in 2003 in the *Journal of the American Medical Association* concluded that "hostility is the one most reliably associated with increased CHD [coronary heart disease] risk."

Scientists can quite accurately calculate individuals' risk of heart disease by examining their diet and lifestyle—what kinds of foods they eat, how much exercise they get, or whether they smoke cigarettes or drink lots of alcohol—and as you might guess, people with unhealthy lifestyles are usually most at risk. But scientists can just as accurately calculate the risk based upon attitude—whether people have a positive or negative attitude or how hostile they are toward others. The good news is that just as you can change your diet and lifestyle, you can change your attitude. It's up to you.

Of course, circumstances in life might be so challenging that it's inevitable that we become *hardened* to some extent, but we still have a choice no matter what. I'm deeply inspired by the story of Viktor Frankl, a survivor of the Nazi concentration camp in Auschwitz. In his nine-million-copy best-selling book, *Man's Search for Meaning,* he writes:

> We who lived in concentration camps can remember the men who walked through the huts comforting others, giving away their last piece of bread. They may have been few in number, but they offer sufficient proof that everything can be taken from a man but one thing: the last of the human freedoms—to choose one's attitude in any given set of circumstances, to choose one's own way.

Frankl's words are a message of hope that no matter what, our attitude is our choice. If we search deep within ourselves, we can always make the highest choice, the one from the softest heart, the one that helps other people to find comfort and happiness; and, in so doing, the one that makes us healthier.

Satisfaction

A study of 22,461 people by scientists from the University of Kuopio in Finland found that the people who were most satisfied with their lives lived longer. They defined life satisfaction as an "interest in life, happiness . . . and general ease of living." Reporting in the *American Journal of Epidemiology* in 2000, they found that the men who were most dissatisfied with their lives were more than three times as likely to die of disease than those who were most satisfied.

It's not so much what happens to us in life that determines our health and happiness—it's what we do with what happens that matters most. If you live in a nice house but see someone with a nicer one, do you feel dissatisfied that your home isn't good enough? Or do you give more thought to what you love about your own house and the people who share it with you?

It's said that the grass is always greener on the other side, but if you notice your *own* grass and don't pay so much attention to other lawns, then you'll experience more happiness and better health. It's what you focus on that matters most. It's *your* attitude that counts.

To Complain or Not to Complain

How often do you complain? In his inspiring book *A Complaint Free World,* Will Bowen encourages us to take up the challenge to go 21 days without complaining. That means to refrain from whining, criticizing, or unfairly judging. He urges us to wear a purple wristband and to change it to the other wrist every time we fuss.

It's an eye-opener. Most people initially have to move the wristband more than 20 times a day, but it's great for making them aware of how they behave. After a short time, people find it quite easy to go four or five days without making a single complaint. That's a huge difference and, as far as I'm concerned, a great boost to their health.

Grumbling about things and criticizing people has become a way of life for so many of us that we don't even notice how often we do it—it's become a habit. Yet we rarely complain about the truth of things, only how they seem to us, which may mean something completely different to someone else.

For instance, say a delivery you were expecting didn't arrive. You moan that this has ruined your day, setting back your entire schedule, and the stress you create brings untold negative effects on your body. Someone else who's waiting for a late delivery might decide that there's something else they can be getting on with and (from personal experience) could find that the delay turns out to be for the best. Is the situation actually a good or a bad thing? That's up to you. But what you decide matters to your health.

Complaining even affects the people around us. We rarely notice this, but we're like tuning forks. When we hit the fork, other things nearby resonate with it. This is also what happens when we consistently gripe around people—we trigger their bellyaching, too, and all of a sudden they're also inspired to find fault with life and the world. Nagging becomes a bacterium that we carry around with us, infecting most people we encounter.

Our thoughts and attitudes inspire our actions, and our actions create our world; so our thoughts and attitudes create our world. What kind of world do we choose? This is Will Bowen's message in his book: if we stop complaining, then we can get to work on creating a better world. And we're doing something positive for the health of our bodies at the same time.

Instead of getting upset, try to focus on what you're grateful for. Gratitude begets gratitude. The more things you focus on that you can appreciate, the more things you notice and experience that you can be grateful for. And that's good for your heart.

"Money Buys Happiness When You Spend on Others"

This was the title of a press release issued on March 20, 2008, by the University of British Columbia in Canada. It describes research showing that people who give money away are happier than those who spend it all on themselves.

The research, conducted by Elizabeth Dunn and other scientists from the University of British Columbia, was published in 2008 in the journal *Science*. The results showed that people who spent some of their money "pro-socially"—as in donating to charities or spending it on gifts for others rather than on themselves—were happier. According to an article on the university's Website:

> The researchers looked at a nationally representative sample of more than 630 Americans, of whom 55 per cent were female. They asked participants to: rate their general happiness; report their annual income; and provide a breakdown of their monthly spending, including bills, gifts for themselves, gifts for others and donations to charities.
>
> "Regardless of how much income each person made," says Dunn, "those who spent money on others reported greater happiness, while those who spent more on themselves did not."

The happiest people were the ones who gave money away. This is contrary to what most people think: that we need to keep all of our money for ourselves "just in case," and that the more we accumulate, the happier we'll be. But it needn't be large sums that we give away. According to the article, Dunn and her team conducted another experiment to test this theory:

> ... [T]he researchers gave participants a $5 or $20 bill, asking them to spend the money by 5 P.M. that day. Half the participants were instructed to spend the money on themselves, and half were assigned to spend the money on others. Participants who spent the windfall on others reported feeling happier at the end of the day than those who spent the money on themselves.
>
> "These findings suggest that very minor alterations in spending allocations—as little as $5—may be enough to produce real gains in happiness on a given day," says Dunn.

Why not decide to give something away today—to whomever and in whatever way you wish?

Many other studies have found that, even though incomes are higher than they were for our grandparents 50 years ago, we aren't any happier. In fact, some polls have found that people nowadays are less happy than people were during that time.

The British Columbia research shows that the level of income isn't as important as what you do with it. Earning a small salary but showing generosity with it leads to greater happiness than earning millions and spending it all on yourself. Money is not the issue. You can be rich and happy, and you can be poor and happy. Happiness lies in what you do with what you have. It's up to you!

Indeed, in another study mentioned in the same article, Dunn and her colleagues did a study that "measured the happiness levels of employees at a firm in Boston before and after they received their profit-sharing bonuses, which ranged between $3,000 and $8,000." The researchers found that happiness was independent of the size of the bonus, and that was a product of what the recipients did with it: "The employees who devoted more of their bonus to gifts for others or toward charity consistently reported greater benefits than employees who simply spent money on their own needs."

Being Positive about Getting Older

Attitude affects how fast we age. In fact, positive people live longer! That's the conclusion of research conducted by scientists at Yale University who studied the responses of 660 people to a series of questions about attitude, such as: "As you get older, you are less useful. Agree or disagree?" People who generally disagreed with these types of statements, and therefore had the most positive attitudes about aging, lived about seven and a half years longer than those who found truth in them. As attitude affects the heart, the Yale researchers even concluded that it was more influential than blood pressure, cholesterol levels, smoking, body weight, and exercise levels in how long a person lived.

A 2006 University of Texas study that examined 2,564 Mexican Americans over the age of 65 found that positive emotions reduced blood pressure. And, in 2004, scientists from the same university even found that frailty was linked with attitude. They studied 1,558 older people from the Mexican American community, and they measured weight loss, exhaustion, walking speed, and grip strength to determine levels of frailty. Over time, they found that the people with the most positive attitudes were less likely to become frail.

In a similar result to the satisfaction study reported earlier, another 2006 study found that people over the age of 80 lived longer if they were satisfied with their lives. Publishing in the *Journals of Gerontology,* scientists from the University of Jyväskylä in Finland examined 320 volunteers who filled out a "Life Satisfaction Index" questionnaire. They found that those who were most satisfied had half the risk of death compared to those who were least satisfied.

Essentially, if you have a positive attitude and keep your mind and body active, you stay healthier, you recover more quickly when you get sick, and your mental and physical abilities stay with you longer. That's the conclusion of much of the research currently looking at the relationship between attitude and the aging process: we don't need to age as fast as we think we do.

Many people cling to the idea that the brain and body decline with age and use it to explain why they forget some things, why they sometimes can't think clearly, and why they feel stiff when they get up. Okay, the brain and body do change, but how fast they change is something that we have an impact upon.

Developing a Younger Brain

A recent study by scientists from Posit Science, a company specializing in brain training, showed that age-related mental decline is actually reversible. Lack of use is the main cause of mental and physical decline, so "Use it or lose it" is an applicable phrase. If you stop using a muscle, it atrophies and becomes weaker. If you keep using it, it becomes stronger. And even if you've lost muscle through lack of use, an exercise regime will restore some, or a lot, of its function. The same is true with mental functions: if you use your brain, even when you're older, it works better.

For the study, the scientists designed a training program that improved neural plasticity, which is the ability of the brain to grow. As you'll see later in the book, the brain is not a hardwired lump of matter—as was once believed—but it's something that's constantly changing in response to our experiences.

Publishing in *Proceedings of the National Academy of Sciences of the United States of America,* scientists reported that elderly adults gained a substantial improvement in memory after doing an auditory-memory program. The study involved volunteers between the ages of 60 and 87 taking part in an eight- to ten-week training that involved listening to sounds for one hour a day, five days a week. At the end of the program, their memories had improved so much that they were performing like adults aged 40 to 60; their mental abilities had improved by around 20 years!

Scientists from Harvard conducted a novel experiment in 1989. They took volunteers over the age of 70 to a retreat center and asked them to act as though it were 1959 for a week. So the environment in the center was a re-creation of what it would have been like in that year: music, magazines, the volunteers' clothing, and even what was shown on TV reflected that era. The volunteers also had to converse with each other as if it were the '50s, discussing topics and current affairs of the time.

At the start, the scientists took a host of physiological measure-ments, including height, finger length, strength, mental cognition, and eyesight. After ten days in the center, they took those measurements again and discovered that the volunteers had gotten physiologically younger by several years just by *acting* as though they were younger. They grew taller, their fingers grew longer, they had improved mental functions, and their eyesight had improved. Some of the volunteers had become mentally and physiologically younger by 25 years!

This shows that how we use our brains and how often we use them really matters. When we were younger, we constantly engaged in mental activities; but as we go through our adult lives, we use our brains less and less. In the early stages of our professional lives we're still highly active, but over time we gradually become less mentally active, just as we become less physically active. Yet we don't need to; we just need to find other things to do. Many of the people who have lived healthy lives way into their 90s have been mentally active right up until their final days.

Recent research in neuroscience has found that one of the best ways to exercise our brains as adults is to learn a new language. We don't need to speak it fluently or even visit the country whose language we're learning (although we may be motivated to once we can speak a little of it), we only need to use our brains to learn it. Research has shown that doing so can actually reduce the risk of Alzheimer's disease. A study published in the *Journal of the American Medical Association* found that: "On average, a person reporting frequent cognitive activity . . . was 47 percent less likely to develop Alzheimer's disease than a person with infrequent activity."

Many adults have such a strong belief that the brain has to significantly decline with age that they enter into a self-reinforcing spiral—like a negative placebo effect—that alters how they behave. They start to act like elderly people instead of remaining young at heart. But part of this attitude comes from looking at men and women around them and observing how they behave. Some of our friends and colleagues who are our same age may act older, while others act younger. How we conduct ourselves should reflect how we *feel*, not how we *think* we're supposed to.

We've come to believe in aging so much that how we think we're supposed to act is deeply imprinted on our psyche. Some authors have pointed out, however, that getting older is cultural. We age at the rate we believe we're supposed to due to misunderstandings about aging, prejudices, and folklore. In the audio program *Magical Mind, Magical Body,* Deepak Chopra, M.D., says, "One of the things that is becoming very clear about the aging process is that what we consider normal aging may be a premature cognitive commitment.

. . . We, as a species, get committed to a certain reality of aging."

An interesting study published in the *Journal of Personality and Social Psychology* showed this. It involved people who were given a list of words with which they were asked to make up sentences, but there were actually two different lists. Some of the people had a few extra words added to theirs, such as: *old, gray, wrinkle, bingo,* and *lonely*—words that are associated with being old. It's called a *priming experiment* because people were *primed* with specific words.

After each person finished their session, they had to walk out of the room and down the corridor to reach the exit. One of the scientists was sitting outside the testing room and inconspicuously timed how long it took each person to walk down the corridor to a mark that was placed on the floor.

The people who used the normal set of words took 7.30 seconds on average to reach the mark. Those who were given the prime version took 8.28 seconds—13.4 percent longer. They also walked more slowly, like an older person would, and closer examination would probably have revealed hunched shoulders or some of them rubbing aching body parts from having sat on a chair for so long while they did the test. One of the things that this study shows is that a degree of aging is all in the mind. So act how you *feel,* not how you *think* you're supposed to.

The comedian Billy Connolly had me in fits of laughter once. He said that he knew he was getting older when he started to get up from his seat and caught himself making the sound "Oooohhh." We sometimes do this out of habit or just because others do, unconsciously picking up on their actions and behaving the way we're *supposed* to. I noticed one of my nephews doing it once when he was four years old, probably because a few of the adults around him had just gotten up from their seats. I had to give him the positive reinforcement that he was really fit (much fitter than the old people) because he could spring up from his seat without making any noises. He never did it again.

In another priming experiment conducted by scientists from North Carolina State University and published in 2004 in the journal *Psychology and Aging,* 153 people were asked to do memory tests after being primed with certain words, such as: *confused, cranky, feeble,* and *senile;* and others with the words *accomplished, active, dignified,* and *distinguished.* When they then did memory tests, older adults primed with the words that connote aging negatively fared much worse than the ones primed with the more positive words. The scientists wrote that "if older people are treated like they are competent, productive members of society, then they perform that way too."

It's not just our own attitudes and how we conduct ourselves that are important, but how we treat other people, too. If we treat others like old, infirm individuals, not only will it probably annoy them that we're speaking to them as if they're children, but it can also gradually erode their spirit and cause them to start believing that how we treat them is how they should be.

It's my opinion that if people believe that they should still be fit and active in their 90s—and if, when we're younger, we treat older individuals as holders of wisdom, life experiences, and stories—then there will be many more members of society who are mentally and physically active in their 90s than we currently see. It's really up to us.

Attitude is everything, they say . . . and I believe this to be true. If we learn to see the positive side of things, then we'll live longer, healthier, happier lives. A good way to do so is to stop complaining and start being grateful.

In the next chapter, we'll see how what we believe can be so powerful that it affects our ability to heal illness.

ကြေးကြေးကြေး

CHAPTER 2

THE POWER OF BELIEVING

"The outer conditions of a person's life will
always be found to reflect their inner beliefs."
— **James Allen**

What if scientists discovered a new drug—just one pill—that could cure or improve the symptoms of most known diseases? It would probably make headlines all around the world and become the greatest-selling drug of all time. Actually, such a thing already exists. Let me introduce you to . . . the placebo!

A placebo is a dummy drug that's made to look just like real medicine. It's used in trials so that the real drug can be tested against a control. Being a control, it isn't supposed to heal—but it does, because patients *believe* that it's real. Their minds actually heal them.

"The placebo effect has evolved from being thought of as a nuisance in clinical and pharmacological research to a biological phenomenon worthy of scientific investigation in its own right." These are the words of Fabrizio Benedetti, a neuroscience professor at the University of Turin Medical School, a member of the Placebo Study Group of the Mind/Brain/Behavior Interfaculty Initiative at Harvard University, and a world authority on the placebo effect.

Since the advent of brain-imaging technology, there's been a surge of interest in the placebo effect. Research now shows that when we take a placebo that we believe is really a drug, the brain lights up as if we were in fact taking that drug, and produces its own natural chemicals.

This has recently been shown with Parkinson's disease. The symptoms of this disease arise from impaired production of a substance called dopamine in part of the brain, which affects movement. Research has indicated that patients who are given a placebo but told that it's an anti-Parkinson's drug are able to move better. Scans have even shown that the brain is activated in the area that controls movement, and the missing chemical is actually produced. The improved maneuverability isn't just a psychological thing; it's a physical release of dopamine in the brain.

Chemicals in the Brain

The production of chemicals in the brain when a person takes a placebo was first proven in 1978 when scientists at the University of California, San Francisco showed that *placebo analgesia* (when a person gets pain relief from a placebo) occurs because the brain produces its own natural analgesics (painkillers). It was found that these are opiates, like morphine, but that they're the body's natural version, which are referred to as *endogenous* opiates. More modern research is beginning to show that the same kind of thing happens when placebos are given for any condition: the brain produces a natural drug that's tailor-made to combat the illness.

There are thousands of natural substances in the brain and body. In the words of Dawson Church, author of *The Genie in Your Genes:* "Each of us holds the keys to a pharmacy containing a dazzling array of healing compounds: *our own brain.* . . . Our brains are themselves generating drugs similar to those that our doctor is prescribing for us."

In a 2005 scientific paper published in *The Journal of Neuroscience,* Fabrizio Benedetti wrote: "Placebo effects seen with different treatments are more likely to track closely with the active treatment to which they are experimentally paired." In other words, if a person is given a drug to treat a condition and then it's secretly swapped for a placebo, the chemicals produced are believed to be natural versions of the drug that was originally used—if it's a painkilling drug, the brain produces natural painkillers.

Similarly, studies on depression suggest that the brain produces natural antidepressants. Brain scans have now shown that taking a placebo in place of the antidepressant fluoxetine (Prozac), for instance, affects most of the same brain areas as the actual drug. The brain always produces its *own* drugs, and this is mind over matter at the molecular level.

No longer can the placebo effect be dismissed as just a figment of the imagination—it really is *all in the mind.* When we believe something, chemicals are produced in our brains that carry out powerful roles that give us exactly what we believe should happen; they're created *because* of a state of mind.

As You Believe

The placebo effect is often quoted at 35 percent—meaning that it works 35 percent of the time—but this is a very broad generalization. It actually varies greatly depending on the illness, the nature of the medical trial, and even the personality of the doctors giving the medicine—and of course the desire of the patients to get better and how much they believe that they'll improve. Effectiveness has been known to vary from as low as 10 percent to as high as 100 percent in some studies. The higher figures indicate that the capacity for healing is within us all, but in some research that ability has been tapped into more than it has in others.

Placebos are particularly effective when it comes to heart medicines, and many scientists believe that this is due to the strong brain-heart link. In 2007, a drug company reported the results of a trial for a new drug for congestive heart failure: while it improved the condition of 66 percent of patients, which is very high, the placebo improved 51 percent of them.

In a 1988 trial on the use of acyclovir as a possible treatment for chronic fatigue syndrome (CFS), which was conducted by scientists at the National Institute of Allergy and Infectious Diseases, 46 percent of people improved on the drug and 42 percent on the placebo. In a 1996 study that tested the steroid hydrocortisone to be administered for CFS, 50 percent of patients improved on the placebo. One woman in her 30s, whose CFS was so severe that she was "very significantly impaired" and had "no energy, couldn't work, and spent most of her time at home," showed remarkable recovery after receiving placebos. Results like these don't mean that the disease isn't real—as some people believe—but that we have the ability to develop a state of mind that can heal it.

Research has even shown that the same substance can act as both a placebo and a *nocebo* (the opposite of the placebo effect, where a patient develops negative symptoms). In a 1969 paper published in *Psychosomatic Medicine,* 40 asthmatics were given an inhaler containing water but were told that they contained allergens that would cause bronchoconstriction (constriction of the airways)—19 of them (48 percent) then suffered considerable constriction of their airways, with 12 people in the group experiencing full-blown asthma attacks. When they were then given another inhaler and told that it would relieve their symptoms, it did, even though it also contained a placebo.

One person in the study was told that the inhaler contained pollen. She then swiftly developed hay fever as well as airway constriction. In a second experiment, she was told that the inhaler just contained allergens but no pollen; this time she only developed asthma symptoms. In a third test, she was again told that the inhaler contained pollen, and once again she developed hay fever as well as asthma. Despite what was actually in the treatment, the woman's reaction to it was totally dependent on what she *believed* it to be.

Performance-Enhancing Placebos

A 2007 placebo study described an experiment that simulated a sporting event involving nonprofessional participants who'd regularly been given morphine in the training leading up to it. But on the day of competition, the morphine was secretly swapped for a placebo. When the athletes competed, their performances were at the same level as they would have been had they actually taken the drug. In other words, they were able to run just as well naturally as they did when they took performance enhancers. Again we see that the body naturally produces its own drugs—although they aren't the same as anabolic steroids, these natural substances do help it perform at high levels.

A 2007 study conducted at Harvard University even found that people who get the same level of exercise receive different benefits from it, depending on whether they believe it's good exercise or not. The study involved 84 hotel-room maids whose job actually provided enough exercise to exceed the U.S. surgeon general's recommendation for daily exercise. However, the women didn't know this and most didn't see themselves as physically active; in fact, when the Harvard scientists surveyed them, they learned that 56 of the women didn't believe that they got any exercise at all. For the experiment, the researchers split the maids into two groups. With one, they went through all of the tasks that the subjects performed during a normal workday—from lugging heavy equipment around, vacuuming, and changing bedsheets to general cleaning; and they explained how many calories each activity burned. They then told the women that their daily responsibilities exceeded the surgeon general's recommendations, but they didn't tell the other group anything.

After a month, the scientists took physical measurements of all the women. The group who now knew that they were getting good exercise had lost weight and had a decrease in their waist-to-hip ratio, body mass index, and body-fat percentage; and had a 10 percent reduction in their blood pressure. The mind is a powerful thing!

It's even been proven that what you believe affects your academic performance. A 2006 study published in the journal *Science* examined the mathematics scores of 220 female students who had each read one of two different fake research reports. Half of the girls read one report claiming that scientists had discovered genes on the Y chromosome (that only men have) that gave males a 5 percent advantage over females in mathematics. The other half read a bogus paper that asserted that men had a 5 percent advantage only because of the way teachers stereotyped girls and boys at an early age.

When the students were tested, the group who believed that the difference was just stereotyping—and therefore felt that they were just as good at mathematics as men were—did much better than the one made up of girls who *thought* that they had a genetic disadvantage.

The Power of Positive Consultation

The placebo effect is often seen as a nuisance in medical trials. Therefore, some companies try to remove it in an attempt to get a more accurate picture of how well the drug works . . . but things don't always go according to plan.

In a typical trial, patients are given either a drug or a placebo. The ones who improve on the placebo—called "placebo responders"—are removed from the trial, and a new trial then begins that doesn't have any known responders. But some studies have shown that if, say, 35 percent of people improve on a placebo in the first trial, then in the second one, even though the placebo responders have been removed, another 35 percent of patients will again respond positively to the dummy drugs.

This is a total enigma for many companies who set up the trials, but the explanation lies in the only factor that hasn't changed between the two studies: the doctors. They still say the same things and communicate with the same enthusiasm from one study to the next. What they say, how they say it, their enthusiasm for the treatment, and how they relate to the people receiving the drugs matter a lot.

For example, in a 1954 study, patients with bleeding ulcers were given water injections but told either that the medicine would cure them or that they were being given experimental injections of undetermined effectiveness. Of the patients who were told that the treatments would cure them, 70 percent showed marked improvement. Yet of the group who were told that it was an experimental drug, only 25 percent improved.

In another study, Fabrizio Benedetti tested the effects of a hidden placebo on arm pain. When a fake treatment was secretly given through a saline drip, the pain level didn't change, but the results were different when it was administered in full view of the patients and a doctor told them, "I am going to give you a painkiller. Your pain will subside after some minutes. Be calm and comfortable and report your pain sensation during the next minutes." The pain diminished substantially.

In a similar study done in 1978 involving dental injections, patients were given either an oversell or an undersell message about a placebo they were receiving before getting an injection in the mouth. In the oversell message, the dentists made the drug sound really great, but with the undersell they explained that the pill might or might not work. The subjects who'd received the positive message had much less pain when they had their injection—as well as less anxiety and fear—than those who were given the more skeptical news.

And then there was a 1987 *British Medical Journal* paper titled "General practice consultations: is there any point in being positive?" in which 200 patients were given either a positive consultation or a negative one for minor ailments. In the positive discussions, the people were told what was wrong and that they'd be better in a few days; in the negative diagnosis, the doctors explained that they weren't certain what was wrong. Two weeks later, the condition of 53 percent of all the patients had improved—but 64 percent of those who had a positive consultation reported that they felt better compared with only 39 percent of the subjects who'd received bad news. So we see that the power of a positive meeting was almost twice as beneficial as a negative one.

Knowing how enthusiastic to be in conveying a message can be a challenge for today's doctors. On the one hand, they know that what they say counts; but on the other, they have to be responsible in conveying the truth about what the drugs have been proven to do, including their limits. But what they say clearly matters, as does how they say it. Current research clearly shows that empathy, warmth, and authority—as well as enthusiasm and confidence—have considerable effects. More research is needed to permit the doctors more freedom in what they can and can't say, as well as the most effective way to convey something. The power of what to believe lies within the patient.

෨෨

Although these results point to the power of a doctor's personality, the disposition of the patients also affects how they receive the message, and therefore, how well the placebo works for them.

Between 2005 and 2007, scientists at the University of Toledo in Ohio compared the responses of optimists and pessimists to placebos. Over a series of experiments, they gave both groups of people a tablet (placebo) and told them that it would make them feel unwell. As one might assume, the pessimists responded more strongly and felt worse than the optimists. Then the scientists gave all subjects a placebo treatment that they said would make them sleep better—this time, the more positive thinkers responded and slept better than the pessimists.

Optimists are more likely to benefit from something that's going to make them better, while those who are negative react better to something that's supposed to make them worse. Again, the key to healing lies within us.

Conditioning—Boosting the Power of the Placebo

We can boost the power of the placebo—it's called conditioning. In a typical conditioning experiment, scientists give patients a real drug for a couple of days and then secretly swap it for a placebo the next day. Of course, the patients don't suspect anything, so when they receive their "medicine" (actually the placebo), they expect to get the usual level of relief that they've been getting during the past few days when they were taking the actual drug . . . and they do. They've been "conditioned" to believe that each injection or tablet will work, just as Pavlov's dogs were conditioned to salivate when they heard a bell ring.

Studies suggest that the longer conditioning is carried out, the more powerful the effect; the deeper into the body's systems the mind can penetrate, the more powerful the placebo becomes. In some conditioning studies, the placebo effect has been boosted to 100 percent.

In one experiment, Fabrizio Benedetti and his research team gave volunteers a placebo and told them that it was a drug that would reduce pain, and their levels of discomfort subsequently did decrease. But when the scientists told the volunteers that it would increase growth-hormone levels, it had no effect.

To alter these levels, Benedetti and the scientists needed to boost the power of the placebo. They conditioned subjects with a substance known as sumatriptan, which is known to boost growth-hormone levels. After a few days of taking sumatriptan, which was effective, the patients secretly received a placebo instead . . . yet their levels still increased. You see, on the first day the placebo had no effect, but, through conditioning, the subjects' minds had associated taking sumatriptan with changing hormone levels, even though they weren't consciously aware of the differences.

The brain contains trillions of neural circuits that are linked to every part of the body. We condition these circuits to fire over and over again so that when we take a pill or get an injection—even though it's a placebo—the same ones fire as when we took the drug. It turns out that our unconscious awareness associates the treatment with immune or hormonal changes, as the last two studies showed.

If we tried to consciously affect our immune systems or growth-hormone levels (without any knowledge of how to do it), we wouldn't have much success. Conditioning boosts the power of placebos, allows us to change systems in the body that we wouldn't ordinarily be able to, and shows that we have considerable power to heal ourselves using our minds. We just need to tap into that power.

Later in the book, we'll learn that we can alter the body's systems another way and thus boost the power of the mind through repetitive visualization of a healing process. But first let's delve further into how the effectiveness of drugs is influenced by belief.

‿‿‿‿

CHAPTER 3

DRUGS WORK BECAUSE
WE BELIEVE IN THEM

"Believe none of what you hear and half of what you see."
— Benjamin Franklin

Some drugs never make it to the marketplace because trials show that they're no better than placebos. In certain cases, the medications' effectiveness is low, while in others it's high . . . but it just might be that the placebo effect is high, too. Thus, a drug that's quite good is deemed ineffective, but completely missing in these examples is the power of the placebo—the influence of the minds of the people who participated in the trials.

This is often the case with antidepressant medications: some of the world's best-selling antidepressant drugs have been regarded as useless because new evidence has shown that most of their ability is due to the placebo effect. In a 2008 meta-analysis (a summary of many studies) of fluoxetine (Prozac), venlafaxine (Effexor), nefazodone (Serzone), and paroxetine (Seroxat)—which covered 35 clinical trials involving 5,133 patients—the placebo effect was shown to account for 81 percent of the effect of the medicine. The only significant difference between the drug and dummy was found in severely depressed patients. With such a high placebo effect, it's impossible to prove that the drugs actually work. They probably do, but the studies show that people have a much greater ability to heal themselves than they'd ever imagined. The fact that millions of men and women all over the world have benefited from one or more of these drugs demonstrates the immense power of the human mind.

It might be that one of the ways in which antidepressant placebos work is that they give people hope. Thus, any placebo can do the same job. Patients feel relief at the knowledge that something might work, and this positive expectation is enough to trump some of the depressive feelings, particularly when the medication is taken every day. In a sense, it's as if people are being given a promise of hope every day . . . but that comes from within, as it's something that we've based on what we believe. Thus, the power to heal lies not just in hope, but in our ability to feel it.

We can put our faith in anything or anyone, and it can heal us. But the key to harnessing the power of the mind is to recognize that it's what we focus upon that matters—what we think and believe—and this comes from within us.

We unconsciously place our trust in things that have meaning for us all the time. But note that, once again, it's the *meaning* that we give these things that causes healing, not the things themselves. The power lies in each of us.

The Meaning Effect

In his excellent book entitled *Meaning, Medicine, and the "Placebo Effect,"* anthropology professor Daniel Moerman, another member of Harvard's Placebo Study Group, refers to many placebo effects as "meaning responses." Apparently, it's the *meaning* that the patients give the treatment that heals them: in other words, much of the power to heal lies in individuals' own perception of a drug or treatment.

Professor Moerman writes: "Meaning responses follow from the interaction with the context in which healing occurs—with the 'power' of the laser in surgery, or with the red color of the pill that contains stimulating medicine. Sometimes, a bandage on a cut finger works better if it has a picture of Snoopy on it." There's no medical reason why a cartoon on a Band-Aid heals a cut faster on a child, yet it does. The image has meaning for that boy or girl, whose thoughts then speed up the mending of the wound.

If we're treated for an illness with a large machine that shoots lightning bolts out of it, then it will probably work better than a pill, even if the machine and the drug are both placebos. It's not the machine or pill that actually heals, but our perception that it will do a better job. Hence, fake drugs work better if they smell medicinal, have a technical-sounding name, or are painful or invasive.

In "Placebos and nocebos: the cultural construction of belief," Cecil G. Helman writes:

> A doctor's office, hospital ward, holy shrine or house of a traditional healer—can be compared to a theatre set complete with scenery, props, costumes and script. This "script," derived from the culture ("macro-context") itself . . . tells them how to behave, how to experience the event and what to expect from it. It helps to validate the healer, and the power of their methods of healing.

It's clear that much of the power to heal ultimately lies within us, in our ability to choose how we look at things, and what meaning we give to them.

Feeling the Blues

Our thoughts about the color of pills affect how well they work. Scientists at the University of Cincinnati tested blue and pink stimulants and sedatives on 57 students where both "drugs" were actually placebos, although this was unknown to the subjects.

Blue sedatives were found to be 66 percent effective, but pink ones were only at 26 percent. The color blue proved to be two and a half times better than pink for creating a relaxed feeling—possibly because blue is considered to be a calming color. But if it has a different meaning in another culture, you'd expect the results to be different—and this is indeed the case.

Daniel Moerman describes some interesting research in *Meaning, Medicine, and the "Placebo Effect"*: he quotes two Italian studies that examined blue placebo sleeping tablets in which they worked well for women but not for men—in men, the pills actually worked as stimulants. Moerman explains that blue is the color of the Virgin

Mary's cloak, so in Italy, blue is associated with peace . . . at least, as far as women are concerned. But the power of this symbol is over-ruled in most men, because blue is the color of the home uniform for the Italian national soccer team, which is a *very* big deal there. (I had the good fortune of being in Italy during the 2006 World Cup—which Italy won—and I can testify to this. I happened to be in a town called Lucca in Tuscany, and every winning game was fol-lowed by a celebration involving most of the town. Local men waved their blue jerseys while driving around on motorcycles, singing and beeping their horns.)

Moerman points out that rather than being a calming color, "blue . . . means success, powerful movement, strength and grace on the field, and, generally, great excitement." Hence, for Italian men, blue sleeping tablets don't work as well as they do for Italian women because of what the color *means* to them.

Our beliefs are influenced by our culture; thus, the placebo effect varies depending on where we live. Take one U.S. study of migraine treatments, for example: 33.6 percent of patients who received placebo injections and 22.3 percent who had placebo tablets experienced relief. This means that dummy-drug injections in the U.S. were one and a half times better than the fake pills. But in Europe, the picture is different: in one trial performed there, 27.1 percent of patients who took tablets received pain relief, but 25.1 percent of subjects who received injections reported improvement. Therefore, in Europe, tablets work better for migraines than injections do.

Moerman points out that getting a shot is much more common in the U.S., so people here believe in it more. But in the U.K., it's more common to take pills, so a placebo tablet works better there.

This type of cultural effect tends to happen with other drugs, too. A trial of Tagamet done in France found it to be 76 percent effective, while the placebo was 59 percent effective. But in Brazil, the drug was 60 percent effective, while the placebo was only 10 percent effective. Amazingly, the placebo worked as well in France as the actual drug did in Brazil—a demonstration of the power of our minds to affect whether medicine works or not.

For Better or Worse, It's in the Mind

Tagamet used to be the best drug for treating stomach ulcers; in fact, a number of trials had shown it to be around 70 to 75 percent effective. But once Zantac was introduced in the 1980s—and was marketed as being much better—patients' (and doctors') opinions about Tagamet wavered. It was no longer the "best drug" on the market, and predictably, the next set of Tagamet trials found its effectiveness to only be at 64 percent. Had Tagamet's chemical formula changed? Had human biochemistry radically altered in the time between the two sets of trials? No. All that had changed were people's beliefs *about* Tagamet. Interestingly, Zantac then took over as the main antiulcer drug, showing around 75 percent effectiveness, which is not really very different from the originally reported power of Tagamet.

Our minds have been shown to affect aspirin, too. A 1981 study involving 835 women, which was conducted at Keele University in the U.K., found that having a brand name on the tablet made a big difference in how effective the drug was.

The study used two types of aspirin tablets: one was labeled with a well-known brand name, and the other as an analgesic; there were also two types of placebo tablets, marked in the same way. The women were then separated into four groups so that they would receive only one type of tablet.

Amazingly, the results showed that the recognizable aspirin tablets worked better than the unbranded ones, even though they were the same drug. And the name-brand placebos reduced pain much more than unbranded ones, yet they were the same dummy drug. Both aspirin and placebo tablets worked better if they were branded, and, incredibly, the unbranded real drug wasn't that much better than the branded placebo.

I've personally seen this type of thing happen with paracetamol (acetaminophen) tablets. Branded tablets (Panadol in the U.K.)— which are shaped and designed differently from the cheaper, mass-market tablets that are sold in supermarkets—seem to work better. When I asked some people their thoughts about the influence of how the drug looked on effectiveness, it turned out that it was the sound of the name, the brand, the price, the appearance, and the packaging of the tablets that gave them faith in Panadol. The mass-market tablets, they said, looked cheap and less powerful, and because of this perception they were indeed (according to my small analysis) less effective, even though they were the same drug.

Pharmaceutical companies often choose names for drugs that enhance their perceived effects. In a 2006 paper published in *Advances in Psychiatric Treatment,* psychiatrist Aaron K. Vallance suggested that the name Viagra actually enhanced the effect of the drug. It sounds similar to the words "vigor" and "Niagara," which creates a perception of vigorousness and power. There's no doubt that the name makes a difference—if it were called "Flopsy," I doubt it would work so well!

And then there's the research that Herbert Benson, Harvard medical professor and author of the bestseller *Timeless Healing,* conducted. He studied angina drugs that were well known and effective in the 1940s and 1950s, helping 70 to 90 percent of people who took them. Yet when they were later retested in higher-quality trials, they were found to be much less effective. From then on, they stopped working so well for people, even though they'd previously proved to be quite potent. Benson suggested that it was mostly because the doctors prescribing the drugs didn't believe in them as much as they previously had. Therefore, they were unlikely to be as enthusiastic as they had been when they initially prescribed them.

In *Meaning, Medicine, and the "Placebo Effect,"* Daniel Moerman refers to these results, stating, "Skeptics can heal 30 to 40 percent of their patients with inert medication, enthusiasts 70 to 90 percent."

Now while there is sometimes little difference between two drugs for the same condition, there *is* a difference in test-tube trials.

Drugs are very powerful. I used to study them as a scientist in the pharmaceutical industry, and I still get excited when looking at the chemistry of how they interact with the body's systems. Designing and developing drugs is a painstaking and highly skilled process that requires exceptional skill in manipulating the chemical structure of molecules. But test tubes don't involve human consciousness. Once people ingest medicine, their thoughts *about* it become all-important. They're either going to think that it will help them or not, but whatever they believe will affect how well it works.

I would like to see this factor taken more into account in medicine. Many doctors do consider that patients have the power to influence the effectiveness of the drugs they take, but it's not universally taught in medical schools as something that they should actively use in their treatments. In many institutions, more emphasis is put on the ethical considerations about giving placebos than on their ability to heal. Some doctors prescribe placebos when they can see no medical reason for the person's complaints. Once the patient receives their placebo, their symptoms frequently reduce.

Placebos heal; that's a fact! But the real power comes from inside us. Placebos are symbols to which we attach our thoughts of hope or relief. The thoughts are ours.

You Must Take All of Your Placebos

For some illnesses, four tablets work better than two, and many studies have shown that this is also true for placebos. In 1999, scientists from the University of Amsterdam summarized the combined results of 79 separate studies of antiulcer drugs involving 3,325 patients. They collected the data together for all of the trials where patients took placebos four times a day (1,821 patients) and found that the ulcers had healed in 44.2 percent of the patients after four weeks. They also pooled the data of the trials where patients took placebos twice a day (1,504 patients), and the healing rate was only 36.2 percent after the same period of time. The study conclusively proved that four placebos were better than two.

Studies have shown that drugs don't work as well if a patient doesn't take the full course of medication that their doctor prescribes . . . but this should be common sense. You need to take your medication when you're supposed to, and always continue to the end of the course of treatment. But studies have shown that placebos also don't work as well if you fail to complete your full cycle of medication.

In a trial involving the cholesterol-lowering drug clofibrate, 1,103 men were given the drug and 2,789 got the placebo. The survival rates were recorded five years later. For the men who received the drug, the rate was 80 percent; for those on the placebo it was 79.1 percent.

Looking more closely at the data, the researchers discovered that the survival rates actually depended upon whether the men stuck to their course of medication or not. They were said to be "good adherers" if they took 80 percent of their medication. After five years on the drug, 85 percent of the subjects who unwaveringly took their medicine were alive, but only 75.4 percent of the poor adherers were. This is common sense and what you'd expect to see. However, looking at the men who received placebos, 84.9 percent of the good adherers were alive after five years, while only 71.7 percent of the men who didn't stay the course were. Even though they received placebos, not taking all that they were supposed to had a significant effect, and for this particular condition, it was a death sentence.

The same type of thing has been shown with antibiotics. A 1983 *Journal of Pediatrics* study reported that people who took their full course of tablets had less fever or fewer infections than those who didn't, regardless of whether the tablets were real drugs or placebos. Of the good adherers, 82 percent were free of infections or fever, while this was only 47 percent true for the poor adherers. In the placebo group, 68 percent of the people who stuck with the medication to the end remained symptom free, but only 36 percent of the "quitters" were so. Amazingly, infections and fevers returned in twice as many people who didn't take all their placebos as those who did.

Sometimes circumstances take over our lives—we get lazy or think we'll be okay now that the condition is pretty much cleared up—and we don't complete the course. But nagging doubts about what we *should* have done occasionally enter our minds, and it's these thoughts that cause the relapses.

Sham Surgery

Studies have shown that, for some conditions, just the knowledge that we've had an operation can heal us, even if we haven't actually had one but just *think* we have. In one study, a group of patients was given ligation surgery for the internal mammary artery—in which arteries were tied off to divert the blood supply to the heart—for angina. Another group was given what's known as sham surgery, in which they still had an operation but the arteries weren't tied. After the surgery, 67 percent of patients reported substantial improvement—they had much less pain, required less medication, and were able to exercise for longer without an angina attack. But amazingly, 83 percent of patients who received the sham surgery experienced the same level of improvement. It was a reasonably small study—21 patients received real surgery and 12 received sham surgery—but the effect was still clear: for the majority of people, knowing that they were getting surgery was at least as good as actually getting it.

Eventually, after this study and a few others, the surgical technique was discontinued. By then more than 100,000 people had done the procedure. And the reason for its discontinuation? Some surgeons didn't believe that it was doing any good. Even so, it had made an enormously positive difference to their patients—in many cases, simply because they *believed* in it.

Just seeing a scar after an operation can also activate the placebo effect. In a sham surgery for arthritis, surgeons merely made an incision in the knee, but patients recovered most of their movement and were able to walk pain free as much as people who'd had actual surgery. Studies have shown that, for some conditions, regardless of whether a surgery is real or not, if patients believe that it is (and why wouldn't they?) and are optimistic about it, they'll receive the same benefit as if they'd actually had surgery. Once again, the power lies within the patient.

It's What You Know

So significant are your thoughts about surgery or an injection that medicines are most powerful when you know that you're getting them. If a treatment or drug is hidden—or even if you're asleep when you get it (so you don't know about it)—it doesn't work as well as when you know you're receiving it. One study of Alzheimer's patients found that they often don't get the full benefit of drugs for other conditions (as in high blood pressure), because they can't remember taking the medicine.

In a 1994 experiment involving a powerful painkiller for cancer pain (naproxen), the drug worked much better for patients who were given information about the experiment. The patients were either given the drug and it was secretly swapped for the placebo after one day, or they received the placebo and it was secretly switched out for the drug. The key to the experiment was that half of them were told that this might happen and half of them weren't.

The study showed that naproxen worked better than the placebo, but both the real and the dummy drugs were substantially more effective for the patients who knew what was going on. Simply having information boosted the power of both the drug and the placebo. And remarkably, in the group that knew about the experiment, the placebo worked even better than the drug did in the patients who weren't aware that the study was taking place.

In other words, as unbelievable as it sounds, a placebo works better for some conditions than a drug that is administered secretly. According to placebo-effect expert Fabrizio Benedetti: "The existence of the placebo effect suggests that we must broaden our conception of the limits of . . . human capability." Human consciousness has the ability to make a poor medicine work much better, an inert substance act as a powerful medicine, or sham surgery work like a real one.

In the next chapter, we're going to learn how our brains actually change as we think: even further evidence that thoughts can heal.

ভাৰভাৰ

CHAPTER 4

THE POWER OF PLASTICITY

"To think is to practice brain chemistry."
— **Deepak Chopra**

Your brain is growing as you read these words. As I mentioned in Chapter 1, scientists call this phenomenon neural plasticity. Everything you see, hear, touch, taste, and smell changes your brain; and each thought causes microscopic modifications in its structure. In a sense, thoughts leave physical traces in the brain in much the same way as you leave footsteps in the sand.

As you think, millions of brain cells (neurons) reach out and connect with each other, molding the actual substance of the brain just as an artist molds clay. These connections between brain cells are called neural connections. Think of the brain as a giant 3-D map showing towns with networks of roads linking them, with new ones constantly being added and expanding.

In a similar way, your brain contains maps, and these are also constantly changing. For instance, if you used your right hand for a few hours without using your left, the "map" for your right would expand as several new roads (neural connections) were forged in it. In this way, your brain map is in a continual state of expansion and contraction as you go through life.

Take a well-known study of symphony-orchestra musicians, for example. Published in *NeuroImage* in 2002, scientists from the Magnetic Resonance and Image Analysis Research Centre at the University of Liverpool showed that years of being a musician had expanded a specific part of the brain known as Broca's area, which is associated with language and musical abilities. It turns out that this area of the brain in people who aren't involved in music is much smaller than it is in those who are. Similarly, studies of blind people who learn braille found that as they practice, the brain map governing the tips of their index fingers expand.

Thoughts Change the Brain

As I've pointed out, it's not just your physical experiences—which are processed through your five senses—that change your brain. Your thoughts shape it, too.

A 2007 scientific study of mathematicians published in the *American Journal of Neuroradiology,* for instance, showed that the area of the brain that controlled mathematical thinking was biggest in those who had been studying the subject the longest. With each year spent in this profession—thinking, abstracting, and analyzing as this field requires—more new branches were added to the "mathematical map."

A recent study of London taxi drivers found the same thing: their brain maps had expanded through years of learning and memorizing routes. Acquiring new information is more than just your brain processing what you see, hear, touch, taste, and smell; it involves what you *think* about these physical experiences. These thoughts change your brain; studying, therefore, changes the brain.

Indeed, research published in the *Journal of Neuroscience* found brain-map changes when students were studying for their exams. Scientists at the University of Regensburg in Germany followed 38 medical students while they prepared for their exams and discovered that the areas of their brains that process memory and abstract information grew thicker.

So, our experiences *and* our thinking change the brain. It's not a static lump of organic matter that delivers genetically programmed instructions to the body, as many of us have come to believe. It's a constantly changing network of neurons and connections, and we are the cause of the transformations. Norman Doidge, M.D., author of *The Brain That Changes Itself,* writes: "The idea that the brain is like a muscle that grows with exercise is not just a metaphor." Just like a muscle, the brain grows thicker as we use it.

As we create new connections in any one area of the brain, their density pushes neurons apart in the same way as if two adjacent trees were to grow thousands of new branches: the space between them would become more densely filled and the trunks would eventually be pushed apart. In this way, the brain gets more crowded as we repeat the same thoughts, ponder the same ideas, or dream the same dreams over and over again.

It comes as no surprise to learn, then, that meditation changes the brain. A study of meditators using the Buddhist technique of insight meditation was conducted at Massachusetts General Hospital in 2005. It showed that meditation had increased the thickness of the prefrontal cortex of the brain—the area that controls concentration, free will, and compassion.

Therefore, when you visualize healing your body (which you'll learn to do later in the book), the first thing that occurs is that you actually change the microscopic structure of your brain. Visualization isn't just a subjective thing or an inert mishmash of mental pictures just there to make you feel good, but a process that causes real chemical and structural changes in the brain. With visualization, mind changes matter almost immediately.

Use It or Lose It—a Leopard <u>Can</u> Change Its Spots

If you repetitively flexed your right hand over several days, the brain map for it would expand because more neural connections would have formed. But if you stopped doing this and then switched to flexing your left hand, the map for your right would shrink because you were no longer using it, causing the map for your left to grow instead.

As Norman Doidge has pointed out, the brain is like a muscle. The more you use a muscle, the thicker it gets. If you stop using it, then it atrophies and gets smaller. Further, anytime you change your way of thinking, many connections that correspond to your old way dissolve and those that identify with your new mode of thinking begin to grow.

So let's say that you've always been someone who complains about things. Inevitably, you'll have built up brain maps that process your negative thoughts and emotions. But after reading this book, you decide that you're going to look at things differently. Since you now realize that your thoughts affect your body, you've decided to think positively and practice gratitude. You'll begin growing new maps that process your new way of thinking, and the complaint-based maps will naturally begin to shrink. In a surprisingly short period of time (many studies have shown it to be around 21 days), your new positive map will become larger than the negative one. At the neurological level, positive thinking and gratitude become a habit. These new ways are now wired into your brain, and you really are a different person.

You needn't think that you or your loved ones are unable to alter your ways. All you need to do is make the effort to change your mind. Your brain responds to the revisions and, in time, as it develops new maps, you don't need to make as much effort anymore. The new behavior is wired and has become routine.

Talking It Through

"There is no longer any doubt that psychotherapy can result in detectable changes in the brain."

These are the words of Nobel Prize–winning neuroscientist Eric Kandel, M.D. They refer to the growing body of evidence that talk therapies cause neuroplastic change in the brain (another way of saying that brain maps change). In the presence of a good therapist or friend, talking about our problems actually modifies the brain.

Psychotherapy that emphasizes conversation helps us view a memory from a new perspective so that we no longer feel pain when we think about something that previously caused us emotional distress. In biological terms, energy is diverted to the front of the brain and away from the area that stores the emotional pain. Millions of new neural connections are born at the front of the brain and, with less energy to feed them, those connections associated with the trauma begin to dissolve. Such is the emotional intensity of trauma, chronic stress, and even depression that some degree of neural damage often occurs. But the regenerative capacity of the brain is so amazing that recent studies have shown that we can in fact repair the damage.

Childhood trauma is linked with a high number of stress-related illnesses in adulthood. It can cause a flood of stress hormones that kill cells in an area of the brain that stores memories (the hippocampus), actually dissolving them. Some scientists view this as a protective mechanism, since neural circuits are literally "burned out" to prevent us from remembering, and thus reliving, the trauma. But recent studies have shown that neurons in the hippocampus can be regenerated: the phenomenon is known as neurogenesis. So not only can we rewire our brain, but we can regenerate it, too. Just ten years ago, such an idea was preposterous to science. Now we know it to be fact, and it's much easier to do and more common than we think.

Neurogenesis

In studies on adult mice living in enriched environments—having a running wheel, the company of other mice, toys, and so on—it was found that the volume of their hippocampi increased by 15 percent compared with mice who didn't live in such environments. Neurogenesis had occurred, and the same is true for humans in conducive conditions.

In 1998, scientists at the Salk Institute in La Jolla, California, first discovered stem cells of neurons in the human hippocampus, which was evidence of neurogenesis and that neurons were being formed.

We now know that living an active life with physical, mental, and social stimulation can regenerate the brain. Research has even shown that when we exercise; feel excited, enthusiastic, and fascinated; are in awe; experience wonder; or even experience spiritual states, then neurogenesis also naturally occurs. Many of these conditions of being are associated with strong positive emotions; thus, thoughts and emotions can cause neurogenesis, and it's likely that talking things through causes it, too.

Studies have shown that neurogenesis continues right up through old age. Scientists at the Salk Institute recently injected terminally ill volunteers with a special chemical that allows newly formed neurons to be seen under a microscope. They discovered that neurogenesis occurred in the volunteers' hippocampi right up to their final days, no matter how old they were.

Research has expanded into other areas of the brain, and neurogenesis has so far been discovered in the parts that process smell (olfactory bulb), emotion (septum), movement (striatum), and in the spinal cord. This suggests that we have a much higher potential for regeneration than medical science ever previously imagined. The human body is a walking miracle that has amazing power to heal and regenerate, and this is influenced by our minds.

Studies have shown that learning new things as adults can enlarge our brain maps and most likely causes neurogenesis. As I pointed out in the first chapter, learning a new language is a great way to exercise our brains as we age because it encourages us to use different brain areas. It's been suggested that if a vaccine for Alzheimer's existed, it would actually be the pursuit of learning a new language as an adult.

Attempting to play a new musical instrument changes the brain, as does playing board games, doing crossword or sudoku puzzles, or taking a college course, no matter how old we are. Learning new dances is also excellent, because it involves exercise of the mind as well. Simply replaying the dances and moves we've done for years, however, isn't as good because we don't have to concentrate on new ways of moving our bodies. We benefit from the novelty of new experiences, and to maximize the positive effects upon our brains, we need to be continually learning.

So as we go through life, no matter how old we are, if we retain our curiosity for new experiences and exercise our bodies and minds, we can mentally grow younger.

ഇരുഇര

CHAPTER 5

THE SCIENCE BEHIND
MIND-BODY HEALING

"Although the world is full of suffering,
it is also full of the overcoming of it."
— **Helen Keller**

As part of the brain-changing process, thoughts produce chemicals in the brain. Many are known as neurotransmitters, and serotonin and dopamine are two that you may have heard of. When you think about something, neurotransmitters are released from the branch of one neuron and make their way to the tip of a branch of another. This creates a bolt of electricity and is what's known as a neuron "firing." When we repeat a thought several times, an additional chemical (protein) is stimulated and makes its way to the center of the neuron (the nucleus), where it finds DNA. It then activates (switches on) several genes of DNA, which make the substances (proteins) that produce new branches (connections) between the neurons. In this way, repeating a thought produces new connections between neurons, and this is how the brain changes with our thoughts and experiences.

The process is rapid. Genes are activated within a few minutes, and a single neuron may gain thousands of new branches in a very short time. One point of significance to note here is that the genes have been activated by a *state of mind* within minutes. This is mind over matter rapidly taking place at the genetic level and has a key role to play in many so-called miraculous healings.

Another type of chemical, known as a neuropeptide, is also produced in the brain. There are many different types of neuropeptides, and these reflect different states of mind, emotions, and attitudes. They interface with neurons by attaching to parts of the surface known as receptors, which are basically docking ports. Imagine several spaceships docking onto a space station. The space station would have several docking ports—of different shapes and sizes—to cope with the different spaceships.

It's quite similar on the surface of neurons. Neurons contain thousands of receptors that allow neuropeptides of different shapes, sizes, and electromagnetic (vibrational) qualities to dock. Another way to think of this is to imagine a child's toy. Remember the one where the child has a colored table containing different-shaped holes? It usually has circular, triangular, square, and star-shaped holes. (On a neuron, these would be receptors of different sizes and shapes.) The child also has circular, triangular, square, and star-shaped blocks, and these fit into the appropriate holes. In the brain, these blocks would be different neuropeptides, each one having its own specific receptor.

But unlike the toy, neurons actually change their receptors. If a certain neuropeptide is produced over and over again in a certain part of the brain, then neurons in that area develop extra receptors to cope. For instance, if an endorphin (a neuropeptide) were produced over and over again, neurons would evolve extra endorphin receptors. Presumably, if they started out with, say, 100, then they might evolve to having 1,000. If production of an endorphin reduced, then the neurons would gradually shed these receptors. Therefore, along with the mind affecting the number of connections between brain cells and activating genes, it also changes their surface (skin).

This is how addiction and tolerance work: If a person keeps taking a certain substance—for instance, heroin—then neurons would develop more receptors for it. Soon, as the brain creates thousands of them, the person requires more of the drug to get the same hit.

Neuropeptides don't just hang around in the brain. Many are released into the bloodstream and travel throughout the body, where they carry out important roles. In a powerful link between the mind and body, our thoughts and emotions produce neuropeptides, which affect the body. Many neuropeptides are even produced in the body instead, and these can make their way to the brain. For example, some immune cells make neuropeptides.

In this way, the body affects the mind but the mind also affects the body. It's a two-way process!

Neuropeptides play an important role in the liver, kidneys, pancreas, gut, colon, reproductive organs, and skin. They also influence blood sugar, blood pressure, heart rate, respiration, body temperature, the endocrine system, the immune system, sex drive, and even appetite. Not only does the mind affect *all* of these organs and systems, it affects our bodies at the cellular level as well.

How the Mind Affects the Body

In his excellent book *Evolve Your Brain,* Joe Dispenza, D.C., discusses the likely changes in cells throughout the body when people alter their thinking. Using the example of a person changing from being impatient to patient, he describes the probable impact upon cells throughout the body.

Just as neurons evolve how many receptors they have, cells in our organs and throughout our bodies do the same thing. Initially, in Dispenza's example, neuropeptides associated with impatience flood the cells in an organ; the cells then evolve more receptors for that neuropeptide. When we become more patient, the flow of impatience neuropeptides ceases, and the flow of patience neuropeptides takes over. The cells then cut back on the number of impatience receptors—because they would no longer be needed—and develop more patience receptors instead. Thus, as we change our minds, we change our bodies at the cellular level.

Imagine the flow of neuropeptides as a colored dye and the bloodstream as a river. As we change our thinking, we change the color of dye that we drop into the river. Downstream, rocks are colored by our different thoughts. For this analogy, think of the rocks as cells—but more like large, spongy boulders that absorb the dyes. As we send different colors downstream, cells adapt to their changing environments by evolving more or less of that color receptor.

As a result, when we move from impatience to patience, relaxed to calm, or one thought to another, we alter the connections between neurons, produce chemicals in the brain, and affect cells and systems throughout our body.

Some scientists believe that thoughts only serve to increase or decrease stress and that the connection between mind and body is just the link between stress chemicals and cells. I can appreciate how they might arrive at this conclusion, but I don't agree. Your thoughts are not black and white; there are an infinite number of thoughts and emotions that you can experience. Both the brain and the body produce thousands of chemicals, many of which are constantly finding their way around the body. As you switch from one state of mind to another—even when you're just making a subtle change— you alter the tone being produced from the mixture of colors that reflects your thinking. (If you're musically inclined, it might help to think of your thoughts in terms of musical tones instead.)

Each state of mind produces a variety of color (or musical) tones. A slight shift in perspective produces a small shift in tone, and this produces a subtle change in cells all over the body. Hence, when we think about healing an illness, there's more than just a reduction of stress chemicals interfacing with cells throughout the body. A range of neuropeptides corresponding to our thoughts will make their way out of the brain and flow around the body, painting it in a variety of tones (or playing different tunes).

The Mind-DNA Interface

Just as the mind affects genes of DNA in neurons, it also affects genes of DNA in cells throughout the body. When neuropeptides connect to their receptors, messages are delivered into the cells. When the information reaches the DNA, genes are either switched on or off or made a little brighter or dimmer.

DNA contains around 25,000 genes. Think of the genes as light-bulbs (I visualize them as flashing Christmas-tree lights, because multiple genes are involved at the same time): When one switches on, a protein is produced. This protein might be involved in building, such as in the construction of new cells for tissues, bones, tendons, blood, or the immune system; or it might be an enzyme that will help change something into something else. For instance, the enzyme pepsin helps convert the food that we eat into smaller units that the body can use. What's produced might even be a hormone that will deliver a message to another cell, because when genes switch on, they produce all that the body needs.

In terms of healing, genes turn on and proteins are made that can be used to make new cells, skin, tendons, blood, or bones. They also generate proteins that are involved in the immune response—for example, if the body has suffered a cut, different ones are produced to help blood clot around the wound. Some genes develop proteins that affect other relevant systems in the body so that the entire organism (your body) is tipped in the direction of healing.

Let's say that a person is irritable and hostile. His or her brain produces the appropriate neuropeptides, and these flood throughout the body, finding cells in organs and tissues that they can interface with and that have the same "color" receptor.

Wound healing is very sensitive to our mental and emotional states, and it's known that hostility and stress slow it down. Neuropeptides of irritation and hostility interface with cells and deliver messages to DNA, then genes are activated and proteins are produced. Some genes that are important to the healing process would only be partially activated (or sometimes not at all)—similar to a dimmer switch only being partially turned on—while others are deactivated or their switches turned down (for instance, growth hormones that are important in healing). Thus, irritation and hostility would mean that the proteins required for healing aren't produced in such high quantities as they would be in a person with a calm state of mind.

Indeed, in keeping with one of the themes of Chapter 1, scientists at the Ohio State University showed that hostility significantly alters healing rates. The study, published in 2005 in *Archives of General Psychiatry* and involving 42 married couples, demonstrated that those who were most hostile healed at only 60 percent of the rate of the people who were more optimistic and relaxed.

In another 2005 study, it was found that stress reduced the levels of growth hormones at the sites of wounds. (Growth hormones—which are proteins—are produced when certain genes are switched on, and they aid healing.) The scientists discovered that wounds take longer to heal when we're stressed.

Looking at the actual genes involved, the scientists observed that more than 100 genes were *downregulated* during stress. This means that, returning to the lightbulb analogy, the brightness of around 100 bulbs was dimmed by stress and more than 70 were *upregulated*, so 70 bulbs became brighter. The scientists noted that "100 downregulated and 70 upregulated genes" tipped the genetic balance toward the death of cells instead of their birth and growth.

If, instead of feeling stress, you're calm—which might be because of your positive attitude, trust in the medical team, or belief that everything is going to work out okay—different genes would be upregulated and downregulated, and therefore speed up healing. More growth hormones would be produced at the site of injury, and these would hasten the process.

Indeed, in another Ohio State University study published in 2004 in *Psychoneuroendocrinology,* scientists showed that social support, which leads to a state of calm, speeds up wound healing. All throughout the body, genes are responding to our minds. In *The Genie in Your Genes,* Dawson Church, Ph.D., writes: "Now we're starting to understand that our consciousness conditions our genetic expression, moment by moment."

In other words, when we visualize our bodies healing—as we shall learn later in the book—our thoughts affect our genes, aiding the regeneration of a damaged or diseased part of the body. As I mentioned, even though the above examples refer to the presence or absence of stress, different thoughts produce different tones. They don't just fit somewhere in the scale between stress and no stress.

The neuropeptides produced by our varied tones of thinking affect a large number of genes. In the example that used the lightbulb analogy to describe downregulation and upregulation, 170 genes were affected. Science used to think that it was one gene, one function—that one gene did one thing. But now we know that a mixture of genes is involved in different functions. We know that it's not black and white with genes—they subscribe to the "variety of tones" way of working.

If each gene were a color or a sound, then different states of mind would produce an infinite variety of tones. This is an area of research that's sure to flower in the next few years.

Trumping Our Genes

So influential is the power of your mind to affect your genes that you needn't live in fear of heart disease or cancer, even if you have a family history of it. A change in attitude and lifestyle could trump many of the "bad" genes that you might have inherited.

Let's say that you're born into a family with a history of heart disease, with genes that make your risk of developing it higher than average. This doesn't automatically mean that you'll develop heart disease. A change in attitude and/or lifestyle will affect numerous genes in the brain and throughout the body, which may cause the "bad" genes to be turned down.

So, returning to the research reported in Chapter 1, developing a positive attitude, being more optimistic, cutting down on hostility and complaining, being more accepting of life and people, focusing on things that you're grateful for, sharing, and even developing a warm disposition toward people will all have beneficial effects.

Lifestyle also influences your genes. A healthy diet, cutting down on toxins and stimulants, and exercising regularly will all make a positive difference. Living like this means that there's a healthy chance that the heart disease or cancer genes may remain dormant. It's your life, so it's your choice.

Attitude, diet, and lifestyle run in families just as much as genetics do. The good thing about this is that you have a choice about these things. If you, for example, have heart-disease genes and adopted the same diet and lifestyle as the people in your family who developed the disease, then your genes would likely be similarly activated. Therefore, you'd be as likely to develop the disease as your family members were. But in many cases, this occurs mostly because of your decisions and not because of genetics—which, in most cases, plays a much smaller role than had previously been believed.

There are, of course, exceptions. Some people with heart-disease genes and a poor diet and lifestyle never develop heart problems, while others without the genes who maintain a great diet and lifestyle do. But trumping our genes is true in a very broad sense.

If your family has a history of heart problems or cancer, examine your attitude, how you treat people, how you feel, your diet, your exercise levels, and how much you drink or smoke; and make any positive changes that are necessary. Consult your doctor and get some good, healthy advice.

The Mind–Stem Cell Interface

The fact that the mind influences genes suggests that it has the power to influence the growth of stem cells as well, since stem cells have DNA. Stem cells are cells that can morph into any type of cells, like flowers without a head: that is, they have only a stem, but they're able to grow different heads. In this way, a stem cell could become a bone cell, an immune-system cell, a skin cell, a heart cell, a blood cell, or even a neuron. As genes are activated, the stem cells grow into the cells that they're required to become.

You may be familiar with the ethical debates over using embryonic stem cells to treat some diseases. Once transplanted into, say, the liver, embryonic stem cells become liver cells. Transplanted into the heart, the same ones would become heart cells instead. Thus, stem cells can encourage the growth of damaged tissue anywhere in the body.

It has long been known that bone-marrow stem cells morph into immune-system cells, which help us fight infection. Earlier we learned about neurogenesis, but there's now evidence to suggest that the stem cells that become neurons begin their lives in the bone marrow, too. Recent research has shown that when skin wounds heal, stem cells travel from the bone marrow and morph into skin cells. There's also evidence that stem cells travel from the bone marrow and morph into heart cells, regenerating damaged heart muscles.

As we know, neurogenesis is accelerated by novel experiences, powerful emotional states, spiritual experiences, and exercise. Therefore, it's logical to assume that in these situations, the mind is having an effect upon stem cells. It's also known that stress can interfere with neurogenesis and slow the healing process. This suggests that tension or strain might turn down the genes on the stem-cell DNA that are required for it to morph into the cell type required for healing.

Based on the evidence, it's highly likely that the mind can either encourage stem cells to morph into new cells or interfere with the process. Indeed, in studies of the heart, high levels of stress are known to lower the levels of endothelial progenitor cells (a type of stem cell), which are destined to become heart cells. Thus, since stress can affect stem cells, it's probable that many tones of our thoughts, emotions, and attitudes do so, too.

If you visualize the healing of a damaged part of your body, I believe that you're certain to have an effect upon the morphing of stem cells into the required cell types for healing. Although there's little research in this area, a growing number of scientists believe that some seemingly miraculous healings and spontaneous remissions (where a person recovers overnight) from serious diseases are actually the results of the movement of stem cells from bone marrow and their morphing into cells that regenerate a damaged area.

Indeed, in his excellent book *The Psychobiology of Gene Expression,* award-winning scientist Ernest L. Rossi writes: "Many of the so-called miracles of healing via spiritual practices and therapeutic hypnosis probably occur via . . . gene expression in stem cells throughout the brain and body."

Precisely how stem cells are involved in wound healing is not yet fully understood. They contain DNA, just as normal cells do. In terms of healing through visualization, it's likely, as Rossi implies, that neuropeptides deliver messages to DNA in stem cells and produce proteins that tell them what cell type they should become.

ဟာ

The mind really does have an incredible ability to affect the body. In the next chapter, we'll learn of some of the new scientific evidence that shows how visualization directly impacts the area of the body that our minds are focusing on.

ဟာ ဟာ ဟာ

CHAPTER 6

THE POWER OF VISUALIZATION

"Visualization is daydreaming with a purpose."
— **Bo Bennett**

I f you visualize a part of your body, you'll note that the part you're visualizing feels it while the rest of your body doesn't. A 1996 scientific paper published in the journal *Psychological Science* featured a very interesting finding by scientists from the University of Connecticut. They reported that when volunteers who had experimental pain induced in certain fingers expected to have less in one, it was indeed less in that finger, but not in any other. The study involved 56 volunteers who had a placebo cream that they believed was an analgesic rubbed on their index fingers on one hand but not on the index fingers of the other. Pain was then inflicted on both fingers, but the volunteers only really felt it in the finger that didn't have the cream. Their discomfort was much less where they had the cream applied, even though it was a placebo.

Fabrizio Benedetti later reported the same type of effect. He induced a burning sensation in the hands and feet of 173 volunteers by injecting them with capsaicin (it's the chemical that makes chili peppers burn). Prior to the injections, some of the volunteers had a placebo cream rubbed on a hand or foot, and again they believed that it was an anesthetic. One group had the cream rubbed on their left hand and another group on their right hand and left foot. Two other groups didn't receive any cream so that they could serve as a control. The study, published in *The Journal of Neuroscience* in 1999, reported that there was much less pain in the areas where the placebo cream was applied. If it was rubbed on the left hand, for instance, there was less pain there, but the levels remained high in the other hand and in both feet. In the groups that didn't get any of the placebo, there was no reduction in pain. Relief only occurred where volunteers *expected* it to.

It seems that when we have an injury and receive a placebo but believe it to be a painkiller, our awareness of where the discomfort is located and our expectation that it will go away cause it to disappear exactly where our awareness is directed, and nowhere else.

In his research, Benedetti showed that endogenous opiates (which we learned about in Chapter 2) were only released in the area of the brain that corresponded to the part of the body where there was an expectation of pain relief (where the volunteer's thoughts were focused). He wrote: "Endogenous opioids do not act throughout the nervous system but *only* [my emphasis] on those neural circuits linking specific expectations to specific placebo responses."

In other words, there's a release of chemicals in specific locations of the brain that brings about what we expect to occur. Our awareness seems to be the directing force that instructs which chemicals should be released and where. So when we anticipate pain relief in any area of our bodies, neural circuits in our brains are activated for that specific part, and endogenous opiates are released there. The whole brain isn't flooded, just the bits that control the areas that our awareness is focused upon.

The same type of thing would most likely occur if we had two different conditions and were given a placebo for one of them, believing it to be a drug. In Chapter 2, we learned of the study where a woman was given an inhaler that she was told contained pollen—but it actually contained a placebo—and she went on to develop bronchoconstriction and hay-fever symptoms. Next, she was given an inhaler and told that it only contained allergens; this time, she only developed asthma symptoms. In the third experiment, she was made to believe that the inhaler contained pollen and, once again, developed asthma and hay-fever symptoms. Her awareness of what was supposed to happen directed which chemicals were released and, therefore, what actually occurred. That means that if people who had asthma and hay fever were given a placebo for asthma and believed it to be a drug, their asthma symptoms would disappear but their hay-fever symptoms would remain. Conversely, if they were told that the placebo was for hay fever, those symptoms would disappear and the asthma symptoms would remain.

Just as in the pain experiments, our awareness of what's wrong with us and what's supposed to happen when we receive medicine seems to be the directing force that instructs the brain and body as to which chemicals should be released; which genes should be activated and deactivated; where chemicals should flow to; and, ultimately, what should happen. Imagine if we believed that we just needed to wish a disease away . . . now that's an interesting thought!

The Brain Is Connected to the Body

Every part of your body is wired to your brain. Nerves connect your brain to your skin, muscles, bones, tendons, and internal organs. This is the reason why when someone touches a part of your body you can feel it, and if an organ is damaged, you experience pain. But along with touch being registered in the brain, just thinking about a part of your body does the same thing. This is how you can increase the temperature of your hands if you imagine them as hotter and why some pain goes away if you're distracted.

Although this was once just the realm of the mystical and dismissed by academics as the stuff of quacks and "alternative types," a great deal of research has recently begun to focus on it. Neuroscience studies have now conclusively shown that if we think about moving a part of the body, the area of the brain that governs it is stimulated. Thinking about moving our hands, for instance, activates the "hand map" in the brain.

Publishing in the *Journal of Neurophysiology* in 2003, scientists at the Karolinska Institute in Stockholm (which is responsible for selecting the annual winners of the Nobel Prize in Physiology or Medicine) demonstrated that when we imagine moving our fingers, toes, or tongue, for instance, the area of our brain that controls each part is activated. In all probability, the brain is activated in the area that governs whatever part of our body that we're focusing on.

If you think about any part of your body over and over again, that has an even more powerful effect. You may remember from the last chapter that repetition of a movement increases the size of a brain map or the thickness of an area of the brain—well, the same thing occurs when you repeat the *thought about* a movement.

In a 1994 Harvard Medical School study, volunteers repetitively played a five-fingered combination of notes on a piano. The sequence was: thumb, index finger, middle finger, ring finger, little finger, ring finger, middle finger, index finger, thumb. They did this for two hours a day for five consecutive days, while another group just imagined playing and hearing those notes for the same duration of time. At the end of the five days, the individuals' brain maps were recorded. The finger maps for the volunteers who had played the notes had grown, as you'd expect, but the maps for the volunteers who had imagined playing them had also grown . . . amazingly, to the same extent.

Further, it's not only the brain that's activated. Since nerves connect the brain to muscles, muscles grow stronger if we picture ourselves using them. A 2004 study by scientists at the Department of Biomedical Engineering at the Lerner Research Institute in Cleveland measured a substantial increase in strength through imagined exercise. Thirty volunteers were involved: Some did physical training of their little finger, but others just envisioned doing it. In each session, the participants did 15 contractions at a time, real or pretend, followed by a 20-second rest period. Each session lasted 15 minutes and took place five days a week for 12 weeks. After the experiment, the scientists tested the strength of each volunteer's little finger. As expected, the group who did the physical training got stronger; their muscle strength increased by 53 percent. But incredibly, the group who did the mental training increased their strength by 35 percent, even though they hadn't actually "lifted a finger."

I know a young athlete, a sprinter named Thomas, who had to have an operation on his shoulder and was advised that he would have to refrain from training for a whole season. Not wanting to lose the strength in his muscles, he went to the gym in his mind, doing lifts as if he were really there. Not only did he recover from his injury much faster than expected, but he returned to training almost as fast and as strong as he had been before his operation. His improvement was rapid: within a short time he was picked to run for his country (Scotland) for the first time.

Recent research has even shown that if we imagine lifting heavy weights, the brain and muscles are stimulated more than if we envision working out with lighter weights. In a 2007 report by scientists at the University of Lyon, 30 volunteers either lifted or imagined lifting dumbbells of different weights. Significantly, it was found that the activation of the muscles was appropriate for the type of weight that they perceived lifting. If they imagined lifting a heavy weight, for instance, their muscles were activated more than if they pictured lifting a lighter one.

Athletes have understood for a long time that muscles are affected by visualization, and therefore, mentally seeing themselves achieving at the highest level frequently separates champions from those whom history doesn't record. But now we know, scientifically, that the brain is stimulated by the visualization, which then stimulates the muscles. This is a fact!

When I was a long jumper, I was jokingly mocked for spending lots of time imagining jumping. But I had the last laugh. My visualization was so effective that I reached the Scottish Championship long-jump final in 1996 after only two months of formal training. This was a high-level competition that attracted U.K. Olympic hopefuls who used it as an event to make the Olympic standard. I often wonder how much I would have achieved if I had kept training at that level, but I was actually more interested in being a coach, and became one the following season.

If you envision jumping far or running fast, your muscles will be stimulated to develop so that you can. But if you set the bar higher, so to speak, and imagine yourself jumping a world-record distance or running a world-record time—and you do this regularly— then your muscles will develop in that direction instead.

In July 2008, the BBC showed a one-hour documentary featuring Colin Jackson, the ex–world record holder for the 110-meter hurdles. Analysis of Colin's blood performed at the University of Glasgow found that he had little genetic advantage, but a study of his muscle fibers found that he had an exceptionally high level of superfast-twitch muscles. On the basis of genetics alone, Colin wouldn't have had such a level of these fibers. It's likely that his determination to be the best played a significant role in how his muscles developed.

If athletes regularly imagine running at a world-record pace, their muscles will be stimulated and grow differently than if they imagined running a time that might just get them selected to run in, say, a city championship. It's what we focus on that counts.

The Power of Watching

Advancements in prosthetics have resulted from research that looked at how imagining moving a hand activates the part of the brain that's responsible for the actual movement. The research uses brain-computer interfaces (BCIs) that record the stimulation of neurons caused by imagined movements. They then convert the stimulation into a computer signal that instructs the limb to move.

In pioneering research published in *Nature* in 2006, a tetraplegic person with a tiny chip inserted into his brain was able to move a cursor on a computer screen and even open e-mail with his mind. He also played a computer game, controlled a robotic arm, and changed the channel and volume of a TV while he was having a conversation. And in a research paper called "Walking from thought," which was published in 2006 by scientists from Graz University of Technology, paralyzed people were reported to be able to walk down a street in a virtual-reality simulator.

Research has now shown that even just watching someone else exercising affects our brains and muscles. In 2001, scientists at the

University of Parma in Italy, publishing in the *European Journal of Neuroscience,* scanned the brains of volunteers as they simply watched people move their hands, mouths, or feet. Amazingly, the areas of the volunteers' brains that controlled the movements of these body parts were activated as if they were the ones making the movements.

Taking it further, in a fascinating 2006 paper called "Bend it like Beckham: Embodying the motor skills of famous athletes," scientists at the Centre for Clinical and Cognitive Neuroscience at the University of Wales found that we don't even have to watch people move; we only need to see a photo of someone known for a particular skill, and our brains and muscles will be stimulated. Looking at a photo of a famous soccer player, for instance, activates parts of the brain that govern leg and foot muscles.

As unbelievable as it sounds, witnessing a great athlete perform makes you better at that event yourself. Watching Tiger Woods play golf makes you a better golfer. Watching someone who isn't an expert also improves your ability, but not as much. If you want to learn a skill, there's a lot to be said for hanging out with people who are masters at it. This is why "modeling," in the NLP (neuro-linguistic programming) sense, works. In NLP, learning from experts is encouraged because neuroscience research shows that your brain and body are then actually stimulated, just like the experts' are.

Visualizing our muscles working improves our strength, but so does watching them. In a similar experiment to the one described earlier in this chapter, scientists conducted a study where volunteers watched other volunteers flexing their little fingers. In the group that performed the actual training, muscle strength of the little finger of their right hand (the one used) increased by 50 percent, but amazingly, in the group that merely watched the training, strength increased by 32 percent.

An interesting by-product of the experiment is that little-finger strength of the left hands in both groups also developed. In the group who did the actual training, the strength of the little finger on their left hand increased by 33 percent, and it was stronger by 30 percent in the group that just watched.

Imagining, witnessing, and actually training all activated neurons in the part of the brain that controlled the muscles of the little fingers. Extending this, if you had impaired movement in any part of your body, just viewing fully able individuals move (without any envy or negative thoughts regarding your own condition) would improve your own movement.

Indeed, in a pioneering study into stroke rehabilitation published in the journal *NeuroImage,* scientists from the University Hospital Schleswig-Holstein in Germany studied eight stroke patients over a four-week period as they watched men and women perform routine actions such as having a coffee or eating an apple, and they also received normal rehabilitation during this period. At the end of the four weeks, the patients who had watched the actions had improved much more than those who hadn't, and MRI brain scans showed that their damaged brain maps were actually regenerating.

Your brain mirrors what you pay attention to. If other people are sad, for instance, and you're focusing on them, your brain will reflect the sadness on their faces. If you spend enough time with them, there's a good chance that you'll get down in the dumps, too. Similarly, if you spend time with happy people, your brain reflects their expressions and actions, and your mood is likely to improve.

The neurons in the brain that are stimulated by what we see are aptly called mirror neurons. They help us learn new things as we watch people doing them. For instance, in a 2004 study, scientists at the Department of Neuroscience at the University of Parma took brain scans of volunteers who had never played the guitar while they were watching someone playing one. The scans showed that their mirror neurons were initiated as if they were actually playing.

Recent studies have shown that such is the power of our awareness and our brains that just listening to sentences describing movements stimulates our minds as if we were actually doing those movements. Scientists have shown that when participants listened to people talking about hand motions, the area of the brain that controlled theirs was activated as well. When they heard people talk about foot movements, the area of the brain corresponding to them was similarly triggered.

Interestingly, studies have shown that when you hear others speaking, your tongue muscles are also aroused, especially if they're speaking clearly. So, if you have impaired range of motion and listen to someone describing perfect maneuverability, your capacity to move would increase and your brain map for the required muscles would expand. Similarly, in sports, if you tune in to an expert tennis player describing a great serve that he or she had performed, for instance, your ability to serve would improve.

I once demonstrated a similar example with a roomful of workshop participants; it's something I learned from a great book called *Neurospeak* by Robert Masters. For about five minutes, I just talked about moving our right arms and rotating our right shoulders. When I finished speaking, I asked each person to stretch both arms and shoulders. To the surprise of the group, their right arms and shoulders were considerably looser and more flexible than their left ones were. Note to sports coaches: what you say really matters!

Extending this, if you're sick, just listening to people talk about perfect health would aid your journey to wellness, especially if they happened to mention how amazing the body's regenerative capacity is. The last thing you need when you're not feeling well is people around you constantly affirming how sick you are.

The brain is incredibly sensitive to what you're aware of. Think of a movement, and the brain is stimulated as if you're performing it. See an event take place—or even just hear about it—and the same type of thing occurs. Even looking at a part of someone else's body increases the sensitivity of that part of your own. Indeed, studies at the University of Wales have shown that looking at another person's hand or neck increases the sensitivity of your own.

This is why we may feel a sudden twinge in our ankles when we watch someone twist theirs or get phantom pains and symptoms of illness when a loved one is suffering. Some men even experience contractions when their partners are in labor. The awareness of the discomfort of those closest to us puts our unconscious attention upon our own body, and neurons in the brain are activated that bring us some discomfort, too. But the fact that we can create distress in our bodies shows us that we can also rid ourselves of it.

Any doctor will tell you that a great many illnesses have their roots in the mind; therefore, the mind should be able to cure them.

The brain doesn't seem to know the difference between real and imaginary, which is great if we want to visualize ourselves recovering from sickness. To the brain, we really *are* recovering—and it's likely that, just as in the placebo studies described at the beginning of this chapter, the right chemicals are released in the right places, and the right genes are activated and deactivated, so we ultimately become what we're imagining.

Guided Imagery

In 2004, medics at Tai Po Hospital in Hong Kong used guided-imagery relaxation to treat patients with chronic obstructive pulmonary disease (COPD). (Guided-imagery relaxation is where people listen to a recording of someone guiding them through a series of relaxing visual images.) There were 26 patients involved in the study: 13 of them had six sessions of guided imagery, while the others just rested during these times. At the end of the study, there was an increase in oxygen saturation in the blood of the group who participated in guided imagery.

A 2006 study conducted at Purdue University's School of Nursing in Indiana found that guided imagery benefited older women with osteoarthritis. Of the 28 women in the study, half used guided imagery for 12 weeks, and half did not. At the end of the period, the subjects who used it had a significantly improved quality of life compared with those who hadn't.

Similarly, a 2008 study at Beaumont Hospital in Royal Oak, Michigan, used guided imagery in the treatment of interstitial cystitis (painful bladder syndrome). Fifteen women used guided imagery for 25 minutes, twice a day, for a total of eight weeks. The imagery focused on healing the bladder, relaxing the pelvic floor muscles, and quieting the nerves involved in the condition. Another 15 women in a control group just rested during these times. The results showed that the women who used guided imagery had significantly less symptoms and pain compared with those who didn't.

A 2008 study published in the *Journal of the Society for Integrative Oncology* found that guided imagery reduced the risk of recurrence of breast cancer. The study involved 34 women who participated in an eight-week imagery program, and it found that they had reduced stress and improved their quality of life. It also revealed that the women's cortisol rhythms, which are indicators of the probability of the recurrence of cancer, were improved.

Guided imagery even affects the healing of wounds. This was shown in a 2007 study at Southeastern Louisiana University's School of Nursing involving 24 patients undergoing surgery to remove their gallbladders. Patients who used guided imagery not only experienced lower levels of anxiety and stress hormones, but they also had much lower levels of surgical-wound erythema, which is the redness around a cut or a sore that's usually associated with infection or inflammation.

Along with its healing properties, guided imagery has also been used in treating fibromyalgia pain. Publishing in the *Journal of Psychiatric Research* in 2002, scientists at the Norwegian University of Science and Technology compared pleasant imagery (which uses enjoyable images to distract the patients from their pain) with attention imagery (patients visualizing the active workings of the internal pain-control systems). Fifty-five women were involved in the study, and their levels of pain were monitored every day for a period of four weeks. The degree of discomfort in the pleasant-imagery group was significantly reduced, while it wasn't in those who focused on attention imagery.

I too have made similar observations. Some people find that actively visualizing their pain reducing is difficult. Thinking like this also causes others anxiety, which only intensifies their irritations. The type of visualization used is important—some of it can be stressful, especially where pain is involved. If you ever find a visualization stressful, stop! With pleasant imagery, stressful daily images are gradually replaced with agreeable ones, thus reducing stress and lessening pain.

Our ability to visualize also affects our success in healing our-selves. In a 2006 study published in *Alternative Therapies in Health and Medicine,* scientists from the Department of Health Promotion and Human Behavior at the Graduate School of Medicine Kyoto University measured levels of stress hormones (salivary cortisol) and mood in 148 people who received two guided-imagery sessions.

First, the study found that salivary-cortisol levels were much less after the first and second sessions. The scientists wrote that, "Unpleasant information, a cause of mental stress, is replaced by a comfortable image, and this replacement affects a person's salivary-cortisol level."

Second, by measuring the vividness of each person's imagery, the study found that those who had the best ability to visualize had the biggest reduction in salivary-cortisol levels.

Don't be concerned, however, if you aren't a good visualizer. The part of your brain involved will expand with practice and your ability will improve. It's just like getting better at a sport—even if at first your ability is low, you're still having a positive effect.

Mental Imagery

Several recent studies have shown that stroke patients and people with spinal-cord damage could regain some movement by imagining themselves moving. Similarly, individuals with Parkin-son's disease could move more easily and accurately.

In a 2007 study conducted by scientists at the Department of Physical Medicine & Rehabilitation at the University of Cincinnati College of Medicine, visualization (scientists call it mental imagery) was used in a six-week study to help stroke patients regain some movement. Thirty-two chronic-stroke patients were involved, half of whom did visualization as well as physical-therapy sessions, while the other half only did the physical therapy. At the end of the experiment, the patients who visualized could move much better than those who didn't. In standard tests, their "arm impair-ment" was much reduced and "arm function" was much better.

When stroke patients imagine moving their arms, their brains are stimulated in the areas that control arm muscles. If these areas had been damaged by the stroke, then the brain maps had begun to regenerate.

Most studies on the use of visualization for recovery from stroke have shown it to be most effective when it's used along with physical exercise. It's important to note that visualization needn't be a substitute for medication or therapy, but something to do *as well.* No matter what drugs or therapies we take for an illness, we have to think *something.* Sometimes we believe that the therapy will work, and other times we don't. Visualization *targets* our thinking in a positive, constructive way.

This ability of the brain to reform itself is important for any kind of injury that requires regeneration to bring back movement. In 2007, publishing in *Experimental Brain Research,* scientists taught visualization to patients who had suffered a spinal-cord injury. Ten tetra- or paraplegic patients were instructed to imagine moving their tongues and feet and gained a better ability to move these parts of them as a result.

Research published in the journal *Neurorehabilitation and Neural Repair* in 2007 showed that visualization could help patients suffering from Parkinson's disease. Twenty-three people were involved in the study; 11 were given one-hour physical-therapy sessions twice a week for 12 weeks, and the rest used visualization as well as having these sessions. At the end of the experiment, tests revealed that the subjects who used visualization were much more improved than those who didn't.

Visualization has also been successfully used to help asthma sufferers breathe more easily. In an Alaskan study involving 70 asthma patients, participants either did visualization where they imagined reduced bronchospasms and inflammations (which was called "biologically targeted imagery") or received education in the management of asthma. After six weeks of two two-hour sessions a week, both groups had substantially improved the symptoms of asthma, but the greater improvement was with the patients who'd visualized.

Most interesting about this study is that, unlike the others, it didn't involve focusing on movements, which most of the recent visualization research has. The peripheral nervous system describes the connection between the brain and the muscles in the body. When we focus on moving muscles, we activate the area of the brain that governs them. The asthma study was concerned with the link between the lungs—an internal organ—and the brain, which are connected by the autonomic nervous system (ANS). Through the ANS, the brain is linked with the eyes, parotid glands, salivary glands, lungs, heart, liver, spleen, stomach, pancreas, intestines, kidneys, bladder, skin, and reproductive organs; and we maintain these systems unconsciously. But as the contents of our conscious minds seep into our unconscious, these thoughts gradually influence the ANS.

Together with placebo experiments, the asthma study shows that it's not only focusing on muscle movements that activates the brain; concentrating on, or even just being aware of, any body part activates the brain, too. All cells in the body are bathed by nerve fibers that connect them to the brain, so when we put our attention upon any part of our body—be it muscle, organ, or cell—we stimulate the area of the brain that's linked with that part and, in so doing, that part itself. Through both the peripheral and autonomic nervous systems, the mind can have an effect upon every part of the body.

The peripheral and autonomic nervous systems are undoubtedly involved in some healing, but it's likely that higher centers of the nervous system also influence some recoveries. These higher centers link our specific thoughts, intentions, mental images, hopes, and wishes with individual processes in the body. Most placebo effects involve the autonomic nervous system, but I'm convinced that many also involve these higher centers. Thus, our beliefs (conscious and unconscious) can influence specific parts and systems of the body in specific ways. What we expect to happen can actually affect what does happen.

In placebo research, people who get better from taking dummy drugs aren't actively visualizing healing. But their attention, either conscious or unconscious, is directed to the parts of their bodies that are injured or in pain, whether these are muscles and linked to the brain through the peripheral nervous system or internal organs that are connected via the autonomic nervous system. When the person receives a placebo, thoughts of wellness, hope, or relief replace sickness sentiments. Different thoughts therefore mentally describe the illness, so the brain and body areas are probably stimulated differently from when the person thought that he or she was sick.

The Power Is Within Us

We know that attitude has a substantial effect upon health. A positive outlook can protect us from illness, especially heart disease, and help us live longer. Placebo studies show that when we take a drug or placebo, what we think really matters. Healing starts with us. The mind has the power to make an inert medicine work or a good medicine seem inert.

We've also learned that our thoughts even change the structure of our brains and that they send chemicals from the brain throughout the body, where they interface with cells and even DNA.

We also now know that when we focus on a part of our body, the area of the brain that governs it gets activated along with it. Through this connection, when we visualize healing, healing occurs.

Before we move on to instructions for the best ways to visualize, the next chapter discusses stress and its role in disease. It's important with any illness to work on reducing anxiety in our lives, because it has a negative impact upon almost every condition.

෴෴෴

CHAPTER 7

TO STRESS OR NOT TO STRESS

*"Do not dwell in the past, do not dream of the future,
concentrate the mind on the present moment."*
— Buddha

I feel that it's very important to devote an entire chapter of this book to stress because it has such a negative impact on the body and has been linked with a large number of conditions. For example, long-term stress has been connected with anxiety, depression, sleeping problems, hypertension, heart disease, stroke, cancer, ulcers, flu, rheumatoid arthritis, obesity, and even a quickening of the aging process. It also depresses the immune system, and as a result, lowers our ability to fight infection. Indeed, that was the definitive conclusion of a 2004 meta-analysis of 293 scientific studies examining the links between stress and the immune system. Our lives will obviously be healthier if we can reduce stress, and this will even help us recover faster from illness and disease.

A 2003 study conducted by scientists at the University of Auckland investigated how stress affected the rate of healing in 36 patients who had undergone operations. The scientists took samples of wound fluid from the subjects after the operation and found that the chemical composition of each person's was different depending on whether he or she was feeling calm or stressed beforehand. The fluid in the more-anxious patients contained fewer substances necessary for healing.

Stress even affects how well medicines work for us. Scientists at the UCLA AIDS Institute, publishing in *Proceedings of the National Academy of Sciences* in 2001, reported that stress not only enabled HIV to spread faster in infected persons, but that it prevented anti-retroviral drugs from doing their job properly.

The scientists measured the viral load and CD4 cell count of 13 HIV-positive men who'd never previously taken combination antiretroviral drugs. They also measured their blood pressure, skin moisture, and heart rates at rest. The patients were then given a powerful regimen of antiretroviral drugs. Over the next 3 to 11 months, their viral loads and CD4 cell counts were measured and compared with the numbers taken before they took the drugs. The results were dramatic: the higher the patient's stress level, the less he responded to the antiretroviral drugs. The average reduction in viral load was more than 40 times for men with low stress, but less than 10 times for men with high stress. This means that the drugs worked four times better for the patients who were calm compared to those who were most stressed. The authors concluded: "Our findings suggest that the nervous system has a direct effect on viral replication."

In another paper, published in 2003 in *Biological Psychiatry,* the same scientists described the results of an 18-month study involving 54 HIV-positive men. They measured each person's "stress personality"—the way he reacted to stressful events—and found that: "Shy people with high stress responses possess higher viral loads." This study showed that the antiretroviral drugs were quite ineffective, and the virus replicated between 10 and 100 times faster in the shy men with high stress than it did in the other patients.

Faced with stressful situations, some individuals tell others how they feel, express their emotions, and explain the challenges they're facing. Doing this really helps them deal with things because it means that they have someone to talk to, and being honest acts as a release valve for their emotions. A problem shared is a problem halved, as they say. Earlier, we learned that talking a problem through can affect the structure of the brain, but many individuals suppress how they feel and don't tell anyone. Either they're afraid that people will think that they're not good enough, or they're worried about the reactions and judgments they might receive.

Much research has found a link between suppressed negative emotion and disease. In my first book, *It's the Thought That Counts,* I referred to several studies showing a link with cancer. One found that tumors were thickest in people with a nonverbal type C personality. This type of person was described as being "cooperative, unassertive, and suppressing negative emotion." This is very similar to the HIV studies above explaining that shy people with high stress responses had higher viral loads, since shyness is often associated with not being able to express oneself. This research tells us that we need to share our problems with other people. Storing our worries and emotional pain does us no good, and will eventually have destructive effects upon our health.

The growth of suppressed negative emotion is like a balloon inflating in the psyche. As it gets bigger, so do the symptoms of disease expressing themselves in the body. We need to find a release valve where we regularly let out a little of the air to relieve pressure.

Let It Out

Some studies have shown that simply writing down how you feel can release the air from the balloon:

— In the 1980s, University of Texas psychologist James Pennebaker had half of the students in one of his classes write for 15 minutes on four consecutive days about their deepest thoughts and feelings regarding traumatic experiences in their lives. The other half was asked to simply jot down everyday things. At the end of the year, the two groups were compared, and it was found that those who had written about their life experiences were the healthier of the two groups.

— In a similar study, published in 1995 in the *Journal of Consulting and Clinical Psychology,* medical students either wrote for four days about traumatic events that they'd experienced or everyday things, and then they received a vaccination for hepatitis B on the fifth day. When blood samples were taken after four and six months, the group who had written on more emotional topics had much higher antibody levels against hepatitis B than the one who just wrote about common occurrences.

— A 2004 study reported in *Psychosomatic Medicine* showed that writing about emotional topics even improved the health of HIV patients. The study involved 37 patients, around half of whom wrote for 30 minutes per day for four consecutive days. Those who wrote about their emotional experiences had significantly lower viral loads and higher CD4 cell counts.

— In a 2007 paper published in the journal *Brain, Behavior, and Immunity,* scientists from Ohio State University showed that emotional-support sessions designed to reduce stress improved the health of cancer patients. The experiment involved 227 breast-cancer patients, and approximately half of them took part. At the end of the one-year study, the women who went through the sessions were healthier than those who hadn't, according to tests on their heart, liver, kidneys, immune system, and even emotional health.

Just as in the previous studies mentioned in this chapter, the ones above also show that talking about our worries and stresses improves our health. And when we do share how we feel with others, it gives them the opportunity to help, which is a deep desire that we as a species crave—that is, the need to be needed. So not only are we doing ourselves a favor by expressing how we feel, but we're helping the human race, too.

How to Relax

As well as talking with people, a well-known antidote to stress is meditation. With regular practice, this technique can have a dramatic impact upon stress levels. If done consistently, it calms the mind and makes it much easier to face life's challenges.

That was one of the first things that I noticed when I first learned meditation: the things that bothered me at the time and caused me stress no longer had the same impact. Since most methods focus on breathing, through meditation practice I was able to induce a state of relaxation in difficult situations just by taking conscious breaths, which means breathing *on purpose*. So when I was challenged in a way that might have previously caused me stress, I would simply breathe, giving the act my full attention. Doing this made me feel differently about the situation I was in; I no longer felt the need to react. Instead, I chose what I would say and do, and I had much more of a sense that I was in control.

What I've just described was my personal experience, but it's one that's shared by millions of people who meditate daily. If you want to meditate and don't know how, then I'd suggest that you sign up for a good class, read a book on it, or just sit for ten minutes and pay attention to your breathing. Listen to how it sounds and sense the feeling as the air goes through your nostrils. This is a very simple technique, but it's very effective.

Such is the recognized power of meditation that it's now frequently used in clinical practice to treat a variety of illnesses and diseases where stress is an aggravating factor. Many studies of meditation involve mindfulness-based stress reduction (MBSR). It's based upon the Buddhist technique of sitting quietly and being mindful of your breathing and any thoughts that arise, and also usually involves gentle yoga sessions. When thoughts emerge, just let them dissolve.

A 2007 study looked at the effects of an MBSR program on the health of early-stage breast- and prostate-cancer patients. It involved 49 participants with breast cancer and ten with prostate cancer. Scientists measured their mood, symptoms of stress, cortisol (stress hormone) levels, immune-cell counts, blood pressure, and heart rates before the study, after 6 months, and again after 12 months. They found a large improvement in stress symptoms, a reduction in blood pressure, a decrease in cortisol levels, and an increase in immune-cell counts.

A 2007 study conducted at the Department of Emergency Medicine at Thomas Jefferson University showed that MBSR could be used to control glucose levels in type 2 diabetes mellitus patients.

After practicing MBSR, patients had lower glycosylated hemoglobin (HbA1c) levels (0.48 percent lower on average); lower blood pressure; and less anxiety, depression, and psychological distress than those who didn't use it.

Meditation has even been evaluated on healthy people. A 2007 study published by scientists at Duke University Medical Center involved 200 healthy adults who learned a simple mantra-based meditation technique over four small one-hour group sessions and then practiced it during the study for 15 to 20 minutes twice a day. The study showed that there were significant improvements in mood as well as reduced stress and anxiety. The researchers also found that more frequent practice produced better outcomes; more meditation was better than less or none at all.

A powerful 2008 Harvard experiment has shown that meditation affects us at the genetic level and clarifies why it has such a profound impact on health. Twenty volunteers were trained in various relaxation-response techniques for eight weeks (the relaxation response is the physiological response to techniques such as meditation, yoga, repetitive prayer, tai chi, qigong, breathing exercises, and guided imagery). After only eight weeks, genetic analysis of the volunteers' blood found that 1,561 genes were expressed differently (switched on or off) after the training: specifically, 874 genes were upregulated ("dimmer switch" turned up) and 687 were downregulated (dimmer switch turned down). More experienced practitioners of the techniques were found to have 2,209 genes affected.

Many of the altered genes were involved in the body's response to oxidative stress, which is stress that can result from mental and emotional pressures and has a negative effect in many diseases. Therefore, this research means that relaxation techniques can have a positive effect on many medical conditions.

It's also clear that meditation benefits us after only a small amount of practice. The above studies show the health benefits even at the genetic level, but we notice almost immediate improvements to our state of mind. I was invited by the Brahma Kumaris World Spiritual University on a one-week meditation retreat in the mountains of Rajasthan in India in 2002. Days typically involved a 45-minute meditation at around 6 A.M., followed by a half-hour silent walk. After breakfast, the delegates attended a few classes, and some free time in the afternoon was followed by another 45-minute meditation, and yet another in the evening after dinner. When I returned home, I realized that my mind had never been so still. I couldn't help noticing that there was an absence of thoughts buzzing around in my head. It was a strange sensation at the time—feeling just emptiness in my mind—although it was quite welcomed. I felt great physically, mentally, emotionally, and spiritually; and I was motivated to make some lifestyle changes that easily became permanent. And this highly peaceful mind stayed with me for about a month before I gradually drifted back into my daily thoughts, but I've never rescinded the lifestyle changes that I made.

Stress can creep up on us. I've worked in a corporate environment where I *had* to get certain things done. But did I really "have" to? Would the world have ended if I hadn't? Sometimes we need to stop our busyness and ask ourselves what's more important, a job or our health.

It's often only when we have a health scare caused by stress that we sit up, take notice, and suddenly realize that it's our choice how we handle situations. Many people have reevaluated their priorities in life after suffering a heart attack or stroke, and they've emerged with a completely different attitude: *Nothing is more important than my health.*

Handling stress is something that can be learned. The skill lies in making a shift in what we think is important. And as we've seen in this chapter, sharing our worries with people and meditation, along with having a positive attitude, really helps.

We should also recognize that it's not so much the events of our lives that cause stress, but our attitudes about them. Recognizing that the stress comes from our own perceptions of situations gives us the ability to control things. Sometimes stuff happens, but how it affects us is up to us.

Just as we have the ability to heal ourselves, we also have the power to see things differently in life, to shift our priorities. When we do, we reduce stress; visualization always works best when we have less stress. And that's when we can really begin to heal—provided we know how to visualize and how to apply it to specific conditions.

This is what the next chapter will show us.

৩৩৩৩

CHAPTER 8

HOW TO VISUALIZE

"Imagination is everything. It is the
preview of life's coming attractions."
— **Albert Einstein**

As we've learned so far, the mind constantly affects the body. Visualization is a potent way to influence this, because it offers additional direction and purpose.

This chapter contains guidance for using visualization effectively so that you'll be able to construct one for any disease or condition. In Chapter 6, I described the results of some research that used visualization, but those studies had been conducted for muscular movements (that is, those involving stroke, spinal-cord injury, and Parkinson's disease). These studies involve the peripheral nervous system, but many recoveries due to the placebo effect involve the autonomic nervous system and its higher centers. They suggest that placing your attention upon any part of your body stimulates it in a specific way that's related to what you'd expect or wish to happen, as well as activating the part of the brain that controls it.

What Happens When You Visualize

The key to using visualization for healing is to imagine the process unfolding inside the body. Having your attention focused upon the diseased area activates the corresponding part of the brain that governs it. I believe that, in response to what you imagine, brain maps change, chemicals are released throughout the body, genes are switched on and off, and stem cells receive instructions on which type of cells to become.

A technique that has helped me visualize more effectively is imagining myself inside my body as a tiny person—I call it a "Mini-Me" (this term was coined by my friend June, along with some women who attended one of my workshops). As a Mini-Me (or a Mini-You), you play a role in the healing process. For instance, if you had a cut, you could imagine yourself as a Mini-You pulling the two sides of the cut together. You could use imaginary ropes or magic thread and pull them together so perfectly that no trace would remain.

While you're doing this, cells around the cut would be getting stimulated, and the brain area that governs it would also be spurred. The more your attention was focused there, the more the brain map for that area would change—because, as we learned from the study that involved individuals who imagined playing a key sequence on the piano and actually increased their brain maps for playing it, the brain doesn't seem to know the difference between what's real or imaginary. Neurotransmitters and neuropeptides would bathe this area of the brain, genes would be switched on and off, and then neuropeptides would be released into the bloodstream.

Genes throughout the body, and specifically at the site of the cut, would be switched on or off as well. In particular, growth-hormone genes would be triggered that would accelerate the healing process. Genes in stem cells would also be activated so that the stem cells can grow into new skin cells. Stress genes would also be turned down, assuming that you feel no stress or tension when you visualize (I will suggest how to easily accomplish this later in the chapter).

On account of your visualization, healing would speed up; and because you imagined the wound closing so perfectly, it's likely that it would heal much more cleanly than if you hadn't. It's also probable that when you fear that a cut will leave a scar, you influence the healing process to tilt it toward what you're imagining.

The exact movement of chemicals and genes that I've just described hasn't been thoroughly investigated in science yet, nor has it been hypothesized in a scientific paper (to the best of my knowledge) . . . but I believe that's just a matter of time. People have been achieving amazing results using visualization for centuries. It's only in the past ten years or so that science has been moving in the direction of exploring the power of the mind-body connection, but it has always existed. Science is now only just scratching the surface in its exploration of why some astounding miracles of healing take place.

In true science fashion, I may be wrong. But that doesn't matter so much. What's most important is that somehow healing is affected by our minds. Visualization is a way to use our heads in a highly positive way and give us a sense of control in our lives. Too often, people feel powerless when they're diagnosed with an illness. Maybe just the feeling of regaining some power and influence by using their minds in such a direct way is all that's needed. Quite possibly, this is why the healings described in the stories later in this book were even possible.

Ultimately the how is not so important—which chemicals go where, which genes go on and off, and so on. Having some knowledge of it helps us build our faith, and that's mostly why I've described it. But perhaps, just the feeling of hope that grows as we visualize on a daily basis moves mountains, in the same way as it plays a huge role in the placebo effect.

The point of much of this book is to give people who want to use their minds something to focus upon when they are diseased or sick. This chapter is about how best to visualize.

Healing Scenes

I call the visualization I just described (imagining myself as a Mini-Me) a "healing scene." It's just like a movie scene, but I'm the main character participating in the healing process. This helps me feel a sense of power over any disease or condition.

When I described healing a cut, I imagined myself actively pulling the two sides of it together. For this, I had some anatomical knowledge of a cut: it has two sides that come together as it heals. For more serious conditions, having some basic information can help. Knowing that a tumor is a lump, for instance, will give you something to build a healing scene around. You could picture it as a block of ice and see it melting until it dissolves to nothing; or you could let it occur gradually in your mind, over several days or weeks, so that it gets smaller every time you visualize. If you're taking medication or receiving radiation treatment, then imagine the chemotherapy agents or radiation as little bullets of heat that are dissolving the tumor.

The key is that your attention is focused upon the area, therefore activating that area and the part of the brain that governs it. Chemical changes consequently take place in the brain, throughout the body, and at the site on which your mind is focused.

Notice that the degree of anatomical knowledge required is minimal. If you do have ample proficiency on the topic, then use it, but it really doesn't give anyone an advantage over others. My understanding is that it seems to mostly depend upon what you believe (just like a placebo). If you know, through science, that a particular thing has to occur for healing, then you can imagine that if you like. It probably doesn't make any difference if you're unaware of the physical process taking place, so it's fitting that everyone can use this method for healing, not just highly educated people.

For example, imagining a tumor melting to nothing would probably have the same effect as picturing growth genes in it switching off and immune-system cells recognizing the tumor cells and ingesting them. Construct your scene with elements that fit your personal knowledge and understanding.

Conversely, sometimes having knowledge and not using it could have a negative effect. In and of itself, it does not; however, if you believe that you *should* be imagining something and don't, then it's your own belief that affects the healing. It would be just like not taking all your placebos, as I described in Chapter 3.

I've noticed that, in some cases, simply using symbolic images is enough. For instance, getting rid of the cold or flu faster than normal by imagining bubbles in a large cavern uses the bubbles as symbols of the illness. Each time Mini-Me bursts a bubble, it symbolizes the illness weakening. Eventually, when I burst all of the bubbles in the cavern, this suggests that the illness has gone.

Perhaps this type of visualization—a symbolic visualization—would work for anything. Imagining popping bubbles of cancer—while even mentally saying, "Cancer cancel!" for extra power—may work miracles. Once again, the feeling of power over the cancer instead of feeling power*less* is the important thing. Or maybe your unconscious mind, which has internal knowledge of the disease, activates the autonomic nervous system appropriately so that cancerous systems in the body are affected. Ultimately, the how isn't too important; the fact that it works is all that matters.

Oftentimes when we're ill, we focus upon the disease or how sick we are. By using visualization, we feel a sense of power or hope and engage ourselves in the mental act of doing something about it. One of the great things about using visualization is that the mind is focused on a positive outcome.

And while thoughts are engrossed in the scene, we aren't giving any attention to suffering or the idea that we won't get better. And, just for a while, we believe in what we're seeing. I mean, we *can* see the disease disappearing, can't we? Sometimes just a few moments of faith a day, or replacing hopelessness with hope, is all we need.

Doesn't the Bible say that if we have faith as a mustard seed, we can move mountains?

How to Construct a Scene

The most important thing is to decide what you want. This means that you can then figure out how to get to this point from where you are now. For instance, resolving that having no cancer is what you want means that you can construct a scene for getting it to leave your body.

This may seem like an obvious thing, but quite frequently we sell ourselves short by shooting for a little instead of going for what we really want. "It would be kind of nice to be rid of this pain" is different from ridding yourself of the condition that's causing it. If you want to do away with something, then let that be your goal.

In one of the previous examples in this chapter, we imagined a tumor being made of ice that we melted until it was gone. If we had a lung or kidney infection, our goal would be to be remove it. As Mini-Mes, we might imagine the infection as ground black pepper scattered over the organ. Then we could use an imaginary vacuum cleaner and suck it all up, seeing the lung or kidney as cleaned and restored to normal.

As I've pointed out, having no anatomical knowledge doesn't matter, but having some can give you a sense of power. It isn't too difficult these days to find information. Public libraries contain books that have pictures of what body parts look like, and you can get information on any disease or condition on the Internet. And I'm sure that your doctor would be happy to discuss your condition in detail with you, and might be quite interested to know that you're taking a positive mental approach to it. If you prefer, though, using a scene that symbolizes healing is great, too. In Appendix I, I shall describe Quantum Field Healing in detail, which is a powerful symbolic visualization.

Once you've decided what images you want to use, go ahead and create a story that involves Mini-Me helping you to get from illness to health. If you have an arthritic joint, for instance, you might imagine two bones painfully rubbing together at first without any fluid separating them, with your goal being a joint that's lubricated with fluid so the bones don't rub together. For your scene, you could imagine Mini-Me walking up to the joint and squeezing lots of lubricating fluid into it. You might then imagine it—now lubricated—moving freely and easily.

You could, of course, imagine the scene unfolding in a different way. At a workshop that I ran, my friend Kevin suggested imaginary diggers (machines used in construction), which had special tools to cut away any excess bone that was rubbing together, driving up to the joint. He pictured the diggers erecting girders to keep the space there so that the bones couldn't rub together again. Then another digger would drive up with a bucketful of lubricating fluid (maybe you could be driving it) and pour it into the gap. The girders were then removed, and the two bones sat comfortably upon the fluid.

Please note that there's no single correct visualization; there's just what works for you. If you're imagining healing a part of the body by repairing damaged cells, you can picture the cells in any way you want. Some people might think of healthy cells as clear blobs with little dots at the center, while others might see them as pink circular jelly balls, rubbery bricks on a wall, or uncooked eggs after they've been cracked in a pan. One person might see a damaged cell of an organ looking shriveled up and dark like a raisin or prune. In their scene, they might imagine cleaning it with a cloth or brush and watching it restored to its healthy shape, color, and texture. Then they move on to the next cell and do the same again until they're all restored to full health.

Another person might imagine nursing the little prune back to full health by taking care of it and giving it magic medicine that would help its strength and color return. At the unconscious level, giving cells magic medicine will probably symbolize their getting all the right nutrients that they need to return to health. This will most likely stimulate the correct brain areas in such a way that they'll indeed receive proper nourishment.

To ensure that your scenes are free of stress, and you have less fear of your condition, it's good to occasionally add some fun to your scene. For instance, in the first arthritis scene that I just described, when you squeeze the lubricating oil out of the can, imagine the squeaking sound as it squirts—you can even exaggerate the noise if you want. Or see all of the individual atoms of oil as little balls with smiley faces, shouting, "Wheeeeee!" as they slide out of the oilcan funnel as if they're having a great time on a slide. Adding bits of humor or lightheartedness to your scenes will often bring a smile to your face.

Because this is *your* imagination, you can imagine anything you want. What's to stop you from using a magic wand to transform one thing into another? To your unconscious mind, all that has occurred is that you've gone from diseased to healed; how you get there in your scene is completely up to you. It might help you to believe that the lubricating fluid is everlasting so that it never runs out and the joint never becomes arthritic again.

Another thing you can do to increase your sense of power is to make the scene feel more real. This can help if you think that you're not good at visualizing. To do this, just engage more of your senses. Notice what your surroundings look like and how the ground and things you hold in your hands feel. For example, if you're cleaning cells, notice how the cloth and fluid feel on your hands. Be aware of the sensation as you move your arms in a rubbing motion. Notice what happens when you squeeze the can of lubricating fluid or when you vacuum up pepper (infection) from an organ. Feel the suction and hear the sound of the vacuum.

Once you're happy with your scene, you can use it as often as you want. You can also evolve it in time or change it altogether if you decide that you can improve it. Each time you elaborate your technique, you make it better for you. Sometimes you may even realize that your condition has improved and that you naturally need to adapt your scene.

How Often Should I Visualize?

Visualize regularly. A tiny hammer can break a huge boulder over time if it continually hits it. Similarly, if you want to be an Olympic champion at a sport, going to the gym just once won't get you there, but going every day might. Remember the earlier report of improving finger strength through visualization? The same level of mental and physical work was required.

If your doctor prescribes some medicine for you, the chances are that the bottle or pack will tell you to take it three times a day. Use the same instructions, then, for visualization. Take your "mind medicine" three times a day. Visualize in the morning, in the afternoon, and at night . . . or more if you wish. I'm convinced that doing it repeatedly has the same effect as conditioning in the placebo effect, which I described in Chapter 2. But, unlike with conditioning, we can powerfully alter systems in the body on purpose. So listen to your own; it will tell you how often you need to visualize.

The length of each visualization session can vary, too. Ten minutes for each one can be a good length of time to thoroughly work through your scene, and this equates to 30 minutes per day. Of course, you can go for longer if you wish. Sometimes you'll get totally absorbed in your visualizations, but you can do them for shorter periods, too. If you do just a couple of minutes at a time, then try a couple of additional sessions. If you find it tiring work on account of your condition, don't stress yourself. Start with just once a day for around a minute. Then build up to two sessions of one minute a day, and gradually work up from there to as much as you're able to do. Many people get good results by doing a sped-up visualization for two to five seconds. They do it every time the condition pops into their minds, which might be as much as 10 to 40 times a day. This can be just as effective as doing three longer sessions.

Some Extra Hints and Tips

Here are some hints and tips that you might also find useful. You don't need to use all of them; they're simply suggestions that can help if you're having any difficulties.

— *Draw or paint your images.* If you have difficulty with visualization, try to draw or paint your scene. Or if you have advanced computer skills and the time, create an animated healing scene. While doing this, you'll still activate the desired area of your body (as well as the part of the brain that governs it) as if you were visualizing. If you aren't so good at art, then trace some images from a medical book or the Internet and make up your scene that way. Then look at your creation at least three times a day while imagining or telling yourself that it's happening in your body.

— *Have patience.* Don't get anxious if you aren't healed in a day or two. Sometimes it can take days, weeks, or months. Some illnesses even take a year or more to heal, depending upon how much reconstruction is needed and whether or not you really believe that it's possible. Be patient with the process—don't lose heart and think that it's not working just because you're not 100 percent healed within an hour of visualizing.

— *Improve your lifestyle.* Try to make some positive changes that benefit your recovery. Examine your diet, habits, and lifestyle. Do you eat a balanced, nutritious diet? Do you drink lots of alcohol, take drugs, or smoke? What kind of attitude do you have? Are you able to handle some exercise? Be honest with yourself.

It's important that you ask your doctor about exercise and try to work in his or her recommendations. Sometimes a few changes can have dramatic results.

— *Ask your body what it needs.* Although some people may find this silly, you can ask your cells, organs, or body what they need. First, get into a relaxed state. By doing so, you'll be conversing with your unconscious mind—just as a hypnotherapist would—and open to receiving more information on the types of changes you may want to make in your life. It might feel like you're having an imaginary conversation, but if you receive any wisdom that makes a lot of sense, trust it.

A diseased organ might tell you, for instance, that it needs the nutrients from a particular food or even that you should cut out a certain food from your diet because it contains substances that are harming your particular biology. You might learn that you should give up smoking, doing drugs, or drinking alcohol.

If you feel your cells telling you to ask your brain to send certain substances, go ahead and ask it to produce them and send them to where they need to go. Or you may get information on the type of visualization that you need to do. Perhaps there's a specific scene that you need to play out.

— *Do a victory dance.* This is something that I personally do in visualizations, since it brings a sense of lightheartedness into what can sometimes be a stressful time. It's just a silly dance that celebrates the success that a scene is showing—I saw it being done in an episode of the hospital sitcom *Scrubs,* as one of the lead characters celebrated a victory, and it made me laugh.

Now, for instance, if I'm vacuuming up some bacteria and notice that I've cleaned up quite a lot, I'll see myself break out into a victory dance in the scene as a celebration of my success. Or I might physically break into my victory dance, and then go back into my scene where I left off (you might find it less embarrassing to do this if no one is around to see you), or I wait and do my dance at the end.

You can do your dance in the bathroom, bedroom, or wherever you wish. I often visualize when I'm out walking. I do much of my writing in coffee shops in Windsor in the U.K., where I live. The walk there from my house takes me around 25 minutes. Along with visualizing healing, I also picture things that I want to happen in my life. But whatever the nature of my visualization, I almost always do a victory dance at the end.

Of course, you might want to be a little discreet with your dance if you're walking along the side of a busy road. I usually do a little dance with my fingers at these times; however, around halfway into my journey I have to walk through an underpass that goes underneath a road. It's almost 100 feet long, so I do my dance as I go through it. There usually isn't anyone around at 6:50 A.M. when I'm passing through, so I can really break out the moves and make myself smile.

One time I'd broken into a few moves that I had seen in the film *Saturday Night Fever* and was totally absorbed in them when I got to the end of the underpass. Suddenly, I looked up to see a line of construction workers staring at me. It was close to Christmas, and they must have been working all night to get a block of apartments finished, and they'd stopped eating breakfast to check out my performance.

This is where I made one of those regrettable split-second decisions. As my right hand was pointing in the air, as in John Travolta's famous dance pose, I drew my hand to my ear and said, "Hello!" as if I was on the phone. They must have thought I was insane. And then, as "luck" would have it, my phone actually did ring as I passed them. I just kept my head down and walked as fast as I could until they couldn't see me anymore. The experience did make me smile, though . . . eventually.

Some of the real power of a victory dance lies in the fact that you can't feel anxiety, stress, worry, or frustration at the same time as you experience humor—it's one or the other. The fun of your dance replaces the worry of a life circumstance. In time, whenever you think of the situation, instead of worrying, you find yourself smiling because you've started to associate the condition with the dance, which is a great way to reduce stress!

Other Ways that Visualization Works

Visualization works on more levels than just having direct biological effects. In addition to giving your body instructions for what you want it to do, the scenes drip into your unconscious mind.

When a thought enters your unconscious mind, it influences how you behave. For example, if the color red were dripped into your unconscious without your noticing and you were later shown some colors and asked to choose one, you'd probably choose red without knowing why. Similarly, if you were to imagine the color red several times a day, you'd start to notice more red things than you normally would. It might *seem* that you accidentally—and without even realizing what you were doing—walked a different path from normal or drove a different route that took you to a place where there was much more red.

So, when we visualize healing, we often change our behaviors without even realizing it. We start to behave in a way that's more conducive to wellness than how we'd normally behave. We may find ourselves in the company of different people who end up sharing knowledge or information that's just what we need to hear. We'll also frequently develop a craving for a particular food, which probably contains some nutrients that our bodies require for healing. Sometimes we'll find ourselves changing the products that we use around the home, because perhaps one of them has an allergen that was having a negative effect upon us.

We might even realize that life circumstances have changed without our having to do anything. It isn't uncommon for us to be directed down a different path at just the right time. While this could be upsetting in the moment, it will probably turn out to be the exact tonic that we needed for our health.

I've noticed that when people recover from illnesses, they mostly put it down to a particular medicine, a change in their diet, or other personal circumstances. Skeptics use this argument to say that visualization doesn't do anything: they point out that it was obviously any of these more socially acceptable factors that led to healing. And, of course, this *is* often true. But what's usually missed is that it was the person's desire to get well again that *inspired* the necessary changes.

Taking medication, changing our diet and lifestyle, *and* having the desire to recover work seamlessly together. It's rarely just one or the other, but a combination that produces the results. At the end of the day, we'll get well. Is it really that important how we get there?

That's why I'd never suggest that you give up your medication. Take your prescribed drugs *and* visualize; at the same time, eat a more nutritious diet, improve your attitude, and adopt a healthier lifestyle.

In the next chapter, we'll move on to another influential tool that aids our minds in healing our bodies.

಼಼಼಼

CHAPTER 9

THE POWER OF AFFIRMATIONS

*"One comes to believe whatever one repeats to oneself
sufficiently often, whether the statement be true or false."*
— **Robert Collier**

The practice of saying affirmations is extremely powerful and can either be used independently of visualization or along with it. Affirmations are statements of fact—or what you intend to be fact—that you make over and over again.

There are three things to remember about affirmations:

1. Repetition
2. Repetition
3. Repetition

When we say something repeatedly, we create neural connections in our brains. The more we say it, the more connections we create, and the stronger they become. As we've learned, we can form the same connections when we're imagining something as when we're actually doing it. Evidence from mirror-neuron research suggests that it's the same for speech. Talking about our hands, for instance, activates the hand area of the brain. Therefore, repeating a statement about something being true will create neural connections as though we were experiencing it as true and making a factual statement.

Let's say that you were holding a sandwich, for instance, feeling and looking at it. Neurons would fire in your brain in the areas that processed the sensory data from your fingers, as well as your thoughts and attitudes about what you're eating. If you didn't have a sandwich in your hands but just imagined what it looked like and how it felt on your skin, then the same neurons would fire in your brain with the same intensity as when you were actually holding it. And in both circumstances, if you affirmed: *I love sandwiches,* your brain would fire in the same areas, regardless of whether you were holding one or not.

Many people, if they've been sick for a long time, affirm their condition with assertions such as: "This is terrible," "I will never get better," or "I feel tired." While these statements might be accurate reflections about how they feel, they also back up the condition on a biological level as neurons are stimulated in the appropriate areas of the brain, chemicals are released, and genes are switched on and off. So the cells linked with the disease are encouraged to produce proteins and other substances that sustain the diseased state.

Of course, it can be difficult to say or even think something different from how you feel, and when you're suffering, the last thing you need is someone badgering you to be more positive. A friend of mine who was having some challenges in her life once made me laugh when she said, "If one more person tells me to think positively, I'm going to punch them." But when you're ready—and you may not be in that space right now due to the overwhelming experience of an illness—then a change of attitude will help.

If you change your attitude and language and affirm, over and over again on a regular basis: *I am recovering, I am getting better, Every day in every way I am getting better and better,* or even *I am determined to recover fully,* then appropriate neural connections will form, and neuropeptides will be released that interface with cells and DNA to bring about healing. The awareness of the illness and which systems of the body are affected ensures that the right neurons are activated to target the right systems of the body. The relief of "knowing" that you're recovering will also assure that stress hormones reduce in quantity, which speeds up healing as well.

Play-By-Play Commentary

You can use affirmations in your healing visualizations, and sometimes it can be helpful to give a verbal commentary on what's happening. For example, during a healing visualization where you sucked up bacteria using an imaginary vacuum cleaner, you might affirm: *All of the harmful bacteria are disappearing from my body.* Since this statement really points out what's going on, the appropriate neurons will fire in your brain as if the bacteria were indeed disappearing . . . which, of course, they are.

Affirmations also draw extra attention to what you're visualizing, helping you focus upon that part of your body by stimulating brain cells and instigating the healing process. They can be useful if your scene isn't very clear in your mind.

As another example, while firing a green laser to burn off cancer cells, you could be affirming: *The cancer cells are being burned off the bone and leaving it intact.* Or let's say that you were visualizing yourself pouring some magical lubricating fluid into an arthritic joint. As you pick up the container of fluid and the rubber tube that you're going to use to pour it into the joint, you could affirm: *This fluid is a magical, 100 percent efficient, everlasting lubricating fluid.* And as you pour the fluid into the joint, point out that: *The fluid is seeping into the joint. The joint is looking totally free now.* Then, as you imagine the joint moving, note that: *The joint is moving freely and easily now.* Basically, you commentate your way through bits of your healing scene. You can add as much or as little narration as you wish, or none at all.

Talking yourself through the visualization is useful if you really can't imagine the situation clearly otherwise, as neurons in your brain will still be excited regardless of whether or not you see the scene. If you can't picture the inside of an artery, for instance, just the awareness of the words *inside an artery* will excite neurons in the brain as if you were actually looking inside one.

How Often Should I Do Affirmations?

Aside from commentary, different amounts of affirmations work for different people, but I've found that the more times I affirm something and the more gusto I say it with, the faster the changes happen. Repeating something ten times a day in the morning and another ten times at night is a good place to start, or you could just do an affirmation whenever the thought arises in your mind. For instance, an affirmation of *I am in recovery* might be something that you say whenever you feel like it, which could turn out to be 20 to 30 times a day.

You don't have to structure your times for affirmations, but it helps to do so. Ten times in the morning and ten at night would be structured. And you would do this for as long as you needed to, until whatever you wanted to change had done so.

You can, of course, affirm more than this if you wish. You might be so determined that you saturate your mind with 50 or more affirmative statements a day. A very personal example of this happened in 1994 when I went to see a doctor because I found a lump on one of my testicles. I was very afraid, especially when he arranged for me to see a consultant in a few days' time. I remember getting into my car and crying, but then I got angry that I'd allowed an aspect of my life to reflect what I didn't want. I committed to make some serious changes after I got through this, which I became totally and absolutely determined to do.

Over the next few days, I affirmed: *It is gone!* with conviction several hundred times. I also made a sweeping motion with my hand as if I were chopping, which was symbolic of actually cutting the lump away. No matter what else I happened to be doing at the time, if any uncertainty that it hadn't left my body crept into my mind, I stopped and did my affirmation and hand movement several times until the doubt was gone.

I was in the second year of my doctorate at the time and was working for the pharmaceutical company that was funding my studies. I recall that I ruined quite a few delicate experiments in those few days because a doubt always seemed to enter my mind just as I was at an important stage, and I was using some rather expensive chemical ingredients. But, to me, my health took precedence over them. It was actually a powerful symbol of what was more important—my work or my health.

When the consultant examined me a few days later, the lump was indeed gone. It might have been a tumor, and it might not have been. Personally, I didn't care. All I was concerned with was that it was gone.

Most of the times that I said my affirmation, I did so with strong belief and really meant it. When I was in a place where I couldn't say it out loud, I would say it firmly and directly in my mind. If I was at home, I'd walk around my room saying it out loud with conviction.

How to Create an Affirmation

So how do you work out what to say for yourself? Affirmations are statements of "fact"—what you intend to be a fact—so write them as positive statements.

Here's a list of some positive statements about healing:

- *I am in recovery.*
- *I am getting better and better.*
- *I am feeling better.*
- *I am improving.*
- *The cancer cells are burning off.*
- *The tumor is dissolving/melting.*
- *It is gone.*
- *I can move freely and easily now.*
- *My blood pressure is returning to normal.*
- *My heart is getting healthier every day.*
- *My breathing is getting easier.*

Also, be sure to make them really positive and create them with no doubt. For instance:

- *I am recovering fast* is more positive than
  My cold is going away.

- *The tumor is dissolving* is more positive than
  My cancer is becoming less severe.

- *I am in recovery* is more positive than *I am not
  feeling as bad anymore.*

Remember, affirmations can be useful together with, or inde-pendent of, visualization. We can see these strategies at work in the next part of the book, which is a collection of true stories from people describing their healing journeys and the roles that their minds played in them.

ക്കെക്കെ

PART II

TRUE STORIES

INTRODUCTION

The following section contains some true stories from people around the world who have used visualization as at least part (if not all) of their journey to recovery from illness. As you will see, many used the technique alongside other modes of treatment. They used it not so much *instead of* but *as well as* their medication or therapies.

In all of the stories that I've collected, I've noticed a striking similarity among them. These are accounts from people who have never met each other, yet each has used a comparable strategy to heal themselves. Each person has created a healing scene—as I called it in Chapter 8—involving some form of imagined removal of unhealthy cells or diseases from the body.

There aren't many books telling us how to do this type of thing, and I've since come to believe that many of us seem to intuitively know what to do. I've found this to be true in my own personal life when I've had to create healing scenes for myself. I may not have been taught it, but I just seemed to know what was necessary to get well.

None of the stories has been medically verified, as I've included them in the spirit in which they were sent to me. People have been kind enough to submit their accounts with the hope that their experiences will inspire others to be able to heal themselves . . . but, most of all, to *believe* that they can.

There's a chance that some of the people featured in the stories would have gotten better anyway in the normal course of their illness. But to say that this is true for everyone would deny the powerful and usually underestimated human mind. As I've stated elsewhere in these pages, there are many factors that influence healing. The mind is one of them, and I hope that through read-ing this book—and indeed this section—we will begin to use our minds in a more positive way.

In the chapters that follow, I've grouped the stories together by similar illnesses or medical conditions. The chapters are as follows: Cancer; Heart Issues; Regeneration; Pain and Chronic Fatigue; and Viruses, Allergies, and Autoimmune Conditions. I hope you find them to be very helpful, no matter what your particular concern may be.

ೕೕೕೕ

CHAPTER 10

CANCER

Iris's Story

I make myself tiny and sit on my shoulder. There's an imaginary spiral slide there that can take me to any part of my body, and I slide down this to reach the area I want. I decided in advance to make a comfortable place there to sit in: some grass or carpet and a soft chair, a place where the sun always shines and I feel calm and peaceful. The grass or carpet and chair is always there every time I do my visualization, and knowing that is very helpful.

I like to work with sound as well as seeing visuals, as that adds to the fun. Because I work with crystals, I always take my pendulum with me, and it acts as a magnet to the cancer cells—I can actually watch it drawing the cells from the area. It's great to see this happening, since I can really achieve the feeling of knowing that I've taken those rogue cells and dispersed them down the slide and out through my toes.

When I sit on my shoulder, I talk to myself and say, "Okay, Iris, it's fun time. Let's go down and see what the rogue cells are up to." As I slide down, I make sounds as if I were a child. Then I find my chair and sit and look at the cells and talk to them: "You know how much I love you all and love talking to you each day, but you know you can't stay here and will have to leave."

I visualize the cells talking back to me and saying, "We love you, too, and we do understand." They start to get excited and ask me, "Did you bring your pendulum with you?"

"Yes, I did," I say, and I take it out of my pocket and hold it up. It starts to spin, and I can hear the laughter from the cells as they fly to it

like a magnet. I check the area in my body to see if it's clear, but I can always find a couple of cells hiding. I call out: "I can see you! You'll miss all the fun going down the slide if you don't hurry up." Chuckling, they rush out to join the other cells on the pendulum.

I keep spinning them around, and they shout out, "Have you opened the taps on your toes?"

I bend over, and open the five taps, and ask, "Are you all ready?" Then I take them to the top of my leg, blow them off the pendulum, and hear them screaming with delight as they go down the slide in my leg and fly out of my toes into Mother Earth. I hear them shout, "Love you, Iris," and I call out, "Ditto."

This Worked Because . . .

Iris had an upbeat, positive attitude, and there was a strong element of humor in her scene. This would have minimized any stress that she might have ordinarily felt relating to her condition. She also created a comfortable place where she always feels peaceful.

In her setting, Iris saw the removal of cancer cells: it went from having cancer cells at the beginning to none when she finished. Her awareness of where they were located would have stimulated those areas as well as the part of the brain that governed them. And the fact that her scene was so clear that she could "really achieve the feeling" that the cancer cells were leaving amplified the power of the scene and the speed of the results.

Note that Iris treated the cancer cells with love and saw them leave her body in a cheerful fashion—some people prefer to do this type of thing rather than use force of any kind. Love is a powerful state and can have really influential effects on a disease. In the end, however, you'll get the same result as long as the scene describes going from the presence of cancer cells to having none.

Petula's Story

I was diagnosed with inoperable breast cancer more than ten years ago and was only given a 15 percent chance of survival, because the cancer had spread into my lymphatic system and my neck. I had chemotherapy and radiotherapy to shrink the tumors, and then if anything was left in my breast, it was to be surgically removed.

While I was having my treatment, I visualized a rabbit—whom I called Pure Health—jumping into my body and eating all of the cancer cells. They were food for the rabbit and didn't harm him; in fact, he looked so healthy and had a really glossy coat. The rabbit loved eating these cells and when he was full, he jumped out of my body and ran off into the woods. There he excreted all of his waste products at a certain spot, where a beautiful tree eventually grew. Everyone who saw the tree or sat under it felt great peace and well-being—it was called a healing tree.

I did this visualization at least two or three times a day and every time I had my treatment. At the end of my regimen, the doctors were amazed at how well I'd responded to it: the cancer had disappeared, and I didn't need an operation.

Another visualization I did was to see the cancer cells as balloons that popped two or three times a day. The empty shells were then flushed through my body and came out as waste products that were sent into the earth to be changed to positive energy for the good of all.

The third visualization was for me to stand under a shower of pure healing water. The water entered through the crown of my head and flowed down the inside of my body, flushing all of the cancer cells out. The water came out of my feet as a thick black liquid at first. This gradually changed to a thinner brown color, and then finally to clear water when the cancer cells had been removed. Eventually, it went down the drain to the earth to be changed into positive energy. After that, I visualized a pure white healing light filling the spaces in my body where the cancer cells had been.

Also, every night before I go to sleep, I affirm: <u>I have a wonderful body that is glowing with perfect health,</u> and <u>Every single living cell in my body is whole, normal, and perfect.</u> I also visualize my body full of pink healing light, as this is the color for love and harmony. Another thing

I do is chant "Om" into my left breast, and at a certain note I can feel the tissue vibrating. I am sure that all of this has helped me, as I'm still alive and well 11 years later. The doctors and nurses continue to marvel at the fact that I'm so healthy.

This Worked Because . . .

Petula's scene described moving from having cancer to perfect health. Notice the creative way that she did this with her first visualization. The use of the "Pure Health" rabbit established a lighthearted mood that would have reduced any stress associated with the condition and made the experience more interesting, which made it easier for her to stay focused. And the name Pure Health was also symbolic of how Petula was imagining herself, as was the fact that the rabbit was so obviously healthy with its glossy coat.

I also like the bit about the cancer cells being recycled. This reflects an attitude of knowing that there's a positive side to everything and a desire for things to work out for the best. And we know that a positive outlook aids health.

Notice also that Petula visualized *and* received chemotherapy. As I've mentioned before, it doesn't need to be one or the other. Putting her attention on the cancerous location would have stimulated it and the brain area that governed it, altering the brain map there and causing numerous chemical changes. Genes in the brain, throughout the body, and at the cancer sites would also have been activated; and the genes in the stem cells would have encouraged the growth of healthy new cells.

Repetition of her visualization played a key role, too; she did this at least two or three times a day.

The use of balloons was a good symbolic visualization and represented the bursting of the "cancer balloons" in her body. To her unconscious mind, the cancer was being eliminated. This stimulated the correct brain and body areas so that this was, indeed, what eventually occurred.

The shower visualization was also powerfully symbolic because, just like the other two, it described the shift from having cancer to not having it. As she progressed with this visualization and the water became lighter until it was clear, this sent a powerful unconscious message to her brain that the cancer was gone. Higher levels of her nervous system would have been working to make that a reality.

The use of three separate visualizations was a very good thing because sometimes we get bored with the same scene. This is where many of us give up, because we can't motivate ourselves to see the same picture time and time again. But when we chop and change our scenes it keeps us fresh.

Last, Petula's affirmations contributed greatly to her healing. They focused her attention upon what she wanted and, just as with the visualizations, stimulated her brain and body in the appropriate ways to bring about healing.

Cathie's Story

Ten years ago I was diagnosed with non-Hodgkin's lymphoma. I had very large tumors in my abdomen and groin, and I was originally scheduled for chemotherapy. Then I was told to wait for five weeks to see how my disease would evolve, since it was believed to be a slow-growing type. However, because the tumors were really large, it was thought that the cancer might mutate into a more aggressive form.

During my wait, I did a lot of reading and had reflexology three times a week. I knew that such treatment could really help, but my reflexologist also told me about the real dangers of chemo—something I hadn't been made aware of. To make a long story short, I decided not to have any conventional treatment and instead relied on an organic diet and vegetable juicing, long walks in nature, and lots of laughter with friends. I also retired from teaching.

I absolutely used visualization to focus my cells on getting rid of the cancer. First of all, I told myself that my body was not my enemy, but that some of its cells had lost their way somehow. I drew a picture representing my cancerous cells as gray blobs without much shape or substance. Then I drew my T cells as little piranhas, with focused, friendly eyes and very sharp teeth. None of the gray blobs stood a chance! I visualized them taking great big bites out of the cancerous cells and devouring them up into their little stomachs; they obviously enjoyed their food because I even "heard" them go, "Miam, miam, miam!" as they ate (that is, "Yum, yum, yum" in my French accent).

At first I had to make a point of going through this visualization several times a day, but very soon it became part of my every waking moment. It was as though I had a little TV screen in the corner of my mind that was constantly showing the same cartoon, and it made me smile a lot.

I also used affirmations, which varied. At the beginning, when I still had a lot of anxiety about being diagnosed and dying, I used one I'd made up. It was a variation of this popular one: Every day in every way I am getting better and better. Mine was: My immune system is very strong and every day my cells are getting cleaner and healthier. My immune system is very strong. Somehow, the repetition seemed to be necessary in order to imprint on my brain.

It worked, because whenever I woke up during the night in a grip of panic, my affirmation would kick in, and I'd be able to go back to sleep after focusing on it for a while. It soon got to the point where I'd hear the words in my brain and go back to sleep immediately, reassured that even in sleep, my body was still working for me. After a while, I would barely open one eye and yet would hear my head filled with my affirmation: the tape was playing without my having to switch it on, so to speak. After I realized that, I never woke up during the night again.

I played with my affirmation during the day as well: I'd take a mirror and pretend to be talking to somebody else, insisting, "My immune system is very strong, you know!" And more often than not, I'd end up laughing at the thought of somebody walking in on me while I was having this weird conversation with my mirror.

I used affirmations to tackle certain emotional issues that were at the root of my cancer, too. The very simple ones suggested by Louise Hay: I love and approve of myself, and All is well, proved impossible at first. I couldn't look at myself and say those things without either crying or laughing hysterically. Still, I continued to use Louise Hay as an inspiration, and I began to look at cancer as being a sign of deep hurt or a long-standing resentment . . . and it hit home. I also did my best with: I lovingly forgive and release all of the past. I still use this one today and feel my heart open up as I say it.

I was diagnosed in April for my 45th birthday; by December, my cancerous tumors had decreased by 70 percent. By the beginning of the following year, they had totally disappeared. You can even check all these facts: my consultant at the Vale of Leven Hospital in Scotland is Dr. Patricia Clarke.

Here's to a life of no limits!

This Worked Because . . .

Cathie created a scene that saw her T cells swallow up the cancer cells, which described moving from a state of having cancer to being cured. This most likely stimulated the cancerous areas of the body, as well as those of the brain that governed them, leading to beneficial chemical and genetic changes in the brain and at the sites where there was cancer.

By affirming that her body was not the enemy, she was treating it with love. When we dwell on things that have gone sour and think that there's something wrong with us, we generate stress, and that has a negative effect on us. Instead, Cathie affirmed that some cells had just somehow lost their way. This showed love and acceptance, which, I believe, made a positive difference.

The use of reflexology certainly helped, too. Although, like many alternative therapies, there isn't yet a great deal of positive evidence that supports it, I do believe that it's just a matter of time before better evidence becomes available. Cathie's belief in it also contributed to its efficacy.

Introducing regular exercise into her routine and switching to a healthy organic diet and vegetable juicing was also advantageous for her. There's evidence indicating that increasing the consumption of fruits and vegetables and decreasing the consumption of meat can affect cancer.

Frequent laughter reduces stress and floods the body with happy chemicals, which most likely play some sort of positive healing role. The little introduction of "Miam, miam, miam" would also have brought a smile to Cathie's face while visualizing.

Giving up teaching was a good idea, as this eliminated a possible source of stress and allowed Cathie to focus more of her energy on healing. It's clear that she had a very positive attitude and was determined to rid herself of cancer.

This woman's strong positive attitude meant that she did lots of visualizations. The scene that she created became part of her every waking moment, which had substantial positive consequences. Also, Cathie's use of affirmations certainly contributed to her healing by improving her immune system.

And by viewing her cancer as stemming from a deep hurt and long-standing resentment, she was empowered to deal with those emotional issues. In my opinion, there's a link between suppressed negative emotions of this type and some forms of cancer, and I mentioned some evidence for this in my book *It's the Thought That Counts*.

Sarah's Story

Following investigatory surgery for a lump in my groin in 2005, I was diagnosed with non-Hodgkin's lymphoma. Further investigations showed evidence of the disease on both sides of my body and also in my bone marrow, and I understood that this categorized the disease as stage IV (in medicalspeak).

It was explained to me that chemotherapy would be the treatment, with the possibility of a bone-marrow transplant in the future. I was also told that, as the lymphoma was low grade, there would be no immediate treatment, only active surveillance until my symptoms changed. I was initially very confused about this course of action, as I'd always understood that early intervention produced the best outcomes in the treatment of cancer. But as I became more knowledgeable about the disease, I felt more comfortable with the situation. I realized that there could be long periods where there was little or no change in my situation, which gave me time to explore other avenues.

Back in the '80s, I bought Creative Visualization by Shakti Gawain, discovered meditation, and lived my life through affirmation and visualization for a while. I even participated in one of Shakti's workshops in London, but for many different reasons, that part of my life has since ceased to exist.

The field of complementary medicine/therapy, however, still remained a source of interest to me, so I started to explore it in more detail in relation to my current situation. Brandon Bays's book The Journey (which describes Brandon's journey of healing cancer through the release of many years of emotional pain) had been sitting on my bookshelf at home for a year or so, but I hadn't gotten around to reading it yet. I decided that there was no time like the present and dived right in.

I set off on my first "journey" two weeks after the diagnosis and found it to be a life-changing experience. I then discovered a holistic consultant who'd developed a complementary approach to cancer treatment. It was there that I began to develop meditation and visualization techniques.

I'd used homeopathy in the past for minor ailments and had been very impressed with the outcome. Therefore, I sought advice and guidance once again from a homeopath. The one I used was able to support all aspects of my current approach to well-being. She also introduced me to Reiki, which I recognized as the most profound method of intervention and found that it reinforced the meditation and visualization techniques that I was using.

Over a period of time, the use of Reiki has intensified my visualization to the point where I only need to use initial intention to produce spontaneous visualization—it's become effortless. Vivid visualizations manifest almost as soon as I close my eyes.

I've had many different experiences of visualization through meditation, journey work, Reiki, and even when I'm out walking the dog; and I believe that these have had a substantial impact on my healing journey.

I feel passionately that if those diagnosed with cancer could only change their relationship with the disease, this would have a profound effect on the long-term prognosis. Too many people feel powerless when faced with a diagnosis of cancer and accept doctors' opinions without question. Sadly, this then becomes their reality. I too was in that place for a period of time.

In my situation, however, I did not have to rush into treatment, and this gave me time to explore other options. Two years on, I'm convinced that health is a state of mind. All aspects of my life have improved and I'm in a much better place. I still see my consultant on a regular basis; however, the frequency of visits has reduced significantly as my symptoms remain stable.

I suppose the most measurable results of visualization have been the physical ones. Following a scan in 2005, I was told that enlarged nodes were evident in both groins. I actually didn't have to be told this, as they were quite noticeable and felt like a series of large peas. When I first started visualization, I'd imagine the lumps as blocks of ice slowly melting until they disappeared, and I repeated this every night before I went to sleep. Within six months, the lumps on the left side had reduced significantly—today, they're hardly noticeable. The ones on the right have also now reduced in size.

I practice visualization and Reiki every day. I also receive Reiki from a practitioner once a month for one hour. As I've now undertaken the initial training to become a practitioner (level 1), I'm able to channel the flow of Reiki energy for myself. Since it's a form of visualization, I've developed my own technique where I use the two together, and I believe that it intensifies the experience. I start with an initial intention and, quite frequently, it is to have a perfectly healthy body. The visualization then often starts to manifest itself with little effort from me.

The most memorable visualization that manifested for me is one that I now repeat on a regular basis, where all of the cancer cells in my body are waiting to get on a bus. I watch them get on one by one, and as the bus pulls away, all of the little cancer cells are smiling and waving at me until they're out of sight.

Another noticeable physical result of visualization over a two-year period is the state of my general health and well-being. Before my diagnosis, I experienced frequent chest infections and was prescribed antibiotics on a regular basis. I also had a distinct lack of energy and was always tired.

Now, however, I'm very happy to report that I haven't had a chest infection for more than two years, I'm very rarely unwell, and I have an abundance of energy!

This Worked Because . . .

Sarah believed that health was a state of mind, so she focused on using her mind in a highly positive way. Her "journey" played a key role in her curing herself because it facilitated emotional healing, which impacted the state of the disease. She also used Reiki and found that it intensified the visualizations that she was using. Undoubtedly, the regular sessions helped tilt her body toward recovery, as recent scientific reports on hands-on healing show that it alters the rate of growth in skin and bone cells.

Sarah's scenes featured the enlarged nodes as blocks of ice—which she saw melting—as well as the memorable one of watching the cancer cells leaving on a bus. Thus, they described moving from having tumors to not having tumors. This would have influenced her brain maps in the areas affected by the disease, as well as the disease itself.

Ultimately, as I've said earlier, I don't believe that the brain registers the difference between real and imaginary. As Sarah imagined the tumors melting and the cancer cells leaving on a bus, it's likely that the brain released the proper chemicals, and all the right genes were affected to bring about the real disappearance of cancer, because that's what she was imagining.

Pat's Story (related by her sister, Carol)

My sister, Pat, woke up one morning and found that she couldn't move. She was taken to the hospital and diagnosed with a cancer that was wrapped around her spine between, I think, the third and fifth vertebrae. She was given radium therapy and after several weeks was able to get around with a walker, but the medical opinion was that she would only live six weeks. That was in 2002. My sister now visits me regularly, driving herself, and the walker has long since gone.

Pat, my daughter, several of our friends, and I are all of a spiritual bent. As soon as Pat was diagnosed, we all started visualization. I can only tell you what I did: I used to look into Pat's back like an x-ray. I would use a blue and white laser to burn away the cancer on some days, then on others it would be a special green acid that only burns away cancer cells, not bone. I did this every day for about a year. When I saw my sister in person, I'd always lay my hands on her and ask for God's special healing force to come through.

Whatever we did, it worked; although the doctors told my sister that they couldn't treat all the cancer with radium because of its position, in her last checkup none was found. She was told that she's completely clear.

I do believe that the mind is a powerful tool, but it needs exercise to make it strong. I also believe in God, angels, and the power of prayer—a very strong toolbox for my mind.

This Worked Because . . .

Pat and her family and friends collectively visualized her healing. Carol's scene told the story of the cancer cells being eradicated, and this probably stimulated the cancerous area and the part of the brain that governed it, leading to biochemical and genetic changes in the brain and at the site of the cancer.

Notice also that Carol wasn't even in the presence of her sister much of the time when she visualized. Healing can be sent to people; all we need to do is imagine the healing scene inside their bodies.

Carol also had a strong belief in the power of the mind, which definitely helped. Coupled with her belief in "God, angels, and the power of prayer," it did indeed prove to be a powerful toolbox.

Jeannine's Story

In July 2007, after a Pap smear, I was diagnosed with abnormal cells on the cervix. The degree was mild, but I was asked to go to a colposcopy clinic on October 11. You may be aware that this is quite common with women of my age (52), and it's usually treated quickly then and there . . . but I found it very alarming. So after the initial shock, which I expressed in a poem in my diary and by telling my closest friends, I set out to do something about it.

In September, I wrote to Mr. Jan de Vries (a world-renowned doctor based in Scotland), who prescribed me an herbal remedy (Indolplex with DIM—Estrobalance). I took one tablet per day but realized just two weeks before I was due to go to the clinic that I should have been taking at least two a day.

I believe in the power of the mind and relaxation. For about two weeks before the appointment, I set my mind to erasing the abnormal cells. I visualized the rows of cells (three or four rows) with a huge black spot (larger than it should be) and changed each one into a healthy-looking one, row after row, until I felt that they were all looking like they were in good shape. I also took an imaginary eraser and rubbed out each abnormal one—replacing it with a normal-looking cell—and visualized rows and rows of healthy cells. And I did this process every night.

I arrived at the clinic for my scheduled appointment, and the consultant found that there was no evidence of abnormal cells. The obstetrician even said that my vagina was looking younger than he expected for my age! Mind you, I'm not sure what he meant by that!

I'd also like to mention that I received two distant healings during that time quite quickly after my diagnosis. One was a bi-aura healing, and the other one was a bi-aura friend sending the color orange (bi-aura is a system of bioenergy healing that works to balance the human biofield).

This Worked Because . . .

Jeannine's story describes going from abnormal cells to healthy cells. Her scene involved seeing rows of them with a huge black spot and changing them into healthy cells. She also used an imaginary eraser to rub out abnormal cells. The brain doesn't know the difference between real and imaginary, so it's likely that the appropriate chemical and genetic changes took place to bring that about.

Jeannine also took an herbal remedy, which probably had a positive effect, even though she didn't take it in the quantity that was prescribed.

In addition, she also wrote a poem and told her close friends of her initial shock. This may have facilitated the expression of stored-up negative emotion, which would have aided the process.

And, as I pointed out with Pat's story, we can send healing to other people. Jeannine received two healings in this way (distant healings), which were bi-aura healings. In one of them, her friend sent the color orange. I am a fan of using colors in visualizations. Orange is often associated with joy, sunshine, and enthusiasm, and also commonly attributed to strength and courage—both meanings are positive in the healing sense.

Linda's Story

Healing by visualization has been amazing for me. Five years ago, I was diagnosed with diabetes and had been living with the condition for two years when I went to a doctor to get an inhaler for asthma and was rushed straight to the hospital for a blood transfusion. It turns out that I had colon cancer. Tiredness was the only symptom, but thanks to an observant doctor who interpreted my white hands as a sign of little blood in my body, I'm here today.

While waiting for major surgery, I began my visualization therapy. I'd been studying the mind for many years, and I was also about to open a business when I was hit with this news. Luckily, not only were the visualizations great for dealing with the panic that hit me, but they took the trauma out of hospital treatments and long days in waiting rooms as well. I just escaped to a beautiful place and had no need for the Valium that seemed to be dished out to other patients to avoid claustrophobia during scans and other procedures. During one 40-minute scan in a "barrel," I mentally took myself on a bush walk, and when it was over and I had to stand up, my legs ached as if I'd been on a long hike.

The surgeon said that most people needed to be off work for three months after the kind of procedure I'd had. He said that it only took seven days for the wound to heal, so the rest had to be in the mind. Great, I thought. What a challenge! I was back at work full-time and using public transportation within three and a half weeks.

The cancer had spread to the lymph system, and I was meant to have chemotherapy. But I believed that I'd created this cancer by hanging on to heaps of negative thoughts about past events, so my mind must now heal my body. I did my visualizations three times a day and made sure that I only ate food that I'd prepared myself, so as not to put toxins into my body.

Here is the visualization that I use. It's adapted from the Silva Method (which is a powerful system of healing):

For greatest effect, I either lie or sit in a quiet place, although this still works in busy places such as on a train. Then I count down slowly from 10 to 1, feeling as if I'm diving deeper into water. Moving my eyes from left to right, I see the number 3 . . . 3 . . . 3. Then, moving my eyes back to the left, I repeat 2 . . . 2 . . . 2, and again 1 . . . 1 . . . 1. By now I'm feeling very relaxed.

I tell myself that I am connected to higher powers (God, Buddha, or whomever is in my thoughts). I see myself reaching out grasping the hand of God. Then I feel the vibrations of the universe flowing through my body. I call on archangels and angels of the four corners to help protect me.

I tell myself to let go of all negative past-life experiences. I feel a light, floating feeling as if I'm free. I forgive all those people who have ever caused me pain and sadness. Initially, faces were very close to my own face, but over time these have floated off into the distance—it's now hard to even remember who was there. They changed from angry faces racing toward me to just tiny dots.

I then tell myself that my mind and body are healthy, strong, and working in perfect harmony: "My mind is in perfect condition, working with all my bodily systems. My eyes see clearly; my ears hear perfectly."

I imagine a vacuum cleaner sucking excess mucus from my nose and lungs, as I've suffered from asthma and sinus problems for years. Air flows freely into my lungs, where I celebrate the smell of the seasons changing.

I tell myself that my mouth is healthy and full of mucus to protect my teeth, and it allows me to speak words clearly. My mouth and mind are in perfect harmony, allowing me to speak my thoughts without causing offense, and my esophagus and windpipe are perfectly healthy.

I tell myself that my stomach, colon, and bowels are perfectly healthy and working well. I see a healthy liver, then view my pancreas and blood working in harmony to give me perfect blood-sugar levels.

I tell myself that my gallbladder, bladder, and kidneys are healthy and working perfectly. And also that my heart is strong and healthy—with all veins and arteries open and clear—allowing blood to travel freely to all parts of my body.

Then I affirm that my immune system is strong, constantly fighting, repairing, restoring, healing, and protecting my body. Sometimes I see a little creature gobbling up any foreign germs in my body. These little creatures work throughout my body.

I affirm that my lymph system and all lymph nodes are very healthy (and I quickly scan my body). When I had cancer in the lymph, I visualized that my cells had the cell memory of 15 years before when I felt I was strong, healthy, and happy.

I affirm that my reproductive organs and tissues are healthy and my bones are strong from the inside out; and I go through my body as if I were inside my bones and travel from my tailbone up my spine, head, chest, arms, legs, and toes. Then I affirm that my skin is smooth and full of elasticity.

I imagine a bright, white light shining above me and draw it into my body via the top of my head. As it slowly passes through my body—cleansing and removing any negativity, illness, and dead cells—I feel a warm glow.

I see a picture of my sick self and, starting at my feet, carefully erase this image as if using a giant eraser. Then I see a beautiful white picture frame with myself in it. During the colon cancer, I saw myself nailing up a barricade with the words NO CANCER across the entire image, but this is no longer necessary.

In the picture frame, I imagine doing all of the things that I ever wanted to do—create energy, meet new friends, make money, try different jobs, garden, travel, go dancing, and so on. I live each thought out in detail to extend the relaxation.

Now I retrieve a positive and happy memory. I relive the sounds, smells, and feelings, but I change the intensity to please me. I stay in this state as long as I like.

To finish, I count from one to five, wriggle my toes, and tell myself that I'm wide awake and feeling better than before.

I regularly have scans, and each time the results are the same: no sign of cancer in my body. The doctors are impressed, and I've never been so happy, healthy, and full of energy in my life. I still spend 20 minutes every day doing visualizations, and now I even teach teenagers at a high school the power of visualizations for anger management. The diabetes is all clear as well, and I no longer use inhalers!

This Worked Because . . .

Linda's whole-body-healing visualization stimulated all of the parts of her body that she imagined as well as the brain areas that governed them. The visualization that she used was adapted from the Silva Method, which is a powerful system of using the mind—one in which I have faith and would personally recommend.

Linda gave her body an allover healing as her words and images described healthy scenes. During her visualization, she not only imagined healing the cancer, but also that her pancreas was healthy and that her lungs and airways were clear of mucus. Ultimately, she cured herself of diabetes and asthma, too.

The repetition of Linda's visualization played an important role (remember, she did it three times per day). She had a strong, positive mental attitude and this helped her remain determined to heal completely. The fact that she believed that the cancer was linked to holding on to "heaps of negative thoughts about past events" meant that she had a strong belief that she could heal herself using her mind. In the visualization, Linda felt forgiveness and therefore released any built-up negative emotion. She also ate food that she prepared herself to avoid any additives that often come in prepackaged foods, which could have had a negative effect upon her condition.

Finally, Linda had faith in a higher power and imagined the vibrations of the universe flowing through her. In this way, she knew that a really strong healing power was entering her body, and I believe that it was.

ೋೋೋೋ

CHAPTER 11

HEART ISSUES

Kevin's Story

One day I was getting the ironing board out, when I noticed that my right thumb had become completely swollen and solid.

My immediate thought was that this could be a thrombosis [a type of blood clot], and the last thing I wanted was for it to dislodge and end up in my brain or heart. My thumb had started turning blue, which added to my fear, so I decided to go straight to the emergency room. From there I was referred to a local general practitioner (I was told that a referral from him back to the hospital would be quicker than waiting).

The GP was very thorough and examined my fingers and eyes, told me I had a fever, and said that he could hear a heart murmur. Putting all of these together, he thought that I could have a heart-valve infection, which was potentially very serious and might involve me having valve-replacement surgery. He explained that bacteria can form on the valve, and bits of it can then break off and cause clots (which is what he thought was causing my blue thumb). He telephoned the hospital and told them that he was referring me immediately. By this time, my thumb was completely blue and still swollen solid.

Walking back to the hospital, I thought about how our lives can change in a matter of seconds. I became very aware of my mortality, which isn't necessarily a bad thing, but <u>wow,</u> it sure can bring on lots of anxiety and raw fear!

After further tests in the emergency room, the doctors concluded that it could well be what the general practitioner had thought. I was admitted to the hospital very late that night with an echocardiogram and chest x-rays planned for the next day.

That night it was difficult to sleep. I lay there thinking of the things I still wanted to do in my life, as well as how I didn't want to have major surgery with the possibility of dying. The more I thought along those lines, the more frightened I became. My fear fed on itself and grew until I suddenly shouted, <u>Stop!</u> *in my mind and reminded myself that there was an alternative way of responding to this situation. I made an agreement with myself that it was okay to acknowledge my fear rather than suppress it, and it would do me more harm to let it develop into a downward spiral of negativity.*

I decided then and there that I wasn't going to need heart-valve surgery, allow my fear to have a negative impact on my situation, or die; I could heal myself.

I started to talk to my body, reminding it of how wonderful, powerful, and strong it was and how it had amazing abilities to heal itself. I encouraged it to get into "superheal" mode!

I suddenly got a visualization that was so spontaneous and clear that it surprised me. I was inside my heart, looking at one of the valves. I saw the three parts of it that open and close together to form a seal, and I saw the bacteria on the valve.

I then saw that I had a pressure hose in my hand—the kind used to clean paths—and I knew I was about to blast the bacteria off my heart valve. But I realized that if I did this, some bacteria would then be free in my circulatory system and could cause further clots. Suddenly I visualized big, blobby immune-system cells forming a protective line a short distance away, and I knew that they would envelop and absorb the particles of bacteria that would be blasted off, preventing them from doing further damage.

I started the pressure hose; having used one before, I knew how it felt and anticipated the kickback when the pressurized water hit something. I worked the blast of water over my heart valve and watched pieces of bacteria flying off, to be swamped by my blobby cells.

I drifted off to sleep, but whenever I woke up (which was frequently), I'd replay the visualization and talk to my body in really positive and powerful ways. I'd encourage it and tell it that I had faith in the massive amounts of energy and healing abilities it had. There was also a feeling of determination inside of me to be totally healthy and vibrantly alive, and to remain so for many years to come.

The next morning I was examined by a consultant and a team of doctors. Interestingly, I no longer had a fever, and my thumb was less swollen and had started to soften. I then had my echocardiogram and chest x-rays, all of which indicated that I have a great heart! There was no sign of bacterial infection.

I cannot, in all honesty, say that I definitely had a heart-valve infection before my visualization. However, no consultant or doctor (at the time or in follow-up appointments) has been able to provide an alternative explanation for the symptoms I displayed.

At the very least, my visualization enabled me to get into a positive frame of mind and eliminate my fear. At best, who knows—it might just have saved my life.

This Worked Because . . .

First, I'd like to point out that Kevin displayed total determination. In my research in mind-body science over the past 13 years, I've found that this state can sometimes accompany what we'd describe as miracles of healing.

Kevin began his determination with a simple word, *Stop!* which he shouted in his mind. He decided that he would no longer pay attention to the fear that he was feeling but instead use his mind in a positive way. His determination made it clear that nothing was more important than his health, allowing his unconscious mind and nervous system to work more directly in healing him.

He did quite a bit of self-talk, reminding his body how wonderful, powerful, and strong it was and that it had amazing abilities to heal itself. He even encouraged it to get into superheal mode, and all of this talk activated parts of the brain that, indeed, encouraged the body to do so.

In the superheal mode, images spontaneously arose in Kevin's mind. I've noticed that this sometimes occurs when we're asking the body or brain for direction. By switching his own body into this mode, Kevin was open to any guidance that he might receive.

His resulting scene tells the story of a heart-valve infection being eliminated. Focusing on his heart valve activated the parts of the brain that governed it as well as the actual heart valve and its interrelated parts. His scene was also played out in a light-hearted way—the image of the big blobby immune-system cells that swallowed up the bits of bacteria kept stress and fear to a minimum.

Kevin used a pressure hose in his scene. This was familiar to him because he had used one before. Therefore, he could make his scene more recognizable by remembering how it felt when he turned one on. Keep in mind that, like Kevin, the clearer we can make our scene, the better.

Helen's Story

I was told two weeks ago that my baby had an irregular heartbeat of 167 beats per minute (bpm). After doing healing work every day—going into the cells of my baby's heart and putting in pink hearts with angel wings to represent love, along with the words normal, regular heartbeat— I was told yesterday that the bpm had come down to 147 and that her heartbeat was totally normal and regular.

I'm not sure whether it was all the love and healing that did it, but I'd like to think it was.

This Worked Because . . .

Helen's healing attention was on her baby's heart. I firmly believe that our intentions are picked up by the unconscious minds of those we direct our thoughts toward. The Institute of HeartMath demonstrated a synchronization of heart-coherence waves in two people separated by about a mile when they consciously conjured up a feeling of appreciation (love). As adults, we sometimes get in the way of healing intentions, but babies don't. They haven't learned the rules that we have.

Helen's healing intentions would have stimulated her baby's brain and heart in a healing way. She put a tremendous amount of love into her visualization (pink hearts with angel wings), which she coupled with the intention of a normal, regular heartbeat. Clearly, love is good for the heart!

Flora's Story

About nine years ago I was quite unwell, and I thought I had bowel cancer. All of the tests were negative, but before the results were known, a blood test showed that I had a dangerously high cholesterol level and a blockage in the left carotid artery, which explained why I was having dizzy spells. (The trouble with the bowels had actually been because of the amount of cholesterol in my system!)

One of the doctors had been listening to my heart and around my neck, which I thought was rather weird at the time. He later told me that when he decided to practice in my home country of Scotland, he'd always check for stroke potential. It was thanks to him that the blockage in my carotid artery was found.

At that time I knew nothing of cholesterol problems but, as is my wont, I read everything I could. My cholesterol reading was 425, and I was put on statins. I had a vegetarian diet but was very fond of cheese, butter, and cream; they were all cut out, and I lost almost 15 pounds.

After about nine months—during which time I told the doctor about the muscle pains and tiredness to no avail—I was taken to the hospital with a suspected stroke because I'd woken up with no movement in the left side of my body. Thank God I hadn't actually had a stroke, but my muscles had been paralyzed by the statins.

The doctors wanted to change the drug type, but I refused. I was a great follower of Louise L. Hay and positive thinking, so I began doing visualization exercises. First, I pictured my carotid artery with the blockage, but I thought that it probably wasn't a good idea to blast it, as I didn't want bits floating along the arteries. Many years ago, the very first computer game my daughter had was Parkie, *where you raced to catch these "things" (yellow balls that opened like a mouth) before they gobbled the flowers. So I pictured the blockage dissolving slowly; I also saw the good cells coming along and sucking up the dissolved cholesterol, just like the "gobblers," taking it out of my system and disposing of it safely.*

It worked. I no longer have a blockage and now control my cholesterol by positive thinking, diet, and exercise.

This Worked Because . . .

Flora understood the power of positive thinking and made a determined decision to use her mind in a constructive way.

In her scene, she used images that she was familiar with, which always help make it clearer. By seeing the blockage slowly dissolving and "gobblers" sucking up the dissolved cholesterol, she stimulated her brain and body in such a way that allowed this to occur. Chemicals were released, and genes were then expressed in the brain and the appropriate areas of the body.

Tamara's Story

I've struggled with being overweight all my life. It <u>was</u> my safety net— the barrier to keep the hurt away. Then finally I made the solemn decision that I didn't need the extra pounds anymore. A few months ago, I started to visualize something that resembles Pac-Man eating away at my fat cells. Since then, I've already lost about 20 pounds.

Losing a substantial amount of weight is a long process, and aside from the unconscious changes in my eating habits that I sometimes notice, nothing about my lifestyle has changed—it's still as hectic as before.

I manage, on average, to visualize five times a week, usually before I go to sleep. The visualization consists of these Pac-Man-type beings eating the fat on particular points of my body and then exploding and disappearing into thin air. Others then actually transport the fat from my thighs and waist to my breasts (as you probably know, the first area of the female body to lose weight are the breasts, but I gained half a cup instead by doing it this way, which is just marvelous!). Finally, I try to visualize my skin tightening up. I finish with a whole-body scan and healing to raise my metabolism and check for parts that may not be in tune with the rest.

Here are the results so far:

- *I've lost 21 pounds in around four and a half months.*

- *I've gone from a tight size 22 to a comfortable 20 and gained half a cup in my bra size.*

- *I've gone from needing at least eight hours of sleep to being comfortable with only six and not being tired.*

- *I don't have any new stretch marks at all!*

- *I eat what I want whenever I'm hungry—takeout included (I have a very busy life). Yet it also seems that I've lost interest in things like chocolate and sweets in general, and I feel full quicker when I eat.*

The brain and the mind are two amazing tools!

This Works Because . . .

Tamara's scene tells the story of fat being eaten up, resulting in a slimmer and healthier body. As I pointed out in Chapter 8, "How to Visualize," visualization often results in our being unconsciously inspired to make some lifestyle changes. In Tamara's case, she's lost interest in eating chocolate and sweets. However, this isn't the only reason that she's losing weight. Her scene seeped into her unconscious mind, and the result is that her nervous system has created the weight loss, and her metabolism has become stimulated in just the right way.

જાજાજા

CHAPTER 12

REGENERATION

Tom's Story

In October 1996 I had a serious car accident. A double-decker bus ran full force into the driver's side of my car, and the result was that I broke my collarbone, ribs, pelvis, hip, and back; fractured my skull; and twisted my kneecap around the back of my leg. I remained in the hospital for three months and was told that I'd probably only regain 75 percent of my agility . . . and that was over a long period of time. Even so, I told the doctor that I'd be fit enough to run a full 26-mile marathon the next year in Glasgow and have 100 percent of my agility back. The doctor stated that he'd give £1,000 (about $1,500) to any charity I wanted if I succeeded, and then he laughed.

Day by day, I focused my thoughts on healing. I created a little healing system whereby I visualized a tiny version of myself going inside my body to the affected areas and a team of tiny workers all doing different jobs—sanding down all of my affected bones and knitting together all of my injuries with their special tools. For example, a welder welded the seam on my pelvis, a joiner sanded the rugged edges of my bones, and the polisher polished them.

I got stronger every day. When I received a scan on my hip, the doctor gave me a surprised look and said that it actually looked as though the bones had been sanded down!

I ran the marathon the next year in four hours and eight minutes and received £1,000 from the doctor, which I donated to charity. He was absolutely amazed at the results.

To this day, I continue to heal myself in this way whenever there's anything wrong with me.

This Worked Because . . .

Tom's scene activated each part of his body that he imagined healing, as well as the brain areas that governed them. This led to genetic changes in the brain at the sites of the injury, as well as in the stem cells, instructing them to evolve into whichever cell type was necessary.

He also showed total determination to fully recover, which resulted in dedicated visualization, and this played a major role in his recovery.

Ed's Story

Several years ago, I tore a calf muscle while training for a race. I saw a physical therapist who did some very good work but told me that the muscle would never be the same again. It was a Western-medicine approach based on the fact that I had some scar tissue.

Naturally, I didn't really like this diagnosis! However, I did accept it. And despite resting and stretching, every time I got to a certain speed and intensity of training, I broke down again.

Sometime later I read and very much enjoyed It's the Thought That Counts. *I also heard David Hamilton talk at a firewalking event about an athlete whose shoulder healed much more quickly than predicted with visualization.* [Note from David: I mentioned this in Chapter 6.] *So I decided that my calf would heal itself completely.*

I kept telling myself that my body knew how to grow healthy tissue. I've never consciously analyzed the scene I created, but I guess I actually saw and felt my body repairing the muscle—almost as if tiny workers were fixing me! I definitely sent attention to my calf and clearly felt that the damaged tissue was being broken down and replaced with healthy tissue.

I haven't had the calf reexamined to see if there's still any scar tissue, but I can say that it has healed 100 percent in terms of the way it feels—and it's been that way for a year and a half. During that time I've been running 30 to 35 miles a week training for other races and achieved my goal times with no pain or discomfort at all.

I know that lots of athletes will be told that their injuries won't heal completely. Well, I believe that they can!

This Worked Because . . .

Ed began with the belief that it was possible for his calf to heal itself completely, despite what his physical therapist had told him and the pain that he'd experienced ever since the injury. From this state of positive belief, his healing indeed became possible.

Ed regularly affirmed that his body knew how to heal itself. Undoubtedly, this caused his unconscious mind to direct the right centers of his nervous systems toward a full recovery. His scene helped out by telling the story of his muscle being repaired. And he conjured up tiny workers, which symbolized that work was really being done.

Mary's Story

About ten years ago (I am now 70), I had a very painful swollen knee joint following a fall while walking in the mountains with my husband. The doctor's diagnosis was a cartilage problem, and I was told that I'd need an operation to snip a portion of the cartilage out. I was then put on the list to see a consultant.

Despite this, I was determined to get better using alternative holistic therapies. To that end, I practiced spiritual healing and shiatsu and took various health supplements. I also engaged in an hour of Buddhist meditation every morning before breakfast. Sometimes I got into a very peaceful state where all thoughts subsided and I felt fully aware. When I was in those states, I did my visualization.

I imagined an enhanced blood supply flowing into my knee joint, where phagocytes (immune cells that ingest and destroy foreign invaders) engulfed the damaged cell tissue and carried it away. I then visualized an enriched blood supply carrying the necessary nutrients for repair flowing into the joint, enabling the growth of new cells. After that, I'd see my knee joint completely whole and healed—and myself hiking again.

In addition to the visualizations I was doing, I kept the appointment with the consultant, who sent me for x-rays. Although they didn't show any cartilage, he wanted to see if the ends of my bones were healthy, considering my age. The result: they were all perfect. After manipulating my leg, he found no evidence of the cartilage problem at all.

I told him about my visualization technique and other holistic practices, and his reply was, "Oh, I don't know about all that."

I do know. I'm right as rain now (and if I happen to get a twinge when I walk down a steep path, that's okay, since I use walking poles to help myself).

This Worked Because . . .

Mary saw her knee joint as completely whole and healed, and she saw herself hiking again, too. She also saw blood, nutrients, and immune cells flowing into the joint, giving it all that it required for healing. These regular visualizations seeped into her unconscious mind and stimulated the correct areas of her brain and the area of injury so that her scene became reality.

Lucca's Story

A few years ago, I ate something that had dried herbs in it, and a small piece of herb lodged between my teeth. When I flossed that night, I probably managed to push the herb under the gum line, and by the next morning I had a full-blown gum abscess. I thought it would just go away, but it got worse. Soon, I had a low-grade fever and couldn't chew without a lot of pain.

I saw my dentist, who relieved the pressure and drained the abscess before she sent me home to rinse with salt water. She wanted to give me antibiotics, but I don't like using them unless they're absolutely necessary. I went back a few days later so the dentist could check out the area, and she found that it was getting worse again. She suggested that I see a periodontist. The periodontist told me that I had an infection that extended down the root of the tooth to the jaw. She then cleaned the abscess out by cutting the gum open, scraping the tooth, and packing it with a disinfectant before closing it up again; and the infection cleared up within about four days. The only drug I had was a non-blood-thinning painkiller that was a little stronger than what I'd normally take for a headache.

While I was in the chair, the periodontist tested the tooth for reaction to cold in order to find out whether the root was damaged. She also checked one tooth to the left and one to the right of the one she'd worked on. Her opinion was that I'd need a root canal in all three teeth, and that it was possible that I'd lose the middle one altogether. The gum had receded during the surgery, and she predicted that it would recede farther and therefore wouldn't be able to hold the tooth.

I didn't like this prognosis, and I didn't want root canals or to lose teeth. I'd managed to heal third-degree burns with my mind 20 years earlier, so I decided that I could heal my tooth and gum as well. I set about using the same technique I'd used then.

Just before I went to sleep each night, I pictured a healthy root going into each of the three teeth (in the form of an emerald green light) and healthy pink gums holding them in place. If I recall correctly, I did this for about a month, and my gum healed well, causing no further problems. I told the dentist that I wouldn't need the root canal after all.

I was back in the dentist's office for a routine scaling about three months later, and she had another look at my tooth and gums to see how they were doing. She asked her assistant to check the chart again to make sure she had the right tooth, because she couldn't find any evidence of the abscess. Not only had the gum healed, but it had regenerated as well. Everyone in the office had to have a look at the "incredible regenerating gum"! The dentist said she'd never seen anything like it, but that "seeing was believing."

This Worked Because . . .

Lucca had faith that she could heal herself. She had healed third-degree burns many years earlier, so she had a memory of what was possible.

Her scene described healthy roots going into her teeth, and she used green light in this part of her scene. The color green symbolizes regeneration and healing in some cultures, so undoubtedly this also assisted the healing. She also pictured her gums being healthy.

Throughout her scene, she stimulated her brain, gums, and nerves. Genes activated in the brain and gums as well as in the stem cells, so her gums were able to fully regenerate according to how she'd imagined.

৵৵৵৵

CHAPTER 13

PAIN AND CHRONIC FATIGUE

Lisa's Story

If I have a headache or other pain, I focus my attention on my heart by feeling or seeing it beating. Then I imagine a small bright light pulsing in the middle of it. I hold this for a few minutes, and then I move the light into the part of my body where I feel pain or discomfort.

I hold this intention and watch the light as it sends waves of healing energy throughout the area (and this can be increased until the light and waves are pulsing throughout my whole body) for as long as I wish.

This doesn't always totally take the pain away, but it certainly reduces it.

This Works Because . . .

By concentrating upon her heart, Lisa becomes distracted from her pain. But her scene of the pulsing light also symbolizes loving, healing intention, which she then moves to the part of her body that feels discomfort. This stimulates that part, and the section of the brain that governs it, as well as the neural pathways that are responsible for the pain. Endorphins are most likely released in the brain where it governs the irritated part, therefore neutralizing the pain.

Lisa's expectation that relief will accompany her visualization also encourages this endorphin release, and that expectation builds with every success.

Sasha's Story

A couple of years ago, I became severely ill with chronic fatigue syndrome (CFS). Previously, I'd been a very active individual with a successful career lecturing in the performing arts, and I had several qualifications in holistic therapies.

The descent into CFS was rapid, leaving me completely disabled—I was unable to put on my own socks and had to be lifted out of the bath. But my story doesn't really start there. It starts at the turning point, when I realized the power of my mind to help me heal.

First, it's important to understand that I'm not saying that CFS is in the mind—it's a physiological condition affecting the neurological and immune system. What I am saying is that I discovered the extraordinary power of visualization and intention to aid my recovery.

My turning point was one particular day when I was lying in bed feeling especially miserable. It was what was then an average day—I was spending 20 hours plus per day in bed, rising only to wash, eat, and use the bathroom. And on <u>this</u> average day, I was doing what I always did, although I wasn't aware of it consciously. My subconscious pattern was playing a series of messages to myself over and over again, such as: <u>This is dreadful,</u> <u>I'll never recover,</u> and <u>My life will never be the same.</u> But in the midst of all this, I heard another voice from inside my head asking me who was making it dreadful.

Right then, everything stopped and there was silence. The small voice inside my head suddenly answered, <u>Me!</u> In a flash of understanding, I realized that although the pain I was experiencing was inevitable given my physiological state, the suffering was a choice. I lay in peace and silence for the rest of the day with a huge sense of relief. I was no longer a victim of CFS, and I realized the power that I possessed to aid my own recovery.

What followed was a journey to health and self-realization that was so profound that I'm actually grateful to CFS for the lessons that it taught me and the way it changed the course of my life. I stopped labeling myself as someone who had CFS, and started to refer to myself as "in recovery." I realized the power of my intention and focused clearly on my goal of wellness. I also began to visualize myself in great health and pictured my nervous system and all of my cells and organs healing. Each day I lay in meditation, gently commanding various body parts to heal and sending them positive energy.

I saturated myself with information that supported my new belief system. As I began to do so, all the tools that I needed to heal seemed to fall into my path. Books by Bruce Lipton, Candace Pert, Donna Eden, and David Hamilton helped me to understand that the mind and body are one. Inspiring material such as The Secret, Way of the Peaceful Warrior, and What the Bleep Do We Know!? guided me to focus and visualize my healing. I also stumbled across the Emotional Freedom Technique (EFT), which alleviated my symptoms and cleared my past; and I used a technique known as PSYCH-K, which helped me reprogram my subconscious mind.

Today I am 100 percent healed, and I reached this point in a remarkably short amount of time for someone who has CFS. I've also changed careers and am running my own business. I now work with others who have CFS and help them overcome their self-limiting beliefs by intending, visualizing, and creating health. I've even written a book called Joyful Recovery from Chronic Fatigue Syndrome/ME [myalgic encephalomyelitis].

It was the EFT and the PSYCH-K that did it in the end. I got over the majority of the condition using EFT, but there was still a bit hanging on . . . and then I did a 45-minute PSYCH-K session known as the Core Belief Balance. At the start of the session I still had CFS, and at the end I didn't! I felt the overactive hypothalamic-pituitary-adrenal axis (HPA)— a system connecting the brain and body that controls stress and thus affects many of the body's systems—switch off when I rebalanced the belief that the world is a dangerous place! And interestingly, my resting heart rate, which I'd monitored on biofeedback software for some time, went from its usual 106 bpm to 72 bpm after the session and has stayed there ever since.

I feel that overcoming my illness has helped me find my path in life, and at the heart of this path was the intention to heal and the belief that it was possible.

This Worked Because . . .

Sasha recognized that she was running a daily subconscious pattern that was keeping her sick. Her turning point came when she acknowledged this and realized that suffering was a choice. You see, two people can have an identical illness, but one may suffer much more than another—the difference is in each person's attitude.

Sasha developed a powerfully positive attitude, which she directed toward healing herself. As she visualized her various body parts and systems becoming better, she would have stimulated these systems and the parts of her brain that governed them, tilting her body toward wellness. Undoubtedly, new subconscious patterns started running—such as, *I am getting better* and *I can do this*—which hugely aided her recovery.

Sometimes, when we're in recovery, our belief that we can get better wavers. But when we feed ourselves positive information that supports our beliefs, then they become strengthened and our rate of healing increases. That's what happened to Sasha: she saturated her thoughts with information that supported her belief that she could heal herself.

Finally, she used energy-healing techniques like EFT and PSYCH-K. I've personally witnessed some quite dramatic and rapid recoveries in people who were treated with these healing modalities, and I'm absolutely certain that they played a large role in Sasha's recovery.

Juliette's Story

I've been recovering from a number of physical and mental-health issues for some time now (including CFS/fibromyalgia and a nervous breakdown); although I'm not completely well, I'm a lot better than I was. Some of this may be due to the visualization that I've been doing on and off.

I often lie down and imagine water pouring through my body, clearing out all of the debris and illness. Images of a beautiful rose can also benefit me when I imagine them in my body, usually my heart center, by helping my emotional side heal from any hurts. In addition, I hold images of myself functioning optimally in my head; for example, I often envision myself walking in the mountains, as I used to enjoy this before I got sick. Sometimes this last visualization is a little vague, and I find it hard to see it clearly at times, since I've been through so many changes.

For the last six months, I've been working with a therapy called GIM (guided imagery and music) that has been very powerful. Images arise naturally in response to the stimulus of the music, and I've found the sensing and experiencing of these mental pictures extremely effectual in both my physical and emotional bodies. As the images formulate during the session, I find that it's easier to maintain them with an awareness throughout their duration, and I use them when I need to feel strong.

One of the prominent visualizations for me is seeing myself as having white angel wings and a light luminescent body. I've found this quite spiritually strengthening; in fact, remembering that I'm a spiritual being on this Earth who has dignity, value, and inner composure has helped me feel stronger every day.

Scenes of myself among mountains; on beaches; and with a healthy, vibrant body are often present. And the unicorn is an image that's been coming up a lot in the GIM therapy, so I use it often. Whenever I see myself riding it on a long beach, this image always give me strength. In between sessions, I like to visualize a unicorn near me, and again I find that this brings me a source of support in a spiritual way.

Since I'm currently doing this work, I'm still in the middle of seeing how I progress, but my life is definitely moving forward. This year I've visited places that I haven't been able to go to for 12 years—such as actual beaches and mountains!—and I've started to swim a lot more. I've also become more assertive with others and developed the spiritual and emotional strength to deal with the changes that I've been trying to make for a long time.

I do the GIM treatment once a month and then regularly visualize/ sense the images during the weeks in between. My therapist is now encouraging me to draw the images, which reinforces them and gives me something tangible to look at. All of this has been incredibly beneficial to my recovery.

This Works Because . . .

Juliette uses some powerful symbols in her scenes. Imagining water pouring through her body and clearing out the debris and illness filters into her unconscious mind and stimulates her brain along with its relevant areas of the body. In this way, illness will indeed be flushed out of her body. And the image of the rose at her heart, which symbolizes love, undoubtedly helps heal the past hurts that may have contributed to (or even caused) her current health issues.

The use of GIM has also been powerful for Juliette, as music often helps people get clearer images. One of the powerful symbols that it has given rise to for Juliette is the image of herself as a light luminescence. This is helping spiritually strengthen her and establish the belief that she has value and is worthy of health and fulfillment (lack of self-worth can be an underlying cause of some illnesses). Drawing or painting her images will further establish their power as well.

Finally, the symbol of the unicorn is highly invigorating. Like all of us, when Juliette feels spiritually strengthened, she feels powerful, worthy, and like she can achieve anything that she puts her mind to—including healing herself. She also feels emotionally more complete. These states of mind will stimulate Juliette's brain and body in such a way that healing is inevitable.

عنصرعنص

CHAPTER 14

VIRUSES, ALLERGIES, AND AUTOIMMUNE CONDITIONS

Barbara's Story

I'm fairly new to the conscious level of realizing that the power of our subconscious mind is available to us. On a number of occasions—but now more than ever—I've realized that the important question to ask isn't "How is life treating me?" but "How am I treating life?"

I am generally a healthy person and have developed the understanding that it's the power of my subconscious that's keeping me full of life. My thought process regarding wellness has always contained positive wording, and I simply see myself as always healthy.

As I assume is the case with most people, I don't like pain and suffering. For me, getting sick isn't an option, and the fact that I'm self-employed is a good enough motivation for keeping my body functioning well.

I'm in an industry where I see clients at close quarters and touch their hands on a regular basis. Because of this, people used to phone me to cancel their appointments if they'd fallen ill. I knew this meant that it would be very difficult for me to make a living, so my response to them was always: "Don't worry, I don't do viruses. As long as you're up to it, I'll be there."

While my clients tend to be amazed by my reaction, I've just never fallen prey to the bugs they might have. Like I said, I simply don't do flus and colds, and that's the way it is . . . and I'm sure this is all to do with what I tell my subconscious.

This Works Because . . .

Barbara has a positive attitude. Her comment that it's far more important to ask how she's treating life than how it's treating her is very empowering. Having such an attitude gives her the power, which is far better than seeing life as something that she has no control over.

This mind-set has helped Barbara to strengthen the belief that she "doesn't do" viruses. This is a very effective assertion and contributes to the strengthening of her immune system, which is keeping viruses at bay.

Susan's Story

I woke up feeling pretty lousy with what I immediately labeled as the start of the flu, but I decided that I didn't want it. I pictured my immune system kicking into gear—I saw all of my fantastic white blood cells multiplying like crazy and devouring the ugly, dark, unwanted germs with speed and ease. I also envisioned my immune system like tiny soldiers (I pictured something like the soldiers from The Nutcracker), and they kicked into action and destroyed and eliminated all of the rubbish.

Then I saw tiny sweeping brushes and pans cleaning up any remaining mess so that there was nothing left to reignite any infection. I imagined every cell working perfectly, just as it was designed to, and I sent love and gratitude to every tiny molecule in my body.

I also believe in something bigger, so I pulled down pure divine healing energy from the heavens through my crown and let it spread to every part of my body. I then balanced this off by sending down roots from the soles of my feet right into the healing earth.

The outcome of all this? Well, I've been feeling surprisingly okay today—not 100 percent perfect (yet!)—but I've had a really productive day at work. Now that I'm home, it's time for some TLC: a nice dinner, a hot bath, and an early night!

This Worked Because . . .

Susan's scene described her immune system "eating up" any unwanted germs. This stimulated her unconscious mind and autonomic nervous system so that her body's defense system would be strong enough to tackle any unwanted germs.

The use of "tiny sweeping brushes" also brought a slightly light-hearted feel to her scene. And her focus on the complete removal of any debris in this way ensured that there were no unwanted germs left over.

In addition, she generated feelings of love and gratitude, which is a powerful healing state. She then sent this into her cells, symbolically —and, therefore, actually—which strengthened them.

Susan's belief in something bigger also contributed to her healing. She illustrated her faith by imagining divine energy from the heavens flowing through her body, connecting her to the divine source.

Kevin's Story

Somehow I developed a wart on the inside of my right big toe. It exhibited all of the typical signs—a raised area of skin with a black center where the virus that caused it had taken hold—so I was tempted to use one of the freeze kits you can buy at the pharmacy. However, the location of the wart was on a sensitive part of my toe that made me squirm, so I decided to try visualization instead.

I sat down, closed my eyes, relaxed, and created the intention of a visualization that was appropriate in this case. Almost immediately, I had a clear picture in my mind of being underneath the wart, with its black center above me. Suddenly, the lower area resembled a building site—a crisscross mesh of protective skin formed between the wart and the skin below. It looked like rebar (the metal framework around which concrete is poured to strengthen it), and there was a clear inner intention that the virus would never be able to penetrate it. In fact, this protective layer was slowly moving up to push this unwanted growth off my toe.

Although I had this visualization only once, it was very clear and powerful, with a strong feeling of intention behind it.

About a week later, I thoroughly examined my toe after taking a shower. To my disappointment, the black center of the wart was still there. However, when I put my fingernails on either side of it, I was delighted to see it come right off! The skin is now almost healed.

This Worked Because . . .

Kevin used a scene that described a mesh of skin growing underneath the wart, which prevented the virus that caused the wart from penetrating the skin. This visualization gave instructions to his nervous system for the healing to occur.

I also like Kevin's use of having an intention to create an appropriate visualization. This caused his unconscious mind—which had a detailed knowledge of the growth on his toe, what caused it, and how to get rid of it—to show him what he needed to imagine. His visualization therefore stimulated the brain and his toe in just the right way so that the wart could be lifted off. That also explains why his images were so clear—he was seeing exactly what he needed to see and nothing else.

Interestingly, Kevin only envisioned the scene in his mind once, and sometimes that's all that is necessary. It's likely that this was helped by his intention to have the appropriate visualization.

Tomek's Story

I had two giant warts on my feet, and the one on my left foot was taking up almost the whole surface of my big toe. I learned from David Hamilton that I could heal them with visualization, and when I tried this, they disappeared! Wow! I'd had these warts for five or six years and had tried everything—I burned them, took drugs, and even tried herbs—and they're finally gone. Now I think I'll go and have a foot massage. Ha!

This is how I visualized: First, I imagined that I was burning the warts with acid. Sometimes I was just brushing them with an acid brush, but I also used a gun that fired it on them. The results were impressive after only one week. Next I tried also to visualize my feet and toes without any unpleasant growths, just nice skin. Finally—and this is the best part—on a regular basis (a couple times a day) I did a victory dance in the bathroom at work, at home, or in the car. Good fun!

I also noticed that I was always negative about the warts in the past. Every time my girlfriend told me to try to do something with them, I'd say, "No, it won't work." So thank you very much, David, 100 million times.

This Worked Because . . .

Tomek created a scene that told the story of the disappearance of his warts. This stimulated the areas of his brain where the warts were situated, along with his immune system—so that the growths quickly disappeared despite their large size.

You can also see from Tomek's description that he has a good sense of humor, and this certainly minimized his stress. I met him after a talk I gave in 2008, and I found this to definitely be true.

He did a regular victory dance, too, which reduced anxiety and helped his brain develop the neural patterns of belief that the warts were indeed shrinking. Ultimately, his body was stimulated to release all of the right chemicals to ensure that this was indeed what occurred.

Lynn's Story

In December 1978 I had the flu, which left me feeling achy, useless, and thoroughly miserable. After that I made a vow that I'd never have it again . . . and I never have!

I've managed this with the use of visualization and affirmations; each year I state that I have no use for being laid up with influenza and that I am healthy. Ever since '78, whenever I feel what might be the beginning of a simple illness, I visualize my immune system as my own personal army.

In the beginning, "Lynn's Army" was equipped with bows and arrows, but over the years it's evolved into a battalion of fighters that use beams of red light to annihilate the attacking enemy, followed by blue light for healing and green light for regeneration. I visualize myself inside a bubble that alternates between blue, green, and all the shades between.

This Works Because . . .

Lynn's story describes how her "army" defeats the enemy of cold and flu. This visualization ensures that her immune system is strong and, indeed, attacking any enemies.

However, Lynn's story has another part to it. As you'll see in the following pages, her opinion is that viewing her immune system as an army that attacks an enemy has had some negative effects. Compare this with how some of the previous visualizers showed love toward diseased cells.

Lynn's Story, Part II

Unfortunately, my "anti-flu visualization" didn't prepare me for another illness, diagnosed on Christmas Eve 2002. I was admitted to the hospital after suffering from kidney failure, and a biopsy revealed systemic lupus erythematosus, an autoimmune disease that's caused by the body's immune system turning against itself. My army had turned mutinous!

During my four-month stay in the hospital, I was too ill to do anything other than sleep. I was treated with a toxic cocktail of nuclear drugs, including chemotherapy; I also had to spend four hours, three times per week, on dialysis.

I'm a very spiritual person, and during this time I felt as if I were surrounded and protected by angels; I guess this was how my subconscious interpreted the feeling of trust I learned to have in those who were in charge of my care and well-being. During my waking hours, I was convinced that I was surrounded by an aura of rainbow colors that was healing and protecting me, and I never doubted that I'd recover from my ordeal.

When I was eventually discharged from the hospital, I couldn't walk due to muscular atrophy. I hated being confined to a wheelchair, and this resulted in a recurring dream in which I was enjoying the freedom of being able to run with the wind in my hair. Considering that all of my hair had fallen out due to chemotherapy, this was a rather positive dream!

This dream started the deliberate visualization of seeing myself walking, which was followed by actually carrying out the task and taking more and more steps each week—until I was finally able to get rid of the wheelchair altogether. I'm still a long way from being able to walk the eight miles per day that I enjoyed before I became ill, and I'm still considered to be disabled. With the use of visualization, however, I remain hopeful that my ability will improve.

Coping with lupus forced me to review my use of visualization. Mutiny is the result of disharmony among the troops, so I began to see my illness in a different light. Lupus is the Latin word for "wolf," and I guess my interest in mythology played a big part in learning to deal with my affliction. The following is taken from an article I wrote for Lupus U.K.'s official magazine, News & Views, which I entitled "The Beautiful Beast Within":

> *For many years, since childhood, I have been fascinated with mythology, particularly the legends of shape-shifters: humans who can take on the shapes of animals, birds, or fish. I have spent most of my adult life in some form of spiritual training, which has included walking the shamanic path and learning about power animals.*
>
> *I met my power animal many years ago. She appeared to me in the form of a beautiful wolf with silvery-gray fur. We have traveled together, and she has taught me many things. In the Native American Indian tradition, Wolf is teacher, and Rudyard Kipling used this description in his Jungle Book stories. Arkela is the alpha male wolf, who finds the orphaned Mowgli and rears him as his own. This is why the Scout movement adopted the name for their pack leaders.*
>
> *In Celtic mythology, Wolf is the mentor. Wolf is seen as the companion of the God of Nature, Cernunnos, and also the Goddess of*

Childbirth, Bridget; both are thought to take on the shape of the wolf and walk between the worlds. For the wolf, communication and community are of the utmost importance. The alpha male and female are chosen for their abilities to teach and lead the others, so cooperation is of vital importance among the members of a pack. These qualities are things that most people regard as vital in a society that wishes to live harmoniously.

For me, lupus is much more than a disease. She is the beautiful beast that resides within me. Just like any wild animal, I have to be careful how I approach her; she needs special care and consideration, but is happy enough to accept the offering of steak every so often! If I have overworked her, she howls and makes me suffer for my inconsideration, and I know to step back and leave her in peace to rest for a day or so.

Sometimes I step back and take a good long look at her; she is wild and ferocious, yet she is beautiful and wise, and I know she has something of the greatest importance to teach me and those working in the field of learning about lupus. Despite the scars I carry, accredited by my own carelessness in dealing with her, I love her. She is a part of me and I have learned that we can only walk side by side if I learn to consider her needs as well as my own.

Visualizing my illness as an alter ego has helped me to cope with having lupus. Six months after I came out of the hospital, my consultant remarked on how well I was, considering that I had been so devastatingly ill. Now, four years on, I am off all lupus-related drugs and enjoying remission.

This Worked Because . . .

Lynn showed trust and care, and she had no doubt that she would recover. This strong, positive belief characterizes some recoveries that are chalked up to the miraculous, and it also underlies some recoveries of people who take placebos for illnesses.

Lynn visualized herself walking, which stimulated her muscles and the brain areas that controlled them so that she was indeed able to get up and move. In the same fashion, the stroke, Parkinson's-disease, and spinal-cord patients described in Chapter 6 recovered movement through mental imagery.

This remarkable woman viewed lupus as disharmony in Lynn's Army—that they turned on her—and this realization has dramatically helped her healing. Lupus is an autoimmune condition where the immune system attacks the body. Other similar conditions include diabetes mellitus (type 1), multiple sclerosis, myasthenia gravis, and rheumatoid arthritis.

The symbolism that Lynn used to make peace with her condition—that is, learning to love the beautiful beast within—ultimately facilitated her recovery. It stimulated her nervous system in the appropriate way so that all of the relevant parts of her body were able to heal, and the immune system ceased its attack upon her.

I asked Lynn if she felt that her use of Lynn's Army was aggressive and maybe had a link with lupus. This was her reply:

> That is exactly what I was getting at, that perhaps my tactics were aggressive. Something I never mentioned before was that after I learned I had lupus, I started visualizing "it" as Jabba the Hutt and zapping it. But my guides told me that this was wrong because the image represented hate, aggression, negativity, and so on, and that the way to overcome the illness was to send it love. Then the whole wolf thing came to me—and because I love wolves, it was much easier to learn to love my illness.
>
> I think that maybe instead of fighting illnesses, we need to embrace them and learn what they're trying to teach us about ourselves. In my case, I've meditated on it and done some past-life regression with the help of my partner, Matt. Louise Hay says that lupus is about "giving up . . . anger and punishment," and this goes along with what I've been learning about myself. I'm working on trying to love my body instead of resenting it. I guess what I'm saying is that we can't fight fire with fire, but by "starving" the flames, as in taking away whatever feeds them, the fire will go out, and the illness will subside. We can only do that by surrounding ourselves with unconditional love, and visualization can help.

When we visualize, we don't need to use fear, hate, or violence in the sense that we see something suffer. It's okay to see the removal of an illness, but we don't need to use violence to do it. So firing lasers or bullets is okay when it's not done in an aggressive, enemy-hunting way. For instance, Carol (Pat's sister, from Chapter 10) mentally used a blue and white laser beam or green acid to dissolve cancer cells, but she wasn't viewing them as enemies or imagining them suffering.

Seeing an illness or diseased cells as enemies that need to be vanquished through violence may defeat the illness, but the internal use of aggression could open us to further attacks. This won't always happen, of course, and it really depends upon our personal beliefs and the strength of our own will. Nevertheless, there are real benefits in making the scene more lighthearted while still working with removal, cleaning, or imagining the healing symbolically.

Drew's Story

In October 2004 I contracted myasthenia gravis, which is a breakdown of the immune system that's considered incurable but controllable with medication. Then, in October 2005, I went on a two-day vibrational-medicine workshop in the north of Scotland.

At the end of the second day, my condition had become extremely acute. My eyelids drooped, I was seeing double, and I couldn't move my jaw. It got so serious that I couldn't speak, eat, or swallow; and the myasthenia started to close down my lungs. A woman named Dr. Petrow came up to me and said, "Drew, I'm afraid that you're too ill to travel. You will have to come home with me and stay with my family, and I will treat you."

At this stage of the condition, the only orthodox treatments available to me to counteract the symptoms were steroids and blood transfusions. However, I received three or four holistic, vibrational-medicine treatments per week from Dr. Petrow with no medication. I was able to go home in February 2006, three months later! (How many doctors do you know who would take a patient home with them for three whole months?)

On Christmas Eve 2005, after I'd been incapacitated for 50 days and lost 60 pounds, I attended a service at Pluscarden Abbey where the monks were conducting a service in Gregorian chant. As I sat in a pew and listened to the singing, my eyelids suddenly lifted. I could see, I could move my jaw freely, and, hey, I could speak! All of my symptoms just fell away! They returned shortly afterward, but at that point I knew that I'd be healed.

Myasthenia is triggered by antibodies in the bloodstream, which lead to the breakdown of the immune system, so I made sure to regularly use visualization in my recovery. (I asked David Hamilton how to visualize eliminating antibodies, and his recommendation was to imagine being at an air-gun stall at a fairground and shooting ducks [antibodies] off a moving conveyor belt. This image worked wonderfully for me.) It's difficult to assess the precise contribution of visualization to my recovery, yet my own view is that it supported the intensive vibrational-medicine treatments that I was receiving three or four times a week.

I had total faith in my doctor, the treatment, the visualization, and that one day I could and would be well. Where this absolute faith came from I do not know, but I have no doubts about the power of the mind being a major contributory factor in the healing of the body.

After my return home in February 2006, I had 11 months of blood, muscle, and eye tests. In January 2007, the head of neurology said to me, "Mr. Pryde, you're the only person I've heard of who has fully recovered from myasthenia gravis." I was told that no further treatment would be necessary.

This Worked Because . . .

There are a number of factors that most likely contributed to Drew's complete recovery. One was his absolute faith that he *would* recover. Considering that myasthenia gravis is considered incurable, this demonstrates how the power of faith profoundly affects the body. Faith such as Drew's is a state often associated with miracles of healing.

The love and care of Dr. Petrow also played a huge role, as did the vibrational-medicine treatments that she administered. Vibrational medicine is based on the fact that all matter vibrates at a certain frequency. It's not too hard to grasp this if you consider that all atoms, by their very nature, are pure vibrations of energy. Although there's little scientific evidence of the effectiveness of this type of medicine at present, it's my opinion that this is a very powerful system of healing that works at a deep level in the body. Keep in mind that many breakthroughs in science take years to be fully embraced by the scientific community. Likewise, doctors who pioneer new techniques are often called "mavericks" or even "quacks" by the medical community until evidence eventually silences the critics.

Yet in mainstream science, one of the key vibrational frequencies of water (around 3300 to 3500 cm^{-1}) is used in laboratory analysis in the technique known as infrared spectrophotometry, which is done routinely in university, pharmaceutical, and medical-research laboratories all over the world. Vibrational medicine administers frequencies that aim to neutralize diseases in the body. And since sound is a vibration, it's a form of vibrational healing; that's why Drew experienced such a dramatic improvement while listening to the Gregorian chants.

In myasthenia gravis, antibodies block the acetylcholine receptors in a key movement-control part of the brain. Drew imagined these antibodies being neutralized by an air gun on a fairground conveyor belt, which was a powerful symbolic visualization. The meaning seeped into his unconscious mind, resulting in activation of his nervous system in such a way that the presence of antibodies actually diminished. So Drew's healing scene obviously played a big part in his recovery.

Now even though you could consider the use of a gun as violence, please note that Drew's scene didn't use extreme force. The location of the fairground set a lighthearted scene, as did the children's game of shooting the ducks. The visualization was largely symbolic in that it not only represented the expulsion of the antibodies from the specific area of Drew's brain, but it also portrayed the removal of myasthenia gravis.

Elizabeth's Story

I had terrible hay fever for years and had to take antihistamines daily. I decided to try visualization, and after doing it only once or twice, I've since had to take an antihistamine two or three times in the last eight months and had no hay-fever symptoms for the rest of the summer.

In my visualization, I saw a "little me" going toward my immune system, which I imagined was made up of hundreds of little soldiers. As I moved in their direction, we couldn't see each other properly because there was quite a bit of fog. It turned out that this lack of visibility was the reason my immune system was attacking me: it feared that I was an enemy. However, as the fog cleared, my immune system and I saw each other. I told it, "Hey, it's me, there's no need to fight. Just chill out and do only what you have to in order to keep me healthy. Take the rest of the day off."

I then saw the "head guy" shout to all of his troops, "Hey, it's just Elizabeth—we don't need to fight." His troops let out a cheer and started to play tennis and lie down on beds to sunbathe. I hugged the head guy and then walked off.

This Worked Because . . .

Elizabeth communicated with her immune system and asked it to relax and chill out. Allergies arise when your body's natural defense system overactively responds to allergens (substances that cause an allergic reaction). Elizabeth simply asked hers to do just enough to keep her healthy. She then imagined her immune characters relaxing and enjoying a game of tennis. This communication seeped into her unconscious mind, stimulating the immune system to indeed calm down its sensitivity.

The presence of fog in her scene symbolized that things were not clear with her immune system, and that's why it was overactive. Once she mentally cleared the fog, communication was able to take place and the immune system could function normally again.

There's a biochemical similarity between some allergies and autoimmune conditions, so this visualization could be adapted and applied to autoimmune conditions as well. I've done just that and listed it in the Visualizations section toward the back of the book (Appendix II).

৩৩৩৩

CHAPTER 15

YOU CAN DO IT

These stories in Part II show that the mind has a powerful ability to heal the body. I'm aware that some people might want to see medical records in order to believe that these "miracles" actually occurred, but I'd like to suggest that they take place every day, all over the world. Relying too much on the medical evidence in front of us reduces our ability to open our minds and believe that such amazing healings are possible. Our own belief, or lack thereof, can enhance or block healing; therefore, we need to open our minds and accept the possibility that people's visualizations really did play a significant role in them curing themselves.

I believe that the mind plays a major role in many of the recoveries that people experience, even when they're simultaneously using the drugs that their doctors have prescribed. We feel hope when we take medicine, which alters our biology and also means that part of the influence of a drug is the placebo effect.

Our visualizations change the microscopic structure of our brains: they expand and contract our brain maps; stimulate cells in the area that we're envisioning being healed; and produce neuropeptides that are released, which causes chemical changes in many other organs as well. Genes are switched on and off all throughout the body, tipping its genetic balance toward healing. And as I've mentioned, it's highly likely that genes in stem cells produce proteins that cause the stem cells to morph into the exact type that are required to replace damaged ones. As I've said, the science of this hasn't been fully investigated yet, but I'm totally convinced that it does occur. Eventually, the body is healed in accordance with the images, real or symbolic, that we've held in our minds.

Many of the unexplainable healings, including spontaneous remissions, that have been documented throughout history have most likely involved this process. The miracle really begins in the mind, which then brings about the necessary biological changes that allow individuals to cure themselves.

Indeed, when he healed the blind, Christ said, "According to your faith it will be done to you" (Matthew 9:29).

တတတတ

PART III

IN CLOSING

CHAPTER 16

THE POWER OF LOVE

"Where there is great love there are always miracles."
— Willa Cather

There's one more topic that I want to explore in this book: love. Such is its power to heal the body and mind—as well as nurture the soul—that I think it deserves a chapter of its own.

A perfect example of what I'm talking about here comes from Aaron. He was so terribly stressed: He was struggling financially, the recent pay raise he was expecting hadn't come through, and he wasn't getting along well with his boss. Every day was like a nightmare for him, and he just couldn't shake the constant feelings of anxiety, fear, and dread.

Then, completely unexpectedly, the woman Aaron had secretly been pining for declared her love for him. In an instant, all of his problems disappeared. Of course the stressful situations still existed, but his *experience* of them drastically changed. The negative emotions he was feeling dissolved overnight.

Experience Love

Love shifts our perception of things. Miracles occur inside us when love reaches in and stirs our souls. Its light then shines upon our lives, totally changing them. My research into the mind-body connection has convinced me that emotional pain is at the root of many illnesses, but it can be cured with love. Therefore, love has the power to heal our physical conditions, too.

The most obvious place to experience love is in relationships— either with family, friends, or a romantic partner. We all need relationships because they're the foundation for our experience of life. Without them, life has less meaning.

In *Aikido and the Harmony of Nature,* Mitsugi Saotome, founder of the Aikido Schools of Ueshiba, writes:

> If you were all alone in the Universe with no one to talk to, no one with which to share the beauty of the stars, to laugh with, to touch, what would be your purpose in life? It is other life, it is love, that gives your life meaning. . . . We must discover the joy of each other, the joy of challenge, the joy of growth.

I believe that our main purpose in life is to deepen our experience of love. To that end, when people who are dying reflect on what was most important in their lives, most of them say that it was the quality of their relationships and the time they spent with their loved ones that tops the list . . . while everything else was just details.

As we experience love, we also experience healing of the mind, emotions, and body. I'm not suggesting that all we need are relationships to cure ourselves of serious illnesses. But love, real love, will change our experience of them. As a result, many of the things that mattered before won't seem to mean as much because we'll have discovered for ourselves what's really important. Stress, which accelerates disease of the mind and body, will fade away and be replaced with gratitude and a deep reverence for all forms of life. And from that space, if there's anything practical that we need to do in order to facilitate any physical healing, we're perfectly suited to do it, with more energy, vibrancy, and motivation at our fingertips than ever before.

Love enhances us. It makes us so much more. With it we become who we've always wanted to become, and our loved ones are able to see in us so much more than we see when we look in the mirror. From that space, we expand into ourselves.

In his poem "Love," Roy Croft writes:

> I love you,
> Not only for what you are,
> But for what I am
> When I am with you.

Of course, like all things, relationships require continual attention and work. How would growth occur if we weren't occasionally challenged to work at things? Molleen Matsumura recently wrote on her popular Website entitled Sweet Reason:

> Love is like a campfire: It may be sparked quickly, and at first the kindling throws out a lot of heat, but it burns out quickly. For long-lasting, steady warmth (with delightful bursts of intense heat from time to time), you must carefully tend the fire.

Ursula K. Le Guin puts it another way: "Love doesn't just sit there, like a stone, it has to be made, like bread; re-made all the time, made new." And there is a skill to remaking love, which is understood through experience. For example, we learn that we have to occasionally put our own desires on the back burner for those of another: in romantic relationships, as our love deepens, we put our own needs aside so that we may contribute to the fulfillment of a loved one; the desire to listen replaces the need to be right. The outcome is that we discover great joy and experience deep healing.

I've realized that love is both the most complex thing imaginable and also the simplest: it allows us to learn what we should and shouldn't do, what's best, and how to deal with the emotions of those we care deeply for. These things can be tricky, but when we make a choice that's based in love, the right solution is always simple. We may have wanted to get our point across because we perceived it to be vitally important or thought that it could help our loved ones so much. But in the period of time when we stay silent and give those special people in our lives our full and undivided attention—when we really listen without our minds attempting to figure out what we think we need to say next—we discover great happiness. What we thought was so important often turns out not to be so. In the moments that follow this choice, love shines from our soul and illuminates the faces of those we are closest to, along with our hearts and our lives.

❧❧

We don't need to wait to be in a romantic relationship to experience love. It's all around us. In fact, it's inside of us. It's how we choose to experience the moments of life, in whichever form they come in, that allows us to feel love.

You can experience love in many ways: by showing kindness to a stranger, smiling at someone on the street, or allowing someone to pull out ahead of you on the road while driving. Notice how you feel when you do these things. The more you do them, the more they will affect you—and it will become easier for your soul to illuminate your path and show compassion and gratitude.

The Power of Gratitude

"Happiness cannot be traveled to, owned,
earned, worn, or consumed. Happiness is the spiritual
experience of living every minute with love, grace, and gratitude."
— **Denis Waitley**

A friend once told me that gratitude changed his life in 30 days. He was depressed at the time and had been for a while. One day he decided to try a simple exercise: every day he wrote down 50 things that he was grateful for, and he did this for a full month.

It was hard at first, but he always managed to find 50 things. Sometimes it took him all day; he'd do a bit in the morning and then add to it throughout the day, but he'd always have his list completed by the time he went to bed. As the days passed, it got easier. After two weeks, he was feeling so much better that he was writing 75 items on his gratitude list. By the end of the month, he was a different person.

What's funny is that often when we change from the inside out, our deepest hopes and dreams move toward us. After completing the exercise, for instance, my friend met the woman of his dreams and got the job he'd always hoped for.

Why not try this exercise for 30 days and see just how much of an impact it can have on your own life? It might be difficult at first if you're really struggling with things, but it *will* get easier. As the power of gratitude causes a crack to appear in the veil of life's difficulties, the light of your soul will shine through. The first thing you'll feel is a tickle around your heart—not a physical tickle, but an emotional one. You'll just feel better. But then more cracks will appear and your light will get stronger until soon, as if by magic, your *experience* of life will change . . . and then your life itself will change.

Go the Extra Mile

My partner, Elizabeth, and I were recently driving to visit our families in Scotland when we stopped at a restaurant to have breakfast. We were both a little tired because we'd left really early in the morning and, due to being very busy in the few days leading up to our trip, we hadn't had very much sleep . . . but the fatigue left us when we encountered the woman who served us. She was working behind a long counter and got us our order before we moved along down the line to pay. She greeted us with a warm smile and some friendly comments, and her genuinely kind and positive attitude was like a refreshing shower. I think she could tell that we were feeling tired because she gave us an extra large portion of breakfast to accompany the big portion of joy, which was just what we needed. Within a few seconds, Elizabeth and I were feeling much better, and we hadn't even eaten yet!

When we got to our table and tucked into our meals, I noticed a feedback form featuring a new initiative being run by the restaurant that was called "Go that Extra Mile." The form gave customers the opportunity to comment if a staff member had gone that extra mile in providing good service. Since Elizabeth and I had just experienced great service, we happily filled out the form.

However, when prompted to include the staff member's name along with the time and date, we realized that we hadn't noticed the woman's name. We went back to the counter and tried to read her name tag—the problem was that the restaurant was filling up and she was quite busy, so we just couldn't see her name.

At this point, I have to admit that we thought of leaving, because it was a little bit uncomfortable to be standing alongside a line of hungry people, some of whom thought that we were trying to cut in. But in life, love often stretches and presents us with opportunities to burst out of our comfort zones. We either act on these opportunities and grow a bit more, or we walk away and wait for another one to present itself.

I decided to shout across to the woman and ask her name. I told her that I was filling out the feedback form and that we were really grateful for the way she'd made us feel when we had arrived earlier. Right then, her face just glowed and her smile almost stretched the full width of her face. I suddenly felt inspired to point out the form to some of the customers in line, too. I said, "Doesn't she have a lovely smile? What a great way to be served . . . with a smile!" And before I knew it, they were all smiling.

Then, as fortune would have it, the woman's manager appeared. I was on a roll now and had no intentions of stopping. I told her what I'd written on the form, right in front of the woman and the customers. The manager's smile suddenly broke through, too. And none of the customers seemed to care that I was momentarily keeping them from their meals. This was a little moment of magic, and everyone was participating in it—I don't think anyone wanted to interrupt.

The manager said it was a great pleasure to receive some positive feedback; apparently we had been the first (I don't know when this initiative had started). She said that all they'd received so far was complaints, so it was really special to receive positive comments, especially in such a personal way.

I'm sure that many customers had been pleased with their service in the past but hadn't bothered to say so. Isn't it funny how most people reserve their feedback until they have something negative to say? How many individuals do you know who send a card to a restaurant when they've had a nice meal, just to say thanks? But how many complain when a meal doesn't meet their expectations?

In the absence of some form of positive feedback, people don't realize what a great job they're doing or what a gift their job is to others. We deprive them of knowing this, and I think it's up to us to tell them.

I've said on so many occasions that those who complain have the loudest voices. Too often, things are changed to suit the minority because those who frequently make their displeasures known usually create a big fuss. I think it's about time that we start to show more gratitude in the world. Let's make a fuss about the good things. Let gratitude have the loudest voice so that things change for the better. I feel that we could make a huge difference in others' lives, and our own, by going that extra mile to say or do something really nice for someone. Don't wait until something bothers you before you offer feedback.

And have you ever noticed how good it makes you feel when you do something nice for another person? After that experience in the restaurant, I felt on top of the world. Amazing, isn't it? One simple act of kindness had the power to radically change Elizabeth's mood, my mood, and how we felt about the world; it also inspired good feelings in a staff member, her manager, and a whole line of strangers as well.

"Pinging" Kindness

> *"Love cures people—both the ones*
> *who give it and the ones who receive it."*
> **— Karl Menninger**

I love to "ping" kindness. I might be walking down a busy street, and when I see someone who looks sad, I imagine pinging a little ball of kindness toward them, then watching it land. For effect, I usually flick my finger as if I'm projecting the ball at them.

I like to get quite creative with this gesture at times. Usually, I give the ball of kindness a color—whichever one I'm inspired by at the time. I also ping whatever quality I feel the person needs. Sometimes, instead of kindness, I might ping happiness; in other situations, it might be fulfillment, love, joy, or forgiveness. I look at the person and just ping the first quality that pops into my mind.

Sometimes I ping more than a little ball. I've also been known to send it to several people at once. When impelled to do so, I'll break a large ball into smaller pieces and shower people with them. Other times, I send a ball rolling down the street and watch it blow through a whole line of people.

And a funny thing tends to happen: When I ping, people often look toward me and smile. There have been several occasions when those who were looking sad or troubled just suddenly appeared different. I like to think that there was an exchange between us in these moments and that the person did actually receive something that was helpful to him or her.

But it's always helpful to me, too. We get back what we give out, as they say. To ping kindness puts me in a state of consciousness of having kindness to ping.

In *Romeo and Juliet,* Shakespeare wrote:

My bounty is as boundless as the sea,
My love as deep; the more I give to thee,
The more I have, for both are infinite.

Love is infinite. When we give it out, in any form whatsoever, we receive some in return. From the consciousness of kindness, compassion, joy, or whatever quality we ping, our soul shines out from us, passing through our heart first. That's why it makes us feel good. And when we feel good, healing begins.

Kindness, of course, is also practical. Demonstrating it to others helps them, but it also helps us. For example, joining a charity makes a real difference in the lives of those who receive its benefits, but there's something immensely healing in the act of dedicating ourselves to helping others. Charitable work often takes away our own pain, as our inner dialogue of suffering gradually changes from "How can I receive?" to "How can I give?"

Many people have recovered from depression by launching themselves into charitable work. This reminds me of how Patch Adams (the doctor featured in the movie of the same name that starred Robin Williams), once advised my dear friend Margaret McCathie to "Go out and serve and see your depression lift." She did, and it did!

I really believe that spiritual and emotional healing occurs in this way. The more love we can consciously spread in the world, the more we heal ourselves. The word *heal* comes from the Old English word *hælen*, which means "to make whole." So when we give love, we make ourselves whole.

Change Yourself and You Change the World

I've often spoken about the similarities between people and tuning forks. When a tuning fork is struck, other things around it begin to vibrate. Similarly, when we're in a bad mood, we perpetuate a gloomy mood around us—people start to act as we're acting. The same, of course, happens when we feel happy: we inspire others around us to be happy, too.

I believe that we send out mental and emotional vibrations everywhere we go, and neuroscience is beginning to shed light upon this phenomenon. It turns out that we unconsciously perceive other people's moods, and our mirror neurons reproduce these sentiments in ourselves.

Imagine if these vibrations were colors. Some days we would send out red and other days we might send out gold. I think that we all have a color that represents our average state, the person we tend to be most of the time. And the more we give love, the more our color is "love-colored."

I've written in other books that science is painting a picture of an interconnected world—a world where we're all connected on a deep level. This brings to mind the way Carl Jung described a collective field of consciousness that connected everyone, which he called the collective unconscious. Each of us has an unconscious mind that overlaps with everyone else's, and the edges between them are blurred. Therefore, at some level, we share a connection, just as the Internet forms a connection between all of our computers.

I've also used the analogy of a spider's web to describe this connection, but it's actually more similar to a web of intelligence. The interesting thing about this is that to change the color of the web, all we need to do is change ourselves, and then our vibrations will ripple along its strands. If we want to see more love in the world, we must start by becoming more loving ourselves. If we want to see more peace in the world, we need to start by becoming more peaceful inside ourselves. His Holiness the Dalai Lama said:

> Responsibility does not only lie with the leaders of our countries or with those who have been appointed or elected to do a particular job. It lies with each of us individually. Peace, for example, starts within each one of us. When we have inner peace, we can be at peace with those around us.

It's Okay to Suffer

I've noticed that one thing that distances people from happiness is the word *should*. We think that we should do this or that, or that we should have done something different—or, more painfully, that we should *be* something different. But I think that we start to feel happiness and peace and experience healing when we love ourselves—when we say, "It's okay to be me!"

If you're suffering right now, that's okay. Don't torture yourself by thinking that you shouldn't be. If you're not happy right now, don't beat yourself up by convincing yourself that you should be happy. People who read self-help material often think that they aren't enlightened enough, loving enough, forgiving enough, or peaceful enough. Then they criticize every little thing they do wrong and, even worse, beat themselves up for every negative thought. I know this to be true, because I still do it sometimes. But it's okay; that's all part of growing up. We'll all get there in the end. In the meantime, lighten up, for your own sake.

My dear friend Stephen Mulhearn, a shamanic teacher who runs a retreat center called Lendrick Lodge in Scotland, has a great sense of humor and often makes light of the way we beat ourselves up. One time he had me in stitches of laughter when he was talking about a friend who was working hard on maintaining a new nutritious diet. Stephen told me that his friend had shaken his head and said, in a deadly serious and grave voice, as if confessing to a murder, "My only vice is milk."

The way Stephen described all of this to me was just so funny—he has that talent. But it got me thinking about how we're our own worst critics. In fact, other people don't need to criticize us; we do a good enough job of it ourselves.

But it's when we can say the following statement that we move toward wholeness: "It's okay to be me. I don't need to be perfect, healed, or enlightened right now; I just need to be me today." This is love for ourselves, and it's the space that inner peace grows from. On the power of love, Hermann Hesse, winner of the 1946 Nobel Prize for literature, wrote:

> You know quite well, deep within you, that there is a single magic, a single power, a single salvation . . . and that is called loving. Well then, love your suffering. Do not resist it, do not flee from it. . . . It is only your aversion that hurts, nothing else.

When we make peace with who we are, we begin to love ourselves. And from this space of not running away from that person we see in the mirror, healing can be profound.

At the end of the day, love, in any form—for ourselves and for others—is powerful medicine. Therefore, I'd like to end the book with an inspiring little exchange. I couldn't find the source of it, but I'm grateful to the author:

> A wise physician said to me, "I have been practicing medicine for 30 years, and I have prescribed many things. But in the long run, I have learned that for most of what ails the human creature, the best medicine is love."
>
> "What if it doesn't work?" I asked.
>
> "Double the dose," he replied.

I think that about says it all!

လူာလူာလူာလူာ

APPENDIX I

QUANTUM FIELD
HEALING (QFH)

*"An ocean traveler has even more vividly the impression
that the ocean is made of waves than that it is made of water."*
— **Arthur S. Eddington**

I was once a scientist with one of the world's largest pharmaceutical companies, but I resigned in 1999, partly due to my fascination with how healing could be achieved by using the mind. I had been playing around with visualization for years, researching the topic of mind over matter and reading many spiritual writings in my spare time. Coming from a scientific background, with an understanding of the placebo effect, I knew that the mind powerfully affected biology. But I was curious to know at what level thought could do this. Was a thought a force that originated in the gap between the branches of neurons? Did it shift molecules around?

I had achieved very high marks in the classes on the quantum sciences I'd taken in college, and had read a lot more on the subject since then on my own. I didn't believe that thoughts arose out of interactions between chemicals in the brain back then, and I still don't. Of course, chemical changes do alter how we think and feel, but the actual thoughts are ours, and I believe that they originate independently of chemicals.

Science says that thoughts are products of chemicals because chemical changes can alter the mind, but now we know that thoughts cause chemical changes, too. The question then remains: which comes first, the thoughts or the chemicals? Each affects the other, but one has to come first. I'm sure that thoughts ultimately come first and influence the very core of reality, at the level where the tiniest particles are created.

If you look inside your body, you see cells. If you look inside cells, you find molecules, of which DNA is one. Looking at what DNA is made of, you learn that it's atoms. But if you look inside an atom, it's mostly empty space. Most people have heard of protons, neutrons, and electrons—the subatomic particles that compose atoms (there are actually many, many more particles)—but they don't realize what they look like and how far apart they are. If a proton were the size of a grape, then an electron would be smaller than the thickness of a hair and approximately two miles away from the proton. That's how much space is between them inside an atom, and atoms are what your body is made of. At this quantum level, reality is mostly empty space . . . we are mostly empty space.

And it gets even weirder, because the subatomic particles (protons, neutrons, electrons, and so on) are not particles at all. You see, they aren't solid but are actually vibrations of energy; in fact, the latest research in quantum physics tells us that they're tiny vibrating strings. When a string vibrates at a certain speed, our instruments detect the vibrations as specific particles (a proton, for instance). But when it vibrates at a different speed, or when two vibrations interact with each other, then we detect a different particle (possibly an electron). Think of it as one vibration creating a red particle and another, at a different speed, creating a blue one. The bottom line is that reality is not solid, but is constructed from vibrations of energy. Scientists believe that these vibrations originate in a larger field of energy, sometimes called the quantum field. Therefore, subatomic particles—which make up atoms, which make up molecules, which make up cells, which make up humans (and our diseases)—are born in the quantum field.

The Quantum Field Healing Visualization

Although I was still working as a scientist, I believed that this was where thoughts interfaced with matter—at the level where matter was created—because ultimately the mind was the instrument that created our picture of reality. Our brains allow us to see matter where really only vibrations of energy exist. If we could align our minds with that level, I reasoned, then our thoughts could be much more powerful—we could consciously shape our reality and thus eliminate disease. While our subconscious thoughts have always interacted at this level, our many beliefs and assumptions about reality distort the quality of our conscious thinking. That's why, in terms of healing results, we tend to get only what we're prepared for: when we have faith in or believe that something is possible or will happen (such as in the placebo effect), we bypass some of our previous suppositions and align ourselves more fully with our unconscious and the deeper level of reality.

I came to believe that faith was extremely powerful, and that this could explain some miracles that mystics and great spiritual masters had performed. At their level of knowledge and understanding—their level of consciousness—their thoughts, uncluttered with conventional beliefs and assumptions, influenced matter much more powerfully than most people's.

A few years after I left the pharmaceutical industry, I wanted a powerful visualization that anyone could use, that could be done quickly, and that would symbolically align the mind with the core level of reality, bypassing our limiting judgments. I actually awoke one night in 2001 with a series of images running through my mind. I wrote them down, and this became what I called Quantum Field Healing (QFH).

Quantum Field Healing works symbolically at the source level of an illness or disease. Its main principle is to look at a disease or illness not as a physical thing but as the energy waves (or vibrations) that it originated from in the quantum field. In this way, you don't see a disease as a physical thing, but rather as patterns of energy vibrations that can be changed, just as you could change a wave on a pond by dropping a pebble in it. In QFH, the stone represents a thought.

Let's say that you have a specific disease (or illness, condition, or pain). Visualize the afflicted body part and then imagine that you were taking a camera inside so that you could see the bones, muscles, flesh, tendons, and joints. Now go deeper inside the part until you see the cells that it's made of, and then into a cell itself to see the proteins, enzymes, and DNA. Enter the DNA and see the atoms that compose it; then pick an atom and go inside it. See the subatomic particles—protons, neutrons, electrons, and whatever else you can identify. Imagine them as stars in the night sky.

The quantum field is a field of energy from which particles condense, analogous to the way in which raindrops condense from clouds. The particles begin their lives in the quantum field. Now, rather than imagining that you're going inside the particles, go to their source—the quantum field itself. See it as a place of total stillness in deep space or a motionless lake of energy, like a pond early in the morning.

Visualize the waves (vibrations) of disease and then mentally remove them, emblematically removing the disease in the process.

Mentally say, "Show me the waves [or vibrations] of _____," and state the name of the disease if you know it, or just call it "the disease." You're asking your unconscious mind to symbolically show you the waves. See the vibrations in any way that comes to mind. I usually see them as stormy seas.

Mentally state, "Cancel!" and watch the waves collapse and disappear. You are now back to your place of total stillness and have just canceled the disease.

Next, replace the old vibrations with new ones. Imagine dropping a pebble into the still lake of energy, only make it a pebble of light, which represents your intention. It may be white or any color that comes to mind. In the state of higher awareness that QFH brings, you may even see symbols—I've seen a face once or twice myself. You can imagine pebbles of anything you want, and be as general or specific as you wish. For my own purposes, I sometimes use "perfect health" or "healing," and I usually add one or two extra qualities as well. For instance, I often add pebbles of peace, love, compassion, kindness, or forgiveness; or any other emotional or behavioral quality that I would like to see, think would help, or sense is related to the disease.

So, see yourself dropping the first pebble into the energy lake. Be aware if you hear any noises (a "peace" pebble, I find, often makes a "ping" or "om" sound in my mind). Watch the pebble make a small splash and then see light (of your color) fanning outward in the energy lake. These are waves of perfect health, peace, or whatever your intention is.

Now, observe the same process for each pebble that you drop. You can add as many or as few as you wish and spend as much or as little time as you can—even adding several pebbles with the same intention. I've found that dropping two or three just once is often enough. But how often you do it is up to you.

☙❧

We've now removed the waves of illness and replaced them with waves of health. The healing is technically done, but I like to further cement it, so to speak. Now we gradually return to where we started, noticing along the way that things are different because there are different waves at the source. This reinforces our belief that the healing is done.

Imagine coming back out from the quantum field to see the subatomic particles. Mentally say, "Show me that it is done." This is giving you confirmation that the healing is complete. Visualize something slightly different from before—for example, instead of the particles being white like stars, see them take the color of the pebbles of light that you added. They are particles that make up the now-healed body. You may even wish to watch them shimmer or see a fine blanket of colored light ripple across the sky, a bit like the northern lights (aurora borealis).

Now come back out to the atoms. Mentally say, "Show me that it is done." See the atoms take the colors of the pebbles of light you added. If you wish, also see them shimmer or move around.

Come back out to the DNA and say, "Show me that it is done." Once again, see the DNA shimmer in the colors of the pebbles of light you added. You might even see some healing genes light up with great brightness.

Come back out to the cells and say, "Show me that it is done." Watch the cells shimmer with the colors of your pebbles of light.

Now come back out to the actual body part and say, "Show me that it is done." Again, watch it shimmer in your chosen colors. And you don't need to just see the shimmering colors at every stage. You can imagine a change in any way, maybe as your atoms or the DNA flexing like a muscle. Maybe your cells will do the same, as they breathe with new life.

If you're so inclined, at this stage you can visualize the malady being eradicated—a tumor dissolving, a virus leaving your body, or an organ or tissue regenerating. You can add an appropriate visualization from the ones listed in Appendix II or create your own scene. It's not really necessary to add one at this stage, but some people like to do so as if they're able to visibly get confirmation that the healing is complete.

Finally, see your whole body and say, "Show me that it is done," and envision it enveloped with the colors that you chose. You might even see yourself flexing your body in perfect health.

To close, mentally say, "Thank you. It is done. It is done. It is done."

Take a few deep breaths and open your eyes. It is done!

One of the unique advantages of QFH is that it expands your consciousness. At the moment where you go inside an atom and see the night sky, with subatomic particles shimmering like stars, it will feel as if your mind is expanding. This symbolizes bypassing the limitations of your body, beliefs, and attitudes; and it lifts you to a higher state of awareness or consciousness, aligning your thoughts much more with the foundation of reality.

You can also apply QFH to changing deep attitudes and beliefs or removing old patterns of emotions that you no longer wish to experience. You'd mentally ask to see the waves (or vibrations) of the attitude, belief, or emotion and cancel it in the same way. Then add the new one that you wish to have.

To Summarize the Technique:

1. Visualize the diseased area in your body.

2. Go inside and see the cells.

3. Go inside and see the DNA.

4. Go inside and see the atoms.

5. Go inside and see the subatomic particles.

6. Go to the source and imagine yourself at the quantum field—a place of total stillness.

7. Say, "Show me the waves/vibrations of _____ [insert the name of the disease, illness, condition, or pain]," and imagine them in any way you feel represents the reality of the condition.

8. Affirm, "Cancel!" and watch the waves collapse and disappear.

9. Say, "Show me the waves of _____ [perfect health, healing, forgiveness, or peace]," and imagine pebbles of brilliant light (any color that comes to mind) dropping into the stillness and the ripples fanning outward, as when pebbles are dropped into still water. Add one or more pebbles.

10. Come back out to the subatomic particles and say, "Show me that it is done." See them take the colors that you chose or change in some other way (for example, a shimmering sky like the northern lights).

11. Come back out to the atoms and say, "Show me that it is done." Again, see a change in color, some shimmering, or any movement.

12. Come back out to the DNA and say, "Show me that it is done." See a change.

13. Come back out to the cells and say, "Show me that it is done." See a change.

14. Come back out to the body area and say, "Show me that it is done." See a change.

15. Watch a healing scene if you wish.

16. Come back out to the whole body and say, "Show me that it is done." See the body enveloped by your chosen colors, flexing in perfect health.

17. Say, "Thank you. It is done. It is done. It is done."

The entire process should only take about five minutes, or you can stay longer at any part if you feel that it's important. For example, with every out breath, you could imagine a pebble of peace.

For some QFH sessions, you might feel it necessary to add several pebbles of peace, perfect health, or forgiveness over the course of several minutes. This would be to ensure that the majority of the healing time is spent at that stage, heavily imprinting its quality into the quantum field.

In time, when you really become expert at the visualization and have strong faith in the power of your mind, you'll be able to go straight to the quantum field in a split second and cancel the diseased state.

True Stories

The following section contains some true stories of people who have successfully used QFH.

Hayley's Story

I was telling my partner and visiting in-laws about one of David Hamilton's workshops that I'd just come from, and I got to the part about the illness visualization. I have an overactive thyroid and, as a result, a small goiter. It's not that noticeable, but to me it has been a very strong visual reminder of the condition. As I was telling everyone about the visualization, unconsciously I put my hand up and touched the goiter, something I know I tend to do when talking or thinking about it and . . . it wasn't there!

I suddenly became aware of my hand gesture, because the unconscious touch didn't give me the expected result. I just couldn't feel the goiter. It had shrunk, and I had to tilt my neck a long way back to even feel the smallest amount.

In my visualization, I had seen it shrinking back from being a pink fleshy mass that was wrapped around my windpipe to a gray, shriveled, dried-up nothing. By the time I got home, it had already happened.

I managed to totally freak out my partner, my in-laws, and myself in one go. They could certainly see that it had changed, and they're generally quite skeptical people.

It was very odd, but in the last minute of the visualization, I felt an incredible urge to cough. It was just a slight throat clearing, but there was a really heavy tickle just below my thyroid. I really tried to hold on to it as I didn't want to disturb anyone else or break my concentration, but in the end I had to cough because it was causing me to lose my focus. As I did, the weirdest thought came through my mind: that I was coughing out the thyroid (symbolically), and I know now that that's actually what I was doing.

I have also realized that I need to slightly modify my visualization—I need to keep a well-functioning thyroid, so I now see it as a beautiful, healthy, gently glowing gland.

Pauline's Story

I was at one of David's workshops and we did a Quantum Field Healing and DNA visualization. I sent the healing (distant healing) to my daughter, Chloë, who was then four years old. She'd been diagnosed with asthma days before and put on antibiotics, steroids, and an inhaler.

When I was doing the healing, I actually felt it being sent to Chloë and became excited. It was really clear: I could see and feel her DNA change color and shape, becoming yellow and light green.

I was woken as usual the following morning by Chloë's kiss, and almost immediately, she told me that her cough and breathing were better and she no longer needed the inhaler. She didn't know that I'd sent healing to her and, since that day (three years ago, at the time of this writing), she has never used steroids or an inhaler and doesn't need them.

This was amazing, and I've used the method with other people since then. I haven't felt the healing being sent as strongly as when I sent it to Chloë, but I know that in some way the person receiving it will be changing for their highest good.

Ruth's Story

My friend Ruth came along to David's workshop and she was so impressed with the Quantum Field Healing that she began doing it to get rid of a mole/skin tag that she had under her eye. She'd already had one removed by surgery and didn't want to go that route again, so she focused on Quantum Field Healing instead. In addition, she visualized new skin growing from underneath and pushing the mole away until it fell off.

A couple of months later, she was in the shower and it actually happened the way she'd pictured it: the mole just fell off. And she had been told that it shouldn't happen that way!

Liz's Story

The day after I went to the DNA and QFH workshop, I was running an event when I dropped a candle in the middle of the floor and burned myself. I decided to use what David Hamilton had just taught us, and instantly, the pain was gone. The next morning there was no trace of the burn.

ကြာကြာ

These are just a few of the many examples of healing that Quantum Field Healing has produced. Try it for yourself and see what results you get. Its power lies in the fact that your thoughts are aligning with the level of reality that all matter arises from. The limits of your abilities only lie in what you believe is possible . . . so what *do* you believe is possible?

ကြာကြာကြာကြာ

APPENDIX II

VISUALIZATIONS

*"I am enough of an artist to draw freely upon
my imagination. Imagination is more important than
knowledge. Knowledge is limited. Imagination encircles the world."*
— Albert Einstein

This section contains a list of visualizations for common ailments and diseases. For some conditions, there's only one visualization; for others, there are two or more. This is to cater to some of the different ways in which people like to imagine things, because a visual image that might feel good for one person may not have the same effect for someone else.

Many of the visualizations are interchangeable or can be adapted for other conditions. Therefore, if you suffer from something that's not on the list, scan through and see if there's one in particular (or any specific elements of some) that you can use—or even make up one of your own. In fact, the visualizations listed here are best used as guidelines, so I suggest that you try to create your own that have greater meaning for you and how you perceive an illness or disease. You could also adapt these so that cells and other parts of your body are represented the way you see them.

You'll notice that some diseases and conditions are described symbolically, such as bacteria and viruses as black dots or inflammations as inflated balloons. It doesn't matter if you know what something looks like anatomically or not, because symbolic images make it easier to create a scene.

You'll also notice that some visualizations are very similar and repetitive, and many are variations upon themes. However, what's included here is an A-to-Z list so that you can dip into any condition and pick up a visualization without having to refer to other pages too extensively.

You can even use the visualizations to enhance any other treatment that you're receiving. For example, if you're receiving radiation for cancer, imagine the treatment as laser beams burning cancer cells off and leaving healthy cells intact. Or you could picture chemotherapy drugs as little balls of light that dissolve tumors.

It's also beneficial to do these visualizations for other people, either just by concentrating on them or while placing your hands upon them. I personally believe in the power of prayer, and visualization for another person is like an active prayer—with his or her permission, of course.

Remember that although this is a book about visualization, I'm not suggesting that you give up your medications or other treatments. In fact, I'm recommending that it's something that can be done *as well as* receiving treatment. After all, whenever you take medicine or receive treatment, you're going to think something: either that it will work or that it won't. Your mind is always present, so you may as well think something positive. Visualization is a way to target your thinking in a positive way. Just make sure that you don't get stressed while in this process of healing. If you do, then stop. Maybe there's a different scene you could use, or perhaps relaxation or meditation would be better for you.

Imagining the healing of an illness or disease might just prove to be one of the most powerful medical interventions we've ever known. In my opinion, new research is already pointing in that direction. By visualizing, we may be activating pathways to health in our bodies that have never been considered. The mind may be the main factor with some people who live a normal healthy life, even when they've been diagnosed with a serious disease.

Here's the list:

Acne

Acne is caused by a blockage in the oil-secreting glands in the skin, which is usually caused by too much oil (sebum) being secreted. This leads to pus being trapped inside or blackheads forming. To eliminate these blemishes:

1. Imagine a pipe or hose that the oil is coming out of. See the oil flowing at whatever rate feels appropriate, based upon how your skin feels to you. If you feel that your skin is too oily, then you might notice it flowing quickly into the glands.

Envision a valve on the pipe or hose. Now turn the valve down and watch the flow reduce. Decrease it as much as you wish and to whatever level seems appropriate for your skin.

Then imagine being underneath the blemish so that you're looking up at it. Take a suction hose and suck the pus or black stuff out. Feel the power of the suction and listen to the slurping sound. Clear out the pore completely until it looks totally clean.

2. Imagine using a colored acid or dissolving gel (any color you want), and rub or spray it into a pimple. It's a magical acid that only dissolves acne and leaves perfectly healthy skin underneath.

Watch the blemish dissolve. See it shrink. Hear it fizzle as it does so, as if it were melting. Then move on to the next one.

If there's any residue left when a pimple is dissolved, use an imaginary vacuum cleaner and suck it up. Take some pride in your cleaning so that there's absolutely no trace of the spot left—only beautifully healthy skin.

3. Just as pictures of models are airbrushed to remove blemishes, imagine that you're airbrushing your skin. Imagine zooming in on each area and using a mental "eraser" tool (like a photo-editing computer-software program) to erase pimples and scars.

Imagine the sensation of rubbing or gently erasing the pimple or scar, restoring your skin to just the way you want it to be—blemish free.

As a variation of this, use a computer scanner to put one of your pictures on your computer (if you have one), and actually use editing software to airbrush your skin. But as you do, affirm that there's a link between what you're doing and the neurons in your brain.

4. For acne scars, imagine the scar tissue as being made of bricks or similar materials. Now remove the bricks one by one and replace each one with a healthy skin cell. Notice how the scar is converted into perfectly healthy skin.

Aging

To slow down the aging process:

1. Imagine stretching out and flattening wrinkles. Use an imaginary iron to make them flat. If you wish, go right inside to the cells, and watch the old, wrinkled ones stretch and flatten as you iron them.

Now take an imaginary oiling can and grease all of your joints. Be sure to do this for each one individually, lubricating them well and making them move with ease. Imagine a light flowing into the top of your head and flooding your entire body so that you have grace in your touch and your movements.

2. Visualize going into your brain and seeing a dial that has AGING SPEED written on it. Note the level that the dial is set to. Now turn it backward to slow down the speed to whatever setting you wish. As you do so, affirm that your body and mind are becoming healthier.

AIDS (see *HIV*)

Allergies

Allergies occur when the immune system is overly sensitive (hypersensitive) to certain substances. For example, a hypersensitivity to pollen is hay fever. Here's how to get some relief:

Imagine that your immune system is made up of hundreds of little cells. You might even picture them as little soldiers. See them on edge, overly sensitive to the slightest movement. When you walk over to them, see them jump.

As you approach them, say, "Hey, it's me. There's no need to be so edgy. Just chill out and do only what you have to for me to stay healthy. Take the rest of the day off."

Then see their chief shout to all his troops, "Hey, it's just [your name]. We don't need to be so agitated." The troops will let out a cheer and start to play tennis (or any game you enjoy) or lie down on beds to sunbathe.

Hug the chief and then walk off.

Anger

To calm your anger:

1. Imagine anger as a large ball of fizzling light inside of your head or any part of your body where you feel your unrest is situated (sometimes people feel anger focused in different parts of their bodies). Picture it like a sparkler or some other type of firework and let it be any color that's appropriate.

Envision a dial that represents the anger level and notice where it's set to. Now turn it down to the level you want (presumably zero). Watch the light shrink until it completely disappears with a tiny "pop."

2. A powerful version of this is to see some of the things that anger you in your mind's eye and then do the visualization. Place the fizzling light inside the scene that you're imagining. This way you symbolically reduce the anger you feel about each thing, so that if the situation arises again in the future, you won't feel angry. You may need to do this several times (10 to 20) in a row to neutralize your feelings about some situations, but it will be worth it.

If a person is your focus of displeasure, once you've popped your anger, say something to them that reflects your new state—perhaps, "I forgive you."

3. Imagine all of the anger in you as being contained inside a pressure cooker. See it swirling around in you.

Now open a valve and let the pressure out. Hear it hissing and feel the pressure inside you dropping until the hissing has stopped and the anger has disappeared.

4. Use the victory dance. Imagine the thing that angers you, and get the thought really clear in your head. Once you can feel anger or irritation, break into your victory dance.

Now think of the thing that angers you once more, and again, break into your dance. I'd recommend that you do this about 10 to 20 times in a row.

You can also apply this to things that you feel emotional pain or trauma about. Doing a victory dance will bring about measurable changes in the brain by diverting blood supply away from areas that process anger, but it will help to build neural connections in areas that process humor and dancing as well.

Anxiety

To calm your anxiety:

Imagine an anxiety dial inside your brain. At one end it says CALM, and at the other it says ANXIOUS. Note what it's currently set at.

If you're feeling a little anxious, then imagine slowly turning the dial down. And as you do, take deep, steady breaths.

Arrhythmia

An arrhythmia is an irregularity in the normal beating of the heart. There are different types, but the most common are palpitations, which this section refers to. They're usually harmless.

1. Visualize little pink hearts with angel wings (to represent love) and the words <u>Regular heartbeat</u> on them. Watch the little pink hearts float gently down onto your heart. Imagine your heartbeat returning to normal.

2. Imagine that the timing system of your heart is faulty and you're going in to repair it. See it like a clock mechanism or a metronome. Conjure up some magical tools and restore it to working order. Take great care and attention as you fix the timing mechanism, and even give all of the individual parts a good cleaning, returning the workings of your heart to a state of perfection. Hear the ticktock of the clock in a beautiful-sounding, perfect rhythm.

Arthritis

Arthritis is characterized by damage to the joint cartilage and lack of fluid between the joints. Pain and inflammation arise as bones rub against each other. To relieve the pain of arthritis:

1. Imagine holding a big syringe or an oilcan full of magical, frictionless, and everlasting fluid. Think of it as either clear or colored (whatever feels best to you).

Now see yourself injecting it into the joint. Watch the viscous fluid go into it and the two pieces of cartilage move apart.

While looking at the fluid-filled joint, see it move freely and effortlessly. If it's your knee, for example, then imagine painlessly walking or running. See into your joint as you visualize this, and be aware of the two pieces of cartilage that are now comfortably kept apart by the fluid.

Celebrate your success with a little victory dance (real or imaginary).

2. A slight variation of this would be to imagine going inside the actual fluid and seeing the atoms that it's made of. View them as little bubbles with smiley faces on them, and as they flow out of the syringe or oilcan, imagine them crying, "Whee!" as if they were on a waterslide. See the excited looks on their faces—they're obviously having lots of fun as they slide into the joint.

See the little atoms flood into the joint and flow right up the sides of a cavern that represents the gap between the two bones (if you're seeing the actual atoms—which are microscopic—then the gap between the bones will be as big as a cavern). See more and more atoms enter the hole until it's comfortably full. They're soft and squishy, so they'll form a spongy fluid.

Now imagine moving back out of the joint so that you no longer see the atoms, but only a frictionless fluid holding the bones apart.

3. Visualize mechanical diggers driving up to the joint. They have special cutting tools that create space by cutting away any excess bone that was rubbing together.

Now see the diggers erecting girders to maintain the space so that the bones no longer rub together.

At this point, another digger drives up with its bucketful of magical, everlasting, lubricating fluid. Watch it pour the fluid into the joint and fill the gap.

Asthma

Asthma is characterized by an occasional constriction of the airways, which limits breathing. In order to breath easier:

Imagine being inside one of your airways, like being in a small tunnel. Now visualize teams of little workers expanding the insides of the tubes and making them wider. Then see them adding magical strengthening rings to help support the increased size and keep the tubes from constricting again.

Atherosclerosis

Atherosclerosis is often called hardening of the arteries. The walls of the arteries become thickened with scar tissue and cholesterol, and calcium deposits eventually build up. This ultimately restricts blood flow. To reverse these effects:

1. Imagine the inside of one of your arteries. If you've been diagnosed with atherosclerosis, then you might imagine lumps of white globular cholesterol lying around that look like big chunks of lard. You may also see large buildups of rocky calcium—white jagged rocks littered all around the top, sides, and bottom of the walls. Use any other image that represents atherosclerosis for you.

Picture yourself holding a laser. It has a label on it that says Bad-Cholesterol and Calcium-Deposit Dissolver. *Switch it on and fire away. Melt the cholesterol or rocky calcium. See them dissolve in much the same way as warm water from the tap melts an ice cube. Clean out all of the bad cholesterol and calcium deposits from your arteries. Then take an imaginary suction hose or vacuum cleaner and suck up any melted residue.*

2. Arteries are supposed to be flexible like pieces of rubber. With atherosclerosis, the "tubing" becomes hard and stiff. Imagine the cells that form the walls of your arteries as rows of soft rubber bricks, some of which are hard, discolored, misshapen, and cracked.

Remove the brittle, damaged bricks from the wall one at a time and replace them with new rubbery ones. With each section that you refit, see the artery as really flexible. See it effortlessly bend and flex.

Athlete's Foot

Athlete's foot is characterized by dry, itchy skin on the feet and toes. To cure this fungal disease:

1. Imagine flaky, hardened skin cells that are cracked and separated from each other—think about photos you may have seen of a riverbed or a lake that has dried up.

Go into the cracks and vacuum up little particles of fungus (athlete's foot is caused by infection with the tinea pedis species of fungus). Picture them in any way that you wish—for instance, like little balls of moss.

2. Start to moisturize the cells, one by one, using a magical gel that also dissolves any stray bits of fungus. As it soaks in, watch each cell change shape—bending, stretching out, and being restored to health. See the cracks disappear as the cells sit comfortably next to each other.

Autoimmune Conditions

Autoimmune conditions—such as type 1 diabetes, lupus, rheumatoid arthritis, and multiple sclerosis—occur as the body's immune system attacks parts of the body. For example, in diabetes, the immune system attacks beta cells of the pancreas.

The following visualizations are intended to reduce the sensitivity of the immune system to the body. The first visualization resembles the *Allergies* visualization because there are biological similarities between some autoimmune conditions and how the immune system reacts to allergens.

1. Imagine that your immune system is made up of hundreds of little people. You're walking toward them, but as you do, you can't see each other clearly because of dense fog. Since they can't make out who's coming at them, they begin to attack your body, fearing that you're an enemy.

Now imagine the fog lifting so that you and your immune-system cells can see each other perfectly. Go over to the chief and say, "Hey, it's me. There's no need to fight. Just chill out and do only what you have to for me to stay healthy. Take the rest of the day off." Then see the chief shout to all his troops, "Hey, it's just [your name]. We don't need to fight."

Watch his troops let out a cheer and start to play tennis (or any game that you enjoy) and lie down on beds to sunbathe.

Hug the chief and then walk off.

2. Imagine that the cells of the immune system are wild dogs attacking the healthy cells. Now walk among the dogs. They won't harm you. Command them to sit down. Mentally state, with absolute conviction: Down, boy.

Watch each dog stop its attack and sit. Then see them totally change in personality and become playful, well-behaved dogs— totally obedient and loving. Pet and give hugs to each one.

Blood Pressure

— **High Blood Pressure (Hypertension).** Use the following visualization to lower your blood pressure.

Imagine a balloon representing your blood pressure, and notice how inflated it is. Now untie it and watch it deflate. Listen to the whooshing and rasping sound as the air rushes out of the balloon. See it get smaller and smaller, and as it diminishes in size and loses pressure, affirm that your blood pressure is reducing.

A great way to reduce blood pressure is meditation, where you just sit quietly and breathe, so try to add mindful breathing to your visualization. You can even do it as you walk or for a couple of minutes as you sit at your desk—just take deep, even breaths.

— **Low Blood Pressure.** Use the following visualization if you need to raise your blood pressure.

Imagine an underinflated balloon representing your blood pressure. Notice how deflated it is. Now use a pump to add air to it. As the air enters the balloon, watch it get bigger and bigger, and be sure to affirm that your blood pressure is increasing. Expand the size of the balloon until it's at the level that you feel is normal and healthy.

Broken Bones

These two visualizations can be used once the bone has been set by a doctor. Even though it's been positioned correctly, there will still be a microscopic break, where new bone material will grow. To increase the rate of healing:

1. Picture the two ends of the broken bone and imagine construction workers repairing both sides. See them build scaffolding and construct hundreds of fibers that connect the two ends, forming a 3-D net of bone between them. As more and more fibers are added, see the net gradually become denser and denser, until the workers have completely healed the fracture.

Affirm that the bone is stronger than it was before the break.

2. This version is a bit more fun and might be preferred by children. Imagine the two ends of the broken bone. Now envision yourself with the powers of Spider-Man, giving you the ability to shoot a web. Stand at one side of the fracture and fire a web strand to the other. Once it sticks, attach the part that's connected to your wrist to the side of the fracture that you're standing on so that the two ends are connected by your web. This is no ordinary web—after a few moments, it hardens and turns to bone. Fire hundreds of strands between the two sides of the broken bone until they're completely fused together. You can have some fun doing this by seeing yourself swing from one side to the other so that you can shoot from both ends.

Bronchitis

With bronchitis, the bronchi (tubes in the lungs that air passes through) are inflamed and produce mucus. To reduce the effects of bronchitis:

Imagine yourself inside your bronchial tubes. See them as red and inflamed, containing deposits of mucus. Now use a suction hose or vacuum cleaner to remove the mucus. If the bronchitis is a result of smoking, then also clean up any little flecks of black residue that are peppered throughout the walls of the bronchi.

After you've eliminated the mucus and cleaned the walls, spray the bronchi with a green magical healing liquid. As it's absorbed into the walls, see the inflammation reduce to nothing and the walls return to a healthy pink color.

Imagine calmly breathing in air that soothes the bronchi.

Burns

Here's how to get some relief:

Imagine using a soft brush and a bucket of magical, ultra-cool, soothing skin paint that has hints of blue and green light in it. See yourself gently brushing the burn with this calming paint. As it soaks in, new cells are going to set up camp underneath the burn. As you continue to cover the tender area, more and more new cells will grow until the burn has completely disappeared and been replaced with healthy skin.

Cancer

I've included more visualizations for cancer than for most other conditions because it's such a widespread disease that manifests itself in different ways in the body. In addition to the following examples, you can read people's stories in Chapter 10.

1. If you're undergoing chemotherapy or radiation, see the drugs or particles of radiation as balls of light that land on the tumor and melt it. Envision globular immune-system cells with smiley faces lapping up the residue.

Notice the tumor getting smaller and smaller. See it shrinking until it disappears with a tiny "pop." For extra smiles, while it's dissolving you could yell, "I'm shrinking! Shrinking!" similar to how the Wicked Witch of the West screams "I'm melting! Melting!" in The Wizard of Oz when Dorothy accidentally throws water on her. You might even wave your arms and shiver your body as you act out the process (especially if no one is around to see), which is a bit like a victory dance.

2. Bring to mind the cells in a cancerous part of your body. Notice that some of them are a healthy pink color, while others are discolored and covered in slime or some other substance. These represent the cancer cells.

Now take a brush and some special cleaning fluid, and start cleaning these cells, one at a time, until each is gleaming and restored to a normal, healthy color.

3. Visualize the cancerous part(s) of your body and see the disease as a slimy black deposit. Now take a colored laser beam (whatever color that you feel will work best) and burn off the cancer, leaving the healthy cells around it intact. It's a special laser, so it only burns cancer cells. Now take a broom and dustpan and sweep up any residue, or suck it up with a vacuum cleaner.

4. Imagine using a magic wand to fire a spell at the cancer cells. You can even make up a magic spell, or use one from one of the Harry Potter books. See every cancer cell flex, change color, and transform into a healthy pink cell. Do this for each one.

5. See a beautiful, green, flawless crystal and place it beside the cancer. Watch it give off its green light, which causes unhealthy cells to vanish. Place your attention upon the crystal several times a day, and notice the light dissolve the cancer. Each time you imagine the crystal, you energize it and make it stronger.

6. Some people prefer to see the cancer as part of them, so they treat it with love and affection instead of attacking it. If you choose to do this as well, visualize yourself sitting down with the cancer cells, hugging them and telling them that you love them. (After all, if cancer were conscious, it wouldn't know it was hurting you; it would think it was helping.) Imagine the cells saying that they love you, too. Then tell them that you have to let them go now. See them leaving your body with big smiles on their faces.

The following two visualizations involve visualizing DNA. Around 50 percent of tumors have been found to contain a mutation in a gene called the TP53 gene. (Please understand that having such a mutation doesn't automatically mean that people will get cancer—only that if their lifestyle is cancer promoting, they'll stand a greater chance of developing the disease than someone with a healthy TP53 gene. In other words, attitude, environment, eating habits, and lifestyle play a significant role.)

The TP53 gene is known as a "tumor suppressor" gene in that it helps stop the growth of tumors. It has often affectionately been called the "guardian angel" gene.

1. Imagine the TP53 angel lying on the ground as though it's been hurt. See it as an injured little organism. Now nurse it back to life again, giving it some medicine and nutrients. Watch it growing stronger, giving off a glow of light, and eventually gaining its full angelic strength. Then imagine it diving into your DNA. See a ripple of the angel's color of light go through the length of your DNA. Then visualize the tumor(s) simply deflating or dissolving and vanishing.

2. If you're computer savvy, see yourself writing a software program—one that needs to be translated into a genetic program to instruct your DNA to restore perfect health. The human body has the ability to use many different pathways to wellness. If one gene is defective, then, in many cases, the body has the ability to use a different genetic program that will maintain health.

Go inside the body, to the site(s) of the cancer, and type a genetic program made up of simple written commands on an imaginary computer. For instance, you could type:

- *"Restore the TP53 gene to normal function."*

- *"Create an alternative genetic program to restore perfect health."*

- *"Switch off the cancer-promoting genes."*

- *"Switch on the tumor-suppressor genes."*
- *"Restore the body to perfect health."*

You could even type, "My body is in perfect health," or words of your own choice that represent what you want. Imagine typing the individual letters, and see these words appear on the screen as you do so.

Once you've written your program of commands, press ENTER on the keyboard and see the words float off and merge with your DNA, one command at a time. Notice the colors of your commands, or if they're colored at all.

As they float off, imagine some genes turning on and some turning off, indicating which ones are about to be affected. See the DNA inside the tumor radiating a colored light (according to your commands). Then visualize the tumor shrinking to nothing and vanishing with a pop, as if all of the air was suddenly let out of it.

Candida

Candida is an infection of a yeast fungus, and it often manifests as candidiasis (thrush) in the vagina. It's often noticed in immunocompromised people.

The visualization that follows is what I would suggest if you get this. Alternatively, you could use any of the *Infections* visualizations. If you want to boost your immune system, too, then you could also use one of the *Immune System (Weak)* visualizations.

See yourself walking around the fungal area with a suction hose or a vacuum cleaner and sucking up all of the fungus. Try to feel its force and imagine its sound.

Cellulite

To get rid of cellulite:

1. Imagine the cells in the cellulite-plagued areas, picturing them as rows of blubbery, jellylike bricks. Use an imaginary suction hose or vacuum cleaner to get rid of these unwanted cells. Feel each one resisting as you suck, but note that they're eventually all picked up by the vacuum. Notice the force of the suction as it vibrates the hose and hear the slurping sound as the fat makes its way up into the bag. Be sure to show great care and patience during this visualization, since this is a beauty thing you're working on.

When the cells are sucked up or dissolved, see that there's only perfect, healthy-looking skin left. Watch it tighten and return to your version of perfect and beautiful.

2. Imagine loads of little fat-eating cells that resemble Pac-Man or piranhas gobbling up the cellulite and leaving the skin looking beautiful and healthy.

Chicken Pox

Chicken pox is a skin disease that's caused by the varicella-zoster virus. To rid yourself of the virus itself, use these visualizations. Alternatively, or in addition to these, use any of the ones listed for *Viruses.*

1. Imagine taking a magical dissolving fluid of any color you feel inspired by, and squirt it into a spot caused by the chicken pox. Watch it soak right in. As you stand beside the spot, see it dissolve right before your eyes as if the fluid were an acid, and hear it disappear with a pop.

If there's any residue left at the end, use an imaginary vacuum cleaner to suck it up. Take pride in your cleaning so that there's absolutely no trace of the mark left, only perfectly healthy skin.

2. See yourself use an eraser and going over the spot cells, one by one, until they completely disappear. If the thought of this is uncomfortable, then imagine using Photoshop (or any other photo-editing software) on a computer. Imagine your face, or any other part of your body, on the screen; select the eraser tool; and effortlessly rub the spots away.

If you feel up to it, you could do this exercise for real by taking a photo of yourself, uploading it to your computer, and then editing it. As you do so, affirm that there's a symbolic link between what you're doing, the neurons in your brain, and the cells in your body.

3. Visualize talking to your spots and asking them to leave. Imagine the cells detaching themselves from your body, one by one, and flying away.

When it comes to healing chicken-pox **scars**, use what follows. Or, as in the second visualization for the virus itself above, you could imagine your face on Photoshop and create blemish-free skin.

Since scars are made up of fibers of tissue, imagine cutting the fibers one at a time. As each cut is made, hear them twang. Once the fibers have gone, use a magical skin paint to coat the scars with new, healthy skin. As fresh layers of paint are applied, notice that each one creates perfectly formed skin. Gradually add more and more layers of healthy skin cells until you see perfect skin.

Chlamydia

Chlamydia is a sexually transmitted disease that's caused by infection of the urethra in men or the cervix in women. The *Infections* visualizations are good ones to use here. You could also do the following, either at the end of those visualizations or separately.

See yourself walking through the area that's infected and applying a magical blue healing gel to it. Rub the soothing substance and notice the cooling sensation. As it absorbs, watch the swelling reduce and the redness return to a healthy pink color.

Chronic Fatigue Syndrome (CFS)

CFS is characterized by chronic mental and physical exhaustion. To stop feeling tired and increase your energy level, use the following visualizations.

Some theories of CFS say that it's caused by a buildup of toxins in the body. Therefore, you could also use the *Toxins* visualizations to rid your body of them.

Envision a ball of light inside your brain that represents your power. Notice its size, color, and brightness. You might perceive that it isn't too bright at the moment, which symbolizes your feelings of weakness. However, your true power is much greater than this. With CFS, the light has just been turned down . . . but you're about to give it a boost.

Imagine turning up a dial and seeing the light grow in strength (this is a great image for expanding your power in general). Watch the glow increase its intensity. You might even see a scale or meter beside it that indicates the level of power. As the light gets brighter, notice the meter reading going up, too, and feel the light expanding outward so that it's causing your entire body to glow.

See the glimmer spread through all of your muscles and over your skin. And see it illuminate each organ so that the entire body, inside and out, is aglow with this beautiful radiance that represents your power. It has been suppressed, but not any longer. Affirm that you are strong, fit, and healthy.

You might even imagine yourself running, jumping, and laughing (a lot). Finish with an imaginary victory dance in celebration of your great strength. This will actually produce happy chemicals in your brain. The more regularly you do this, the greater the effect will be—you'll soon be able to do a real victory dance.

Common Cold

The common cold is mostly due to infection by the rhinovirus, and it usually causes a sore throat and mild fever. To rid yourself of this pesky virus use the following visualization.

Alternatively, use the *Infections* or *Viruses* visualizations. Even though the common cold is a viral infection, the *Infections* visualizations are often more appropriate because people don't generally think of the common cold as a virus. And, ultimately, it's what you think that counts. If you wish, also use the *Sore Throat* visualization.

Imagine the cold as hundreds of bubbles floating in a room or cave that symbolically represents your body. See them pouring out of a few large pipes—say, two to five.

Go to the first pipe and imagine that it has a valve on it that's shaped like a steering wheel. Turn the valve and stop the flow of bubbles. As you do, gradually see the flow slow down. When the surge has been completely halted, put a lock on it so that it can't open again, and do this for all of the pipes.

Now burst the bubbles. You can do this with any tool you wish, or you can do it mentally. See each one pop as you burst it. Break every last bubble until the cold has completely gone from your body.

Cuts

To speed up the healing process when it comes to cuts:

1. See yourself inside the cut and noting the two separate sides, like the walls of a canyon. Use magical threads to stitch them together, starting, for example, from the bottom of the canyon and working your way to the top. With each stitch, pull the two ends together and notice how they fit seamlessly. Visualize them closing up so perfectly that they create an exact connection—you can't even see where the cut was.

Stand back and admire your great work. You may even see loads of skin cells applauding you for the great job you've done. Give yourself a pat on the back (this will generate happy chemicals that will speed up healing).

2. Imagine a team of construction workers repairing the cut and building new skin. Watch the immune-system cells mop up any bacteria in the area. Finally, notice the two sides of the wound being pulled seamlessly together.

3. You could also visualize talking to and touching the cut in a kindly manner. Lovingly stroke it, since touch generates the growth hormones that are required for regeneration. Feel that the two sides of the cut love each other and no longer wish to be separated (maybe they have had an argument and that's why they're apart). See them reach out and lovingly embrace each other. You could even do this while listening to some romantic or inspirational music.

Cystic Fibrosis

Cystic fibrosis is a genetic disease that affects the mucous glands of the lungs, liver, pancreas, and intestines, and causes thick mucus to be produced. This leads to airways becoming clogged, and the buildup can cause severe bronchitis and pneumonia.

In addition to the following, you can do the *Bronchitis* visualization (minus the reference to flecks of smoking residue) or the *Pneumonia* visualization.

1. Cystic fibrosis arises out of a mutation in the CFTR gene. Therefore, you could visualize CFTR as a little character lying on the ground who's been hurt. You might even see "CFTR" written on its T-shirt or jacket.

Now nurse it back to life again, showing great care, compassion, and attention. Give it some medicine and nutrients, and see it grow stronger, eventually giving off a glow of light.

Once healthy, imagine the new and improved CFTR diving into your DNA. Watch your DNA flex with great power, and note a pulse of light travel its length. Now visualize the mucus evaporating from your lungs and the other areas where it's causing infection.

You could imagine writing a new genetic program to compensate for the defect, instructing your DNA to find another way of restoring you to health. I believe that the human body is capable of many more miracles of healing that we've never given it credit for. Just as in an airplane, if one engine is faulty, the others can compensate and bring the plane home safely. So if one gene is defective, then the body often has an ability to use a different genetic program that will provide health by another route.

2. Imagine writing a computer program, only it must be translated into a genetic program to instruct your DNA to find a way to restore perfect health. As you write it on an imaginary computer, affirm that your body can take different pathways to health.

Your genetic program should be made up of simple written commands. For instance, you could type:

- *"Create an alternative genetic program to restore perfect health."*

- *"Switch on the healing genes."*

- *"Restore the body to perfect health."*

- *"My body is in perfect health."*

- *"The symptoms of cystic fibrosis are disappearing."*

Alternatively, you could put down anything that you might find more appropriate for your situation. Imagine typing the individual letters, and see the words appear on the screen as you type.

Once you've written your program of commands, press ENTER on the keyboard and watch the words float off and merge with your DNA, one command at a time. As they do, notice some genes turning on and some turning off, indicating which ones are about to be affected. Watch your DNA radiating a colored light throughout the infected area. Then see the infections reducing to nothing and the mucus dissolving.

Cystitis

Cystitis is a bacterial infection of the bladder and urethra, so you can use the *Infections* visualizations. Also, to help tackle the burning sensation:

See yourself inside your bladder, looking at red and swollen cells. Now imagine that you have buckets of magical blue cooling fluid. It's thick and gloopy and feels really cold to the touch. Apply the fluid to each cell, one at a time, and watch all of them relax and return to a healthy pink color.

Depression

To lift yourself out of depression:

1. Imagine a ball of soft green, pink, or white light—or as a little candle flame—in the center of your brain or heart. This represents your happiness. Be sure to notice how big it seems to you.

Now envision a dial and turn it up. As you do this, see the light get bigger and brighter. Mentally affirm that it's a symbol of your inner strength and happiness.

Continue to turn the dial and watch the light grow. Observe it expanding right out of your head or heart and spreading throughout your entire body. Watch the light flow through your arteries, veins, and internal organs. Imagine it tickling your cells, and see them smile. Visualize the light penetrate up through your skin.

Mentally affirm that you're surrounded by this radiant light and that your power and happiness are great.

2. If you're able to, think of a time in your life when you were really happy—really, really happy! Now capture that moment in a little transparent ball of light and move it into your heart or brain. See it multiply hundreds or thousands of times and watch the balls float all around your body so that it becomes saturated with them. I'd also recommend that you then burst into a victory dance to celebrate. It would also help if you can put on some upbeat dance music.

3. See the depressed you. Now walk up to yourself and give him or her a hug. Place your hands upon your depressed self's head, and imagine healing light flooding into it and circulating around the body. As you do this, feel the compassion and love of giving. This makes it a high-energy (high-vibration) light, which helps raise the energy of your depressed self.

Diabetes

There are two main types of diabetes: type 1 and type 2. Type 1 diabetes is an autoimmune condition where the immune system destroys insulin-producing beta cells in the pancreas, resulting in high levels of blood sugar. Type 2 diabetes is the result of insulin resistance or reduced insulin sensitivity, which also results in high blood sugar. Type 2 is more common in overweight adults. Here are visualizations to rid yourself of either:

— **Type 1.** In addition to the two below, you can use the *Auto-immune Conditions* visualizations.

> *1. Imagine flooding your pancreas with a green healing light (green symbolizes regeneration). Visualize some of the damaged beta cells as half eaten; and as you flood them with this regenerative light, see them grow back to full strength.*

> *2. Alternatively, envision a team of construction workers wearing green and rebuilding the cells. See them work to perfectly regenerate the cells, one by one, so that the pancreas is as good as new again.*

— **Type 2.** Some studies have suggested that the reduced insulin sensitivity in type 2 diabetes is due to the insulin receptors on the cells' surfaces. So for this visualization, imagine that the receptors are asleep and you're waking them up.

> *See insulin molecules approach the receptors in any way you wish, but notice that the receptors are asleep. You may even hear them snoring. Give them a little shake and ask them to wake up. Tell them that there's a lot of insulin around that needs to get into the cells.*
> *See the receptors get up and stretch. Listen for anything that they say. Then watch the insulin and the receptors embrace each other before the insulin disappears through a hole in the receptor.*

Observe a line of insulin molecules doing the same, each hugging the receptor before entering the hole.

Diarrhea

Diarrhea often results from some kind of infection; therefore, use any of the *Infections* visualizations.

Emphysema

Emphysema is characterized by a destruction of the walls of the alveoli in the lungs, which limits breathing. To repair the damage that this condition has caused:

1. Imagine that you have a bag of new alveolus cells, and start filling up the holes in the walls using these cells. Use a magical fluid to coat the edges of the new cells and fit them perfectly into the gaps. As you fill in each hole, notice that the cells around the new ones join seamlessly with them.

2. Think of a time in your life when you could breathe effortlessly (it's even better if you can recall a happy time). Remember the feeling of being able to breathe in and out really easily, and turn that feeling into a ball of colored light.
Now bring the light into your lungs and see it multiplying and filling all of the holes in the alveoli. As the light merges with the walls, see it turn into new, healthy alveolus cells.

Endometriosis

Endometriosis is the growth of endometrium (the tissue that lines the uterus) outside or beyond the uterus. The deposits undergo periodic bleeding in sync with normal menstruation, which can lead to inflammation. In ovarian endometriosis, cysts can also develop. They're known as chocolate cysts because of their dark brown color. Use the following visualizations to rid yourself of this condition:

1. If you've been clinically diagnosed with ovarian endo-metriosis, notice your ovaries with dark brown deposits on them. You can actually envision them in any way you like—as which-ever image you feel best represents them. For example, you might see them as rocky or sludgy.

Now use a suction hose or vacuum cleaner and go around your ovaries, sucking up every last piece of these cysts. Make sure that your ovaries are totally clean and are left looking healthy and happy. Maybe even see them with little smiling faces now that they've been restored to such good condition.

You could also use a power hose or jet wash and blast your ovaries clean. Then clear up the residue with suction or using a dustpan and brush.

2. Imagine that there's an animal that just loves eating chocolate cysts. See it devour the chocolate coating, totally clear-ing every last bit until the ovaries are polished clean.

Enteritis

Enteritis is often called gastroenteritis, although the stomach isn't really involved. The same visualization can be used for both, however. Enteritis is the inflammation of the small intestine that's usually caused by infection from a virus or bacteria. To cure your-self of this condition, use the following visualization. Alternatively, use any of the ones listed under *Infections*.

Imagine the inflamed cells as being inflated, and then let air out of them, one by one, as if you were letting the pressure out of a blown-up balloon. Listen to the whooshing sound as the air rushes out and the inflamed cells return to normal size.

Now rub on a magical blue cooling fluid. It's thick and gloopy and feels really cold to the touch. Apply the fluid onto each cell. Watch them cool and see any redness return to a healthy pink color.

Being magical, the fluid has special properties: it's also a paint that neutralizes any infection in the area and prevents reinfection.

Epilepsy

Epilepsy is the name given to any of a number of recurring brain seizures. The following visualization will help you rid yourself of this condition:

Imagine being inside the brain seeing little agitated characters that seem to be on alert, jumpy, and a little afraid. These are epilepsy characters, so notice what they're doing.

Now walk over to the leader. Hold his hand and say: "There's no need to be afraid. Everything is okay. You can relax and leave now."

See the leader stop shaking, smile, and give you a big hug. Watch him go over and spread the good news to the rest of the characters. Then focus on them all leaving your body in any way you wish.

Flu

The flu is caused by an infection with the influenza virus. It usually results in fever, sore throat, cough, and aches and pains all over the body.

Use the *Common Cold, Infections, Viruses,* or *Sore Throat* visualizations.

Gastroenteritis (see *Enteritis*)

Gonorrhea

Gonorrhea is one of the most common sexually transmitted diseases. It's usually characterized by a burning sensation while urinating and sometimes a discharge. Use any of the *Infections* visualizations or the ones written here:

1. Imagine the site of pain or infection and rub a magical blue soothing gel onto each of the cells there, one at a time. Initially, you'll see them as red and inflamed, but once you rub on the gel, see (or hear) them breathe a sigh of relief, then watch the swelling reduce and them return to normal.

2. Alternatively, imagine the irritated cells as inflated balloons. Let the air out of them and hear the whooshing or rasping sound as they return to their normal size and color.

Hay Fever

Use the *Allergies* visualization and, if you wish, add this:

Imagine yourself walking through a field of freshly cut grass where there's pollen everywhere, but you feel great and have absolutely no symptoms of hay fever. Laugh as you revel in the fact that you're no longer affected by pollen. Do a victory dance.

Heart Disease

Heart disease is a collective term for a number of different cardiovascular diseases. Use the following visualizations to rid yourself of any of them.

1. Imagine the heart and some of the damaged cells as shriveled-up prunes—or any other way that you'd assume they look like. Now take a cloth and some magical pink or green cleaning fluid (pink symbolizes love and green symbolizes regeneration), and gently clean the cells, one by one, restoring them to perfect health.

2. The heart symbolizes love, so imagine putting more love into it. Speak to your heart and tell it that you love it deeply and unconditionally. Give it a hug.

Now imagine its beat. Maybe you can actually feel or hear it. See a soft pink or green light at the center of your heart and watch it expand with every beat. Notice it gradually get bigger and brighter a little bit at a time. Also, see some pink or green heart-shaped bubbles floating into your heart (perhaps you can even envision angels blowing them into it). As you do this, feel your heart muscle get stronger and healthier. Now sense the light expand out through your arteries, effortlessly dissolving any plaque or cholesterol deposits.

You could even take the visualization further if you feel that it would be good for you: Watch the light continue to radiate outward until your entire body is engulfed by it. See bright rays moving out through your body's systems. As the light expands through your cells, watch them laugh and hug each other—they're being "tickled pink," so to speak (if you're using pink light).

As the light envelops your organs, watch them beat or flex in sublime health. See large smiles appear on the faces of their cells as the light from your heart is feeding health into every part of your body. Notice the light move through your liver, kidneys, and other organs; watch it travel to your head and make your brain glow. See your brain cells dance with delight as they are bathed in the light.

Returning your thoughts to your heart, feel its muscles flex and pump with the ease and effortlessness of an Olympic champion, pumping blood around the body. Appreciate how beautiful this is, and hear the power as if you were standing right beside the beat.

Hemorrhoids

Hemorrhoids are swollen veins in the anus or rectum. To take care of this painful issue:

Picture the hemorrhoids like inflated balloons. Now untie the balloons and watch them deflate. Hear the whooshing or rasping sound as the air pours out (imagining this sound will make you smile, since it's commonly associated with this area!) and the balloons lose pressure, one at a time. See each balloon get smaller and smaller until they're all completely deflated.

Hepatitis

Hepatitis is the inflammation of the liver through infection, and there are a few different types: A, B, or C (D and E also exist but are less common).

Use the *Infections* or *Viruses* visualizations. Although hepatitis is a viral infection, we tend to think of infections as bacterial. Since this is a common mistake, it's sufficient to use the ones I've described for *Infections*.

Additionally, or alternatively, you can use the following. They will help heal any liver damage that you may have experienced as a result of the infection.

1. Imagine your damaged liver cells looking shriveled and black. Now take an imaginary cloth and some magical green cleaning fluid and clean the cells, one by one, restoring each one to perfect health.

2. Picture your liver cells as fully inflated balloons. Attend to each one individually by letting the air out of them, and listen to the whooshing or rasping sound as it rushes out. See each cell return to its normal size and healthy pink color.

HIV

HIV stands for human immunodeficiency virus. The relationship between HIV and AIDS is often misunderstood. AIDS (acquired immunodeficiency syndrome) is the term normally used when a person's immune-system cell count (specifically their blood CD4 lymphocytes) drops beneath a certain level and they suffer from "opportunistic" infections. Many people infected with HIV are never diagnosed with AIDS; therefore, there isn't an AIDS virus, there's an HIV virus, which lowers the immune system to a level where many infections can occur and a diagnosis of AIDS is made.

The severity of an HIV infection is based on whether or not the virus docks onto receptors on immune-system cells (CD4 T lymphocytes, which are often called T cells). The immune-system cells are then destroyed. But before this occurs, more of the virus is replicated and released into the bloodstream. Thus, the virus multiplies and the T-cell count reduces.

For HIV, use any of the *Viruses* visualizations, the *Immune System (Weak)* visualizations, or any that are used for specific AIDS-related illnesses. Alternatively, use this:

Imagine the receptors that the viruses dock onto on the immune-system cells. Picture them changing their shape so that the HIV can't recognize them, and therefore can't dock and get into the cell. For fun, you could see the receptors disguising themselves by putting on funny wigs, large glasses, or big teeth.

Imagine different ways in which the receptors could prevent the HIV virus from getting into the cell. For instance, they could even turn themselves inside out or emit a sound that confuses the virus.

See the virus eventually giving up and leaving the body.

Hypertension (see *Blood Pressure*)

Immune System (Weak)

To strengthen your immune system:

1. Immune-system cells begin their life in your bone marrow. Imagine being inside that marrow now, and observing a factory that's producing immune-system cells. Watch all of the elements on conveyor belts being assembled and the completed cells popping out of the end, eager to get to work. Visualize them in any shape, color, or size you wish.

There's a big dial on the wall that indicates the speed at which the immune-system cells are being produced. Note the setting. If it's low, then turn it up—feel yourself actually doing this—and watch the conveyor belt speed up as though it's just been given a turbo boost. Observe an increased number of cells being produced.

Pay attention to how these cells move out of your bone marrow, along your arteries and veins, and all around your body. See them move specifically to wherever the infection is located, neutralizing any bacteria, viruses, or pathogens.

2. Imagine teams of little workers making immune-system cells at a large factory—something similar to an aircraft hanger that's made of bone.

See several of the factory workers at each table assembling all of the parts. And when each new cell is created, watch it breathe with life, smiling and eager to get out into the body to start mopping up invaders.

Observe a constant stream of new immune-system cells leave the factory, head out into the body, and gobble up all infections or diseases.

Infections

Many diseases and conditions are caused by infections, so these visualizations can be applied to any of them. While I mention bacteria specifically, these can be used for both bacterial and viral infections.

1. Use an imaginary suction hose or vacuum cleaner and clean up all of the bacteria. See the bacteria in any way you wish (for example, as little flecks of black pepper, brown or black sludge, small brittle pieces of a rocky substance, or little colored organisms). Hear the sound of your device as it sucks up the particles, and feel the force of the suction, making everything as realistic as possible. Continue until the area is free of any remaining bacteria, virus, or pathogen.

2. Switch on an imaginary power hose and direct the jet at the bacteria. Feel the force of the water rushing through the hose and hear the spraying sound. Watch as the bacteria fragments are blasted off the walls of your body parts.

Clean up any residue or fragments of bacteria with a brush, dustpan, or vacuum cleaner; or see globby immune-system cells jump up and gobble the pieces of bacteria like Pac-Man. For extra smiles, when each cell has eaten lots of bacteria and is getting full, notice it burp with contentment.

3. Visualize a shower of crystal clear healing water that pours in through the top of your head and flushes infections away.

Imagine the feeling as the water courses through your body and out the soles of your feet. Initially see it as dark brown as you begin to flush out the infection, but gradually watch it become lighter and lighter, as the infection is completely rinsed out. Eventually, only clear water will flow out of your body as all of the infection is gone.

4. To protect yourself if people around you are sick, imagine being surrounded by a large bubble. If you perceive any infectious agents flying toward you, see them simply bounce off the giant balloon.

If you believe in angels, then you could even ask one to surround you with one of their bubbles of protection. This is useful if you're in a crowded place and see someone cough or sneeze close by, or if a member of your family has the flu or anything that's contagious.

Insomnia

Use the following visualizations to induce sleep:

1. As you lie in bed, breathe deeply. With each out breath, visualize all of your muscles sinking deeper into the mattress. As you do this, mentally say the word <u>sleep</u> in a very slow and soothing way: <u>Ssssslllleeeeeeeeeepppppp.</u>

2. Imagine that you drank something delicious, natural, and healthy that has the effect of relaxing your body with every breath you take. The drink's soothing effects flow into every muscle and relieve it. It calms your mind and allows you to put aside any thoughts or anxieties so that you can peacefully drift off to a wonderfully deep sleep.

Irritable Bowel Syndrome (IBS)

IBS is often characterized by diarrhea, abdominal pain, and bloating. To relieve it, use the following visualization:

Imagine that you're gently stroking your bowel. Treat it the way you would someone who was feeling grouchy. Crabby people just need some TLC; in the same way, your bowel needs some love so that it doesn't feel irritable anymore. Give it a hug, caress it, and tell it that you love it. Picture it saying that it loves you, too.

Strike up a conversation with your bowel, asking it what's wrong and if there's anything you can do to help. Maybe it will tell you to cut out certain items from your diet and give you recommendations for alternatives. Or it might suggest that you don't get so stressed about things. Whatever you hear, listen to the advice.

Your intuitive picture of your bowel might at first appear as something with an angry face that's spitting and hissing, but after some real care from you, see its face soften and give you a big smile.

Even if this sounds silly, no one said visualizations had to be a serious thing. After all, it's the thought that counts!

Lupus

Lupus (systemic lupus erythematosus) is an autoimmune condition. With lupus, the immune system can attack almost any organ or tissue, but it's often known for its negative effect on the skin—many people with lupus have a bright red rash on their face.

Use either of the *Autoimmune Conditions* visualizations. In addition, or alternatively, you could do specific visualizations to heal some of the areas that are affected by lupus.

Malaria

Malaria is caused by infection from the Plasmodium genus of protozoa through the bite of an infected mosquito. The parasite invades and destroys red blood cells, which causes recurring (cyclic) fever and chills, sweating, fatigue, and even jaundice and anemia.

Use any of the visualizations for *Protozoan Infections* or *Infections* to neutralize the symptoms. You could also employ one of the *Immune*

System (Weak) visualizations if you choose that as your strategy. If you use the first one in that section, when the new immune cells reach the protozoa, see them eating it. And for extra smiles, imagine each immune-system cell letting out a loud burp when it's full.

Measles

Measles is a virus that's characterized by fever followed by a red rash. You could use any of the *Viruses* visualizations for this and also, or alternatively, do one specifically for the skin rash:

1. Imagine each cell in the rash as red. Now take a cloth and some colored cleaning fluid and get to work washing the cells one by one. As each is cleaned, it's restored to its normal color.

2. Alternatively, you can take an imaginary eraser and simply erase the red color and irritation from each cell, revealing a nice skin-colored cell underneath.

Meningitis

Meningitis is the inflammation of the meninges, which are the protective membranes covering the nerves of the central nervous system. The two main types that exist are viral and bacterial, viral being the less serious of the two.

Use any of the *Infections* visualizations, and the following can be used in addition to it:

Imagine equipping yourself with a whole host of gear to completely remove the infection. See it on the meninges in any way you wish. Now start shooting, blasting, sucking up, cleaning, and/or spraying, until you've totally neutralized the meningitis, and put in the required amount of determination that's necessary. Just to add a dimension of magical cleverness to this, recognize that all of your equipment can only harm infections— none of it can damage the meninges.

Spend as much time as you need to until the infected areas appear totally healthy. Look around and examine your handiwork, clearing up any debris in whichever way you want— dustpan and brush, vacuum cleaner, or globby immune-system cells eating it all up like Pac-Man.

Once it's clean, you might even give all of the meninges a coat of magical immune paint, which prevents reinfection. Step back and admire the amazing job you've done, as they all look so healthy and beautiful.

Multiple Sclerosis (MS)

MS is an autoimmune disease where the immune system attacks the myelin sheath (myelin is a white fatty substance) that coats axons (the arms of neurons). Therefore, communication down the axons is affected. Use either of the *Autoimmune Conditions* visualizations.

In addition, imagine regrowing the myelin sheath as follows:

Picture a nerve without its protective coating in any way that feels right for you. For example, you could see it as an exposed copper wire from which the insulating plastic has worn off or as a tree with no bark. Or you could get a more realistic picture from a medical textbook or the Internet.

Now see teams of construction workers repairing the nerve, adding myelin all along its length. Or if you wish, add the myelin yourself.

Muscle Tears

To repair muscle tears:

1. Imagine teams of construction workers repairing the tear. Envision them making new muscle fibers and knitting them together to join the two ends. Notice blood flowing into the area and carrying nutrients to nourish the muscle.

2. Visualize being right there beside the muscle tear. See yourself using magical threads to stitch it back together. With each stitch, pull the fibers closer and see them fit seamlessly.

Obesity

For obesity, you can use any of the *Weight Loss* visualizations, or you can try one of the following. These will work best in addition to healthy diet and lifestyle changes.

1. Imagine fat cells melting like blocks of ice. See each one totally dissolve into a pool of liquid, and watch each one do this individually. Then clean up any residue with a mop and bucket or a suction device.

2. A chemical known as leptin produces an "I'm full" signal in the brain, and there's scientific evidence to suggest that obese people are more resistant to that warning, which causes them to overeat. And in some people, the ob gene (the gene that produces leptin) may actually be faulty, which predisposes them to eat more.

If you've been told that you have a faulty ob gene and are therefore not producing enough leptin, then you could visualize ob as a little character lying on the ground as though it's been hurt. You might even see "ob" written on its T-shirt or jacket.

Now nurse it back to life again, showing great care, compassion, and attention. Nourish it with some medicine and nutrients, and see it growing stronger and giving off a glow.

Once it's healthy, imagine it diving into your DNA. See the DNA flex with great power and a pulse of light travel its length.

Finally, watch as the fat evaporates from the places you want it to.

3. If your body has become desensitized to leptin, less able to hear the "I'm full" call, try the following visualization. Note that leptin normally travels to the hypothalamus in the brain, where it docks onto leptin receptors, so here we're going to assume that the receptor can't hear the leptin calling it.

Imagine a leptin molecule, in any way you wish, running about inside the hypothalamus of the brain. Although it's shouting, "I'm full!" it isn't being heard because the receptor is asleep on the surface of the cell.

Envision the receptor in a shape that the leptin molecule could fit into. Go over and nudge it to wake it up. It will suddenly rise and say something like, "Sorry, my alarm didn't go off." It stands to attention as it sees the leptin calling out, "I'm full!" The leptin moves closer and the two hug or shake hands before the leptin disappears down the hole and into the cell.

This visualization is fun to do, which is a good thing.

4. See yourself as being your ideal weight. Infuse that image with fun and appreciation for all of the great things about being that weight. Envision doing some of the things that you would do at your ideal weight and shape, and notice people's reactions to seeing you.

Change the image into a ball of light of any color you wish, and move it to the areas of fat that you want to get rid of. Watch the fat evaporating and specific areas of your body morphing into your desired size and shape.

Pain

Use the following visualizations to relieve yourself of pain:

1. Imagine a dial indicating your discomfort level, and slowly turn it down. If you feel any further waves of pain, decide where they register on your dial, and turn it down again.

2. See pain signals traveling up a nerve from the area that's hurting the nerve cells in your brain (pain actually originates in the brain; it just feels as though it's at the site of an injury). Two nerves correspond with each other by sending signals across a gap between them, so put a piece of insulating polystyrene between the ends of the two nerves to block the signal. Imagine it moving up the nerve like electricity dancing along a wire, and then hitting the polystyrene and just fizzling out so that no communication passes across the gap—this is a magical piece of polystyrene because it only prevents distress indicators. See signals of different colors jump through the polystyrene, and be assured that it's only pain that can't get across; every other type of signal is allowed in and out of your brain.

3. Finally, while not technically a visualization, this is quite effective for many people: Pain intensifies when you try to resist feeling it. So instead of fighting against it, try to focus all of your attention on it. As you become aware of it, you're shifting your consciousness to an awareness that you're not the body; you're the intelligence that's aware of the body and its pain. It's a subtle shift, but a deep, unconscious recognition like this can neutralize pain.

Palpitations (see *Arrhythmia*)

Parkinson's Disease

Parkinson's disease is characterized by muscle tremors and rigidity mostly due to reduced production and release of dopamine in the basal ganglia of the brain, which connects with the movement-control area.

In addition, reread the examples of the use of mental imagery for Parkinson's and stroke rehabilitation described in Chapter 6, and do what the subjects did: for one hour, twice a week, visualize moving your muscles as if you were totally recovered, along with doing your physical therapy—and you can do more if you wish.

1. Imagine brain cells, made of a spongy material, which are supposed to be producing dopamine. Now give the spongy cells a squeeze and see dopamine squirt out in little bubbles of any color you see, and watch them float onto the branches of nearby brain cells (like tree branches).

As each bubble touches a branch, notice a pulse of electricity travel through your brain along the nerves and into each muscle that you wish to control, and move the corresponding part of the body perfectly. If you wish, go inside the area of the brain that isn't producing and releasing enough dopamine; instead of squeezing the sponge, turn up an imaginary dial and see little dopamine molecules being made and squirting out.

2. Imagine a dopamine factory inside the basal ganglia and a supervisor rushing in, saying, "We've got a big order that just came in. We need to increase production."

Then see teams of little construction workers making dopamine and loading it into big trucks where it's then taken out and released into the brain. See the little molecules swim across to the ends of the branches in a part of the brain with a big sign above it saying Motor Area. *(The motor area is what controls movement.)*

Watch the dopamine molecules being absorbed into the branches of the brain cells and electric charges pulsing along the nerves.

Pneumonia

Pneumonia is the inflammation of the lungs that's usually caused by a bacterial infection.

Use the *Infections* visualizations, the first visualization listed in the *Immune System (Weak)* section, or the following to cure yourself of it:

Envision being inside your lungs and noticing the redness and inflammation of the individual swollen cells. Now imagine letting the swelling out of them, just as you'd let air out of a balloon. Listen to the sound as the air whooshes out of the cells, and see them return to their normal size and healthy pink color.

Protozoan Infections

Protozoa are single-celled organisms that can infect the body. They act like parasites because they take over the cells that they infect. For instance, the plasmodium species of protozoa that produce malaria destroy and overrun red blood cells.

Use the following visualizations if you find yourself infected:

1. Imagine surrounding your cells with a protective bubble that prevents any parasites from entering it. Watch the parasites bouncing off the bubble as they try to get in—after a few attempts, see them give up and fly out of your body.

2. Visualize speaking to the parasites, asking them to leave your body because they're harming you. Notice that they didn't know that they were hurting you; they were just looking for food.

Tell them that there's plenty of food in the world for them.

Now see them fly out of your body and land in a distant forest where they can safely eat all they want.

Rheumatoid Arthritis

Rheumatoid arthritis is an autoimmune disease that causes the immune system to attack the joints. Use either of the *Autoimmune Conditions* visualizations. In addition, or alternatively, use either of the *Arthritis* visualizations.

Scars

See the visualizations about scars in the *Acne* section.

Sciatica

Sciatica is caused by compression of the sciatic nerve. Use any of the *Pain* visualizations or the one that follows to neutralize any discomfort.

1. To symbolize sciatic pain, imagine that the sciatic nerve is squashed underneath a boulder. Picture the nerve in any way you wish, perhaps as a taut rope.

Now see yourself rolling the boulder away and freeing up the nerve. Watch the tension reduce as it returns to its normal position.

2. Imagine the sciatic nerve stretched to the right or left (away from its normal position) and pulled too tightly around a bone or muscle. Now gently pull the nerve off of the bone or muscle and help it to gently recoil back to its proper position. As it's rewrapped, feel the tightness relax as you hold the nerve in your hands.

Self-Esteem (Low)

Use the first *Depression* visualization.

Sinusitis

Sinusitis is caused by bacterial infection and leads to inflammation of the paranasal sinuses, which are air-filled spaces within the bones of the face. This can cause a blockage of the small opening from the sinus to the nose, which means that mucus can't drain freely. The resulting pressure buildup causes pain in the face or head.

Use any of the *Infections* visualizations or either of the two that follow to tackle it.

1. Envision a highly inflated balloon, and notice how much pressure is in it.

Now let the air out, and hear the whooshing or rasping sound as it deflates. Then sense the fluids flowing freely in the sinuses again.

2. Imagine red inflated cells that are so swollen they're blocking a tunnel (the passage between the sinuses and the nose), preventing fluid from getting through.

Picture a valve that you can turn to deflate the cells, like letting air out of a balloon. Listen as the air rushes out and the cells return to their normal size. And as they do, see fluid effortlessly pass through the channel.

Sore Throat

You can use any of the *Infections* visualizations if you wish to tackle your sore throat by neutralizing the infection or you could try the following:

Imagine spraying magical, ice-cold vapor all over the infected area. Feel the coolness, and allow the substance to erase the irritation. See the redness fade to a healthy pink color and any swelling reduce to nothing, as if you've released the pressure from a balloon.

Spinal-Cord Injury

With some spinal-cord injuries, the spinal cord is severed, but most of the time it remains intact (although the body experiences a loss of movement).

The following visualizations can be done for either type of trauma, as they're symbolic of reestablishing communication.

1. If you've ever seen a fiber-optic cable, you'll know that it consists of hundreds of individual fiber optics. Imagine the spinal-cord injury as a break in some of these individual wires— which is actually a rupture in the nerves of the spinal cord.

Now see yourself reconnecting the nerves, one by one, with magic thread. Tie it around one end of the nerve, string it across to the other side, and then pull the two together until they connect.

As each individual nerve is repaired, feel a pulse of electricity flow across the newly reconnected section in any color you like. Then notice a pulse flow from your brain to whichever part of your body that you intuitively sense is now connected. As you repair more and more nerves, see them reaching every part of you.

2. Instead of using thread, you could imagine rubbing some magical fertilizer on the end of the severed nerve, and watch it grow toward the other end of the break (as if you were watching a plant or flower grow in time-lapse photography). If it doesn't reach the necessary length, add some more fertilizer until the two ends connect and the break is healed. Then see the pulse of electricity as in the previous visualization.

3. Imagine being inside the bone marrow. Once there, see a room, cave, or cavern full of stem cells resting. Ask them to become spinal-cord cells, and see them excitedly saying, "Yes!" They were there just waiting for instructions.

Watch them move out of the bone marrow and travel to the site of spinal injury. Perceive what the healthy spinal-cord cells look like, and see the stem cells morph into an exact match, fitting seamlessly alongside the existing healthy cells. As the new ones take their place, notice how the damage to the spinal cord becomes fully repaired.

4. Just as with the studies described in Chapter 6, where success was obtained for tetraplegic patients, you can also try some motor imagery. Pick a movement—for instance, a finger movement—and envision moving the finger over and over again. This will help to regenerate your brain maps.

Stress

The following visualizations can be done when you're feeling stressed:

1. Imagine your stress as an inflated balloon, and notice how full it is. Now take a deep breath and let the air out of the balloon. Hear the whooshing sound as the pressure decreases, and watch it completely deflate. For extra smiles, hear the rasping sound as you exhale. Do this as many times as you need to until you feel relaxed and calm.

Once you're relaxed, notice that your balloon is completely flat, which symbolizes that your stress level has reduced to zero.

The more you do this visualization, the more effective it will become; after some practice, you'll only need to do it once to relax.

2. See the stress in your mind as a fizzling, sparking ball of light. Now imagine a dial with the words STRESS LEVEL written above it, and note the level that the dial points to. Take a deep breath, and, as you exhale, turn it down. As you do this, perceive how the light gets smaller and smaller until it completely disappears.

3. Envision a glass of liquid (clear, or any color you wish) that's filled with calm. Now take a drink, and see the calm liquid flow down your throat and spread into every part of your body.

4. Picture all of the people, situations, and things that you feel stressed about. Put the image of them in one place and shrink it down—smaller and smaller—until it's the size of a pea. Then take it in your hands and flick it away. Feel the super-strength within yourself to be able to flick it right out of the city, state, country, or planet.

Stroke

A stroke is the rapid loss of brain function due to a rupture or obstruction of the vessels that supply blood to the brain. It often results in loss of use or debilitation of one side of the body.

The following visualizations are designed to rebuild the affected part of the brain.

1. See the damaged area of the brain as a field of burned stumps of trees and bushes. It looks like a fire has reduced this once-beautiful area to a charred landscape.

Now imagine sowing new seeds. Place one in the ground and watch it grow into a tree, which represents a neuron. (If it will help with your visualization, find a picture of a neuron from a medical textbook or the Internet, and note the similarities between neural connections and the branches of a tree.)

See this happen over several seconds, as if you were watching time-lapse photography of a plant or flower growing from a seed to an adult, and observe the tree grow branches. Now plant another seed, and watch it do the same thing. As its branches grow, notice how some of them reach out toward the branches of the last tree and connect with them.

When two branches (neurons) connect, imagine a pulse of electricity flow from one to the other and then down into a part of the body where movement is impaired.

Plant more seeds, watch them grow, see the branches connect to those of nearby trees, and observe the pulse of electricity as they connect. Repeat this process until you've replanted the entire forest.

Note that there are two ways that you can plant your forest of neurons. First, you could imagine just planting a bit of the forest with each visualization, maybe just a few square feet at a time, and watching the seeds mature right before your eyes. For each instance you do this, you can plant more and more of the forest, so that after weeks or months, you've completely regrown it and watched all of the new connections forge.

The other option is to sow the entire forest in one visualization, and see the trees develop gradually. With this option, you might observe all of them growing over a period of weeks or months from seedlings to tall trees. Show great care and patience as you nurture the baby trees, and perhaps even talk to them as you would to a child, and explain how to connect with the others. Eventually, you'll see the forest fully grown.

2. Reread the examples of stroke rehabilitation that used mental imagery in Chapter 6. Every day, imagine moving your muscles as if you were totally recovered.

Swollen Glands

To reduce the swelling in your glands, use the following visualization. You could also (or instead) use any of the *Infections* visualizations.

1. See your swollen glands as inflated balloons, and notice how overfilled they are. Now untie them and watch the air rush out. Hear the whooshing sound as they deflate (it's fun to hear this, and it will make you smile), one at a time. Watch each one get smaller and smaller until they're all completely flat.

For extra smiles, imagine each balloon shouting, "I'm shrinking! Shrinking!" similar to how the Wicked Witch of the West screams "I'm melting! Melting!" in <u>The Wizard of Oz</u> when Dorothy accidentally throws water on her. If no one is around to see you (or if people are and you just don't care), wave your hands and act like you're decreasing in size. It's a little like doing a victory dance.

2. Picture a bustling nightclub called Glands that's full of people. Go inside and see the bouncers start to clear everyone out. As they do so, notice that there's much more space to breathe and move around. Glands the club is no longer at its bursting point—and, as a result, your glands are no longer swollen.

Syphilis

Syphilis is a sexually transmitted disease that's caused by infection with the Treponema pallidum spirochete bacterium.

Use any of the *Infections* visualizations. The Treponema pallidum bacterium is a spirochete (corkscrew-like) shape; so, to make the visualization more specific to your needs, imagine the bacteria as little spirals, like pasta.

Toxins

There are many substances in the world that are toxic to the body. These visualizations can also be applied to any illness where you feel that there's something in your body that you need to remove. For instance, you could use them to remove cancer, bacteria, viral and protozoa infections, chronic fatigue syndrome, or even pain.

1. Imagine crystal clear water entering through the top of your head and flowing through your body and out the soles of your feet. Feel it rinse out your entire body.

At first, see the water emerge from the soles of your feet as a dark color—in what you feel represents the degree of toxicity in your body. But as it continues to pass through you, see it become lighter and cleaner as it exits your feet, until it's as crystal clear as it was when it entered the top of your head; once you've achieved this, there are no more toxins left in your body.

2. See yourself with a circular net that acts as a filter. Pull it from the top of your head down through your body and out your feet, capturing toxic particles along the way. Notice the toxins in the net and dispose of the loads by transporting them to the sun, where they're burned up.

3. Imagine toxins as little flecks of dust or dirt sticking to tissues and organs throughout your body, and use a vacuum cleaner to suck them up.

Tuberculosis

Tuberculosis (TB) is caused by the mycobacterium tuberculosis bacteria, which affects the lungs. The bacteria are small rod-shaped organisms, which means that you can be quite specific with your visualizations. Use the following to cure yourself of it. Additionally, or alternatively, use any of the *Infections* visualizations.

1. If you notice that some of your cells are sick because they've been hurt by the TB bacteria, you can imagine nursing them back to health one by one.

Give each cell little spoonfuls of special nutrients that are made of everything a cell could possibly need and are really tasty. See the cells smile and say, "Mmm," as they eat. Watch as the normal color returns to their faces and they grow stronger. Picture them glowing with a green regenerative light, which gets brighter as their power increases. See them regain their full health.

2. Imagine that you're inside your bone marrow, and see a room, cave, or treasure trove full of resting stem cells. Go over and ask them to become whichever cells that the TB has damaged. Watch them excitedly respond, "Yes!" since they were just waiting for instructions.

See them move out of the bone marrow and travel to the lungs. Observe what healthy cells look like in this area (there will always be some around), and notice how the stem cells morph into exact replicas of them and fit seamlessly alongside. As the new cells take their place, note how the damaged area fully regenerates.

Ulcers

Most ulcers are caused by the bacterium Helicobacter pylori and are characterized by abdominal pain, especially if fatty food is eaten. Use any of the *Infections* visualizations to neutralize the Helicobacter pylori bacteria. In addition, or alternatively, do this visualization.

See the ulcer as a small pit of gravel that's mixed with goo in your stomach—if you've ever had a mouth ulcer, imagine that it's similar to that.

Use an imaginary suction hose or vacuum cleaner to pick up all of the gravel and goo. Now watch teams of workers filling the space that this mixture left, adding new stomach-lining cells one by one. Notice how the new cells join together perfectly, until the hole has been filled and the stomach lining is restored to its perfect self.

Varicose Veins

Varicose veins are overly dilated veins, most commonly found in the legs. To get rid of them:

Picture an overinflated vein with a valve on top of it. Now slowly release the pressure from it using the valve. Hear the sound of pressure releasing, as if you've let the air out of something. Imagine a balloon deflating as you do so, and use this representation to see the overfilled vein shrinking back to normal. Do this for each vein.

Viruses

The following visualizations can be applied to any viral infection:

1. Imagine the receptors that the virus docks onto in the immune cells. Notice that they're playing a game and changing their shape so that the virus can't recognize or connect with the cell. For fun, you could see the receptors disguising themselves by putting on funny wigs, large glasses, or big teeth.

Be creative by thinking of different ways in which the receptors could prevent the virus from getting into the cell. For instance, they could turn themselves inside out or emit a sound that confuses the infectors.

See the virus eventually give up and leave the body.

2. Talk to the viruses and tell them that they're causing harm to your body. Imagine them saying that they didn't realize they were having a negative effect. Lovingly ask them to leave, and then see them exiting your body with big smiles on their faces.

3. Imagine using a computer that's inside your body. Type the command "Upload universal antivirus program" (or any other instruction that defends against a program that can corrupt your system). Press ENTER. Observe how the words fly off the screen and turn into lights of any color that you see. Watch them multiply into millions and millions of lights and move throughout your body, going wherever your mind takes them. Notice that your whole body is now glowing with the light.

Warts

Warts are small areas of roughened skin that are caused by the human papillomavirus (HPV). They can be flat or raised. To get rid of them:

1. Imagine taking some colored acid and rubbing it on the cells of a wart . . . and then watch them dissolve. Hear the fizzling sound as each cell disappears, and notice the wart get smaller.

2. Talk to your warts and tell them that you don't need them anymore. Thank them for being a part of your life, and watch their cells leave and wave good-bye to you with big smiles on their faces.

Weight Loss

The following visualizations will work best along with some exercise and a healthy diet. Alternatively, you could use either the first or third *Obesity* visualizations.

1. Imagine little piranhas or Pac-Man-like creatures nibbling away at the fat that you want to be rid of. Notice how they're really enjoying eating it, and watch them get fatter. When they're totally full, see them leaving your body with satisfied smiles on their faces, as replacements begin to eat in their place.

2. See the cells in your fatty areas, and carefully suck the fat out of each one with a hose. As the unwanted material is emptied from the cells, notice the skin tightening up and returning to its normal size. See each one looking just the way you want it to.

3. Imagine that there's a little piston inside the fat on your body with a sign above it saying FAT BURN. Picture it going up and down very slowly; this represents the rate at which you're burning fat. Find a dial on the side of the piston with speed settings—turn it up and watch the piston move faster. Or notice a foreman standing beside the piston, and ask him to turn the rate up and hear him enthusiastically reply, "Okay!"

Now envision the furnace chimney of a factory that's burning your fat. Watch the smoke surge out from the top. Previously, it was hardly visible, but now you realize that there must be an inferno down below—the smoke is suddenly billowing out of your body!

Worm Infections

Worm infections are so widespread that they affect around three billion people, especially in tropical and developing countries. Many worms live in the intestines, but some travel to other organs as they mature.

To rid yourself of them, use the following. Alternatively, you could lovingly ask them to leave.

Envision a color or type of light that repels the worms. Now see a glimmer of it inside the body where the worms are located. Turn up a dial and watch the light get brighter and grow in intensity. Watch as it becomes too much for these organisms without hurting them (just like we might move from the hot sun into the shade). Imagine the worms leaving the body.

৶৶৶৶

APPENDIX III

DNA VISUALIZATIONS

*"It is the marriage of the soul with Nature that makes
the intellect fruitful, that gives birth to imagination."*
— Henry David Thoreau

This section contains two DNA visualizations. I created the first one several years ago and thought it would be useful to include in the book because it can be applied to just about anything. The second is more specific and can be used for conditions where a person has been told that he or she has a faulty gene.

DNA is composed of around 25,000 genes, which I like to visualize as blinking Christmas-tree lights that are constantly switching on and off, because this is how the body grows and repairs. When genes turn on, they produce proteins, enzymes, hormones, and many other substances.

The point of the first visualization is to symbolically switch off some protein-producing genes that are causing or sustaining an illness or disease, and then turn on other ones that generate proteins whose functions are to cure or maintain health.

This visualization is symbolic, because nervous tissue isn't connected to DNA and we don't switch specific genes on or off by choice. I believe that when we do a symbolic visualization, we give our body instructions regarding what we *want* to happen. The body then uses whichever biological pathways that are necessary to get there. This is especially useful for those of us who have an interest in the mind-DNA interface, and it also allows us to be more specific in our visualization, which is different from what we may have been doing previously.

The First Visualization

Imagine the body part where the disease, illness, or condition is focused. Go inside and see its cells, and then go inside the cells and see the DNA. (If you don't know what DNA looks like, either get a picture of it from the Internet or in a book. You could also imagine it as organic intertwined strands, similar to braided hair.) In your mental picture of DNA, now add lightbulbs placed along the length of the strands.

Mentally say, "Show me the genetic program that produces the proteins that sustain this disease/illness/condition." Envision some genes (however many feel like the correct amount) lighting up relative to the other genes, as if your body intelligence was highlighting the exact ones that are involved.

Take a deep breath, and imagine turning down a dial to the off position and see the lights dim until they've completely gone out as you fully exhale.

Now mentally assert, "Show me the genetic program that produces the necessary proteins to heal this disease/illness/condition." Envision some genes (however many feel like the correct amount) become slightly highlighted relative to the rest. As you inhale, turn the dial to the on position, and see the lights become brighter until they're beaming as you fully inhale. And as you exhale, see them retain their brightness.

Now come back out of your cells, look at them, and say, "Show me that it's done." Watch your cells breathing with new life, and notice anything else that pops into your mind's eye. (Sometimes visible changes or other images spontaneously arise during visualizations. For instance, depending upon what you apply this one to, you might observe the diseased cells or body part returning to normal. If you have cancer, see the tumor(s) shrink down to nothing, as if all of the infection or disease has just been drained from them.)

Accept these images as confirmation that healing has taken place. See your whole body now move with grace and ease, in perfect health.

Say, "Thank you. It is done. It is done. It is done." This is how I like to finish this visualization. It adds a sense of completion and finality. The whole process should only take you a few minutes.

❧❧

Our knowledge of genetics and how genes create and cure illnesses—although seemingly quite advanced—is always expanding, and we're constantly learning things that would have seemed impossible only a few years ago. I believe that, even with faulty genes, the body has the ability to function much better than expected. In some cases, a person may live in perfect health with few or no symptoms of an illness.

The Second Visualization

The next visualization is almost the same as ones listed for cancer and cystic fibrosis, but I feel that it's important to reproduce it in this section to show that it can be used for other conditions:

Imagine a faulty gene lying on the ground as though it's been injured; see it like a little hurt organism. Now nurse it back to health again, showing great care, compassion, and attention. Give it some medicine and nutrients, and see it growing stronger and giving off a glow of light. Gradually watch as it regains its full strength. Then, once wellness is restored, imagine it diving into the DNA, which, as a result, flexes with great power, and a pulse of light travels its length. Finally, envision the condition disappearing in any way that you wish.

❧❧❧❧

REFERENCES

Chapter 1

For the Mayo Clinic study of optimists and pessimists, see Toshihiko Maruta M.D., et al., Mayo Clinic Proceedings, August 2002, or visit: **www .sciencedaily.com/releases/2002/08/020813071621.htm**.

For the 2004 study involving 999 Dutch men, see E. J. Giltay, J. M. Geleijnse, F. G. Zitman, T. Hoekstra, and E. G. Schouten, "Dispositional optimism and all-cause and cardiovascular mortality in a prospective cohort of elderly Dutch men and women," *Archives of General Psychiatry,* 2004, 61, 1126–35.

For the nun study, see D. D. Danner, D. A. Snowdon, and W. V. Friesen, "Positive emotions in early life and longevity: findings from the nun study," *Journal of Personality and Social Psychology,* 2001, 80(5), 804–13.

For the study where volunteers were exposed to the cold or influenza viruses, see S. Cohen, C. M. Alper, W. J. Doyle, J. T. Treanor, and R. B. Turner, "Positive emotional style predicts resistance to illness after experimental exposure to rhinovirus or influenza A virus," *Psychosomatic Medicine,* 2006, 68, 809–15.

For an article containing the study of 200 telecommunications executives, see Peggy Rynk, "The value of a healthy attitude: how faith, anger, humor, and boredom can affect your health," *Vibrant Life,* March–April 2003.

For the study of 586 people finding that attitude is the best prevention against heart disease, see D. M. Becker, "Positive attitude is best prevention against heart disease," paper presented at the American Heart Association Annual Scientific Sessions, Anaheim, CA, November 12, 2001.

For the study of 866 heart patients and positive attitude, see B. Brummett, "Positive outlook linked to longer life in heart patients," paper presented at the American Psychosomatic Society, March 2003.

For the emotional-vitality study, see L. D. Kubzansky and R. C. Thurston, "Emotional vitality and incident coronary heart disease: benefits of healthy psychological functioning," *Archives of General Psychiatry*, 2007, 64(12), 1393–1401.

For the hard marriage, hard heart research, see:

— T. W. Smith, C. Berg, B. N. Uchino, P. Florsheim, and G. Pearce, "Marital conflict behavior and coronary artery calcification," paper presented at the American Psychosomatic Society's 64th Annual Meeting, Denver, CO, March 3, 2006.

— T. W. Smith, B. N. Uchino, C. A. Berg, et al., "Hostile personality traits and coronary artery calcification in middle-aged and older married couples: different effects for self-reports versus spouse ratings," *Psychosomatic Medicine*, 2007, 69(5), 441–48.

— P. Pearsall, "Contextual cardiology: what modern medicine can learn from ancient Hawaiian wisdom," *Cleveland Clinical Journal of Medicine*, 2007, 74(1), S99–S104.

For the 25-year hostility study, see J. C. Barefoot, W. G. Dahlstrom, and R. B. Williams, "Hostility, CHD incidence, and total mortality: A 25-year follow-up study of 255 physicians," *Psychosomatic Medicine*, 1983, 45(1), 59–63.

For the paper quoting hostility as an indicator of heart disease, see R. B. Williams, J. C. Barefoot, and N. Schneiderman, "Psychosocial risk factors for cardiovascular disease: more than one culprit at work," *Journal of the American Medical Association*, 2003, 290(16), 2190–92.

For the Finnish satisfaction study, see H. Koivumaa-Honkanen, R. Honkanen, H. Viinamäki, K. Heikkilä, J. Kaprio, and M. Koskenvuo, "Self-reported life satisfaction and 20-year mortality in healthy Finnish adults," *American Journal of Epidemiology*, 2000, 152(10), 983–91.

For the "money buys happiness" research, see Elizabeth Dunn, "Money buys happiness when you spend on others: UBC and Harvard research," *University of British Columbia Media Release*, March 20, 2008. To view the media release, visit: **www. publicaffairs.ubc.ca/media/releases/2008/mr-08-032.html**.

For the effect of attitude on aging, see B. R. Levy, M. D. Slade, S. R. Kunkel, and S. V. Kasl, "Longevity increased by positive self-perceptions of aging," *Journal of Personality and Social Psychology,* 2002, 83(2), 261–70.

For the study of positive attitude being good for blood pressure, see G. V. Ostir, I. M. Berges, K. S. Markides, and K. J. Ottenbacher, "Hypertension in older adults and the role of positive emotions," *Psychosomatic Medicine,* 2006, 68, 727–33.

For the study linking frailty with attitude, see G. V. Ostir, J. Ottenbacher, and K. S. Markides, "Onset of frailty in older adults and the protective role of positive affect," *Psychology and Aging,* 2004, 19(3), 402–08.

For the link between life satisfaction and longevity, see T. M. Lyyra, T. M. Törmäkangas, S. Read, T. Rantanen, and S. Berg, "Satisfaction with present life predicts survival in octogenarians," *The Journals of Gerontology Series B: Psychological Sciences and Social Sciences,* 2006, 61, 319–26.

For the Posit Science Corporation study, see:

— H. W. Mahncke, B. B. Connor, J. Appelman, O. N. Ahsanuddin, J. L. Hardy, R. A. Wood, N. M. Joyce, T. Boniske, S. M. Atkins, and M. M. Merzinich, "Memory enhancement in healthy older adults using a brain plasticity-based training program: a randomized, controlled study," *Proceedings of the National Academy of Sciences, USA,* 2006, 103(33), 12523–28.

— H. W. Mahncke, A. Bronstone, and M. M. Merzinich, "Brain plasticity and functional losses in the aged: scientific basis for a novel intervention," *Progress in Brain Research,* 2006, 157, 81–109.

For the Harvard age study going back to 1959, see Ellen J. Langer Ph.D., *Mindfulness* (Da Capo Press, 1990).

For information on using the brain and reducing the risk of Alzheimer's, see R. S. Wilson, C. F. Mendes de Leon, L. L. Barnes, J. A. Schneider, J. L. Bienias, D. A. Evans, and D. A. Bennett, "Participation in cognitively stimulating activities and risk of incident Alzheimer's disease," *Journal of the American Medical Association,* 2002, 287(6), 742–48.

For the priming experiments, see:

— J. A. Bargh, M. Chen, and L. Burrows, "Automaticity of social behavior: direct effects of trait construct and stereotype activation on action," *Journal of Personality and Social Psychology*, 1996, 71(2), 230–44.

— T. M. Hess, J. T. Hinson, and J. A. Statham, "Explicit and implicit stereotype activation effects on memory: do age and awareness moderate the impact of priming?" *Psychology and Aging*, 2004, 19(3), 495–505.

Chapter 2

The quotation from Professor Benedetti can be found in F. Benedetti, "Mechanisms of placebo and placebo-related effects across diseases and treatments," *Annual Review of Pharmacology and Toxicology*, 2008, 46, 33–60. This is also a good review of recent research into the placebo effect.

For the release of dopamine when Parkinson's patients receive placebos, see:

— R. de la Fuente-Fernández, T. J. Ruth, V. Sossi, M. Schulzer, D. B. Calne, and A. J. Stoessl, "Expectation and dopamine release: mechanism of the placebo effect in Parkinson's disease," *Science*, 2001, 293(5532), 1164–66.

— R. de la Fuente-Fernández, A. G. Phillips, M. Zamburlini, V. Sossi, D. B. Calne, T. J. Ruth, and A. J. Stoessl, "Dopamine release in human ventral striatum and expectation of reward," *Behavioural Brain Research*, 2002, 136(2), 359–63.

The first evidence of opioid release during placebo analgesia can be found in J. D. Levine, N. C. Gordon, and H. L. Fields, "The mechanism of placebo analgesia," *Lancet*, 1978, 654–57.

For an account of placebo effects tracking closely the treatments with which they are paired, and a discussion of the similarity in brain scans while patients receive Prozac or a placebo, see F. Benedetti, H. S. Mayberg, T. D. Wager, C. S. Stohler, and J.-K. Zubieta, "Neurobiological mechanisms of the placebo effect," *Journal of Neuroscience*, 2005, 25(45), 10390–402.

For the MRI brain scans of people receiving placebos and high placebo responses, see:

— J.-K. Zubieta, J. A. Bueller, L. R. Jackson, D. J. Scott, Y. Xu, et al., "Placebo effects mediated by endogenous opioid activity on m-opioid receptors," *Journal of Neuroscience*, 2005, 25, 7754–62.

— T. D. Wager, D. J. Scott, and J.-K. Zubieta, "Placebo effects on human m-opioid activity during pain," *Proceedings of the National Academy of Sciences, USA*, 2007, 104(26), 11056–61.

For some clinical trial results, visit: **www.clinicaltrialstoday.com/ centerwatch_clinical_tria/clinical_trial_results/**.

For the chronic fatigue syndrome study that tested acyclovir, see S. E. Strauss, J. K. Dale, M. Tobi, T. Lawley, O. Preble, R. M. Blaese, C. Callahan, and W. Henle, "Acyclovir treatment of the chronic fatigue syndrome. Lack of efficacy in a placebo-controlled trial," *New England Journal of Medicine*, 1988, 319(26), 1692–98.

For the study using hydrocortisone, visit: **www.hhs.gov/news/press/ 1996pres/961013.html**.

For the placebo studies on asthma, see:

— T. Luparello, H. A. Lyons, E. R. Bleecker, and E. R. McFadden, "Influences of suggestion on airway reactivity in asthmatic subjects," *Psychosomatic Medicine*, 1969, XXX, 819–25.

— E. R. McFadden, T. Luparello, H. A. Lyons, and E. R. Bleecker, "The mechanism of action of suggestion in the induction of acute asthma attacks," *Psychosomatic Medicine*, 1969, XXXI, 134–43.

For the study of performance-enhancing placebos, see F. Benedetti, A. Pollo, and L. Colloca, "Opioid-mediated placebo responses boost pain endurance and physical performance: is it doping in sport competitions?" *Journal of Neuroscience,* 2007, 27(44), 11934–39.

For the study involving the hotel-room maids, visit: **www.npr.org/templates/ story/story.php?storyId=17792517.**

For the study of women's beliefs affecting their mathematics performance, see I. Dar-Nimrod and S. J. Heine, "Exposure to scientific theories affects women's math performance," *Science,* 2006, 314(5798), 435.

For information on placebo responders, as well as lots of information on a range of placebo studies, see Daniel Moerman, *Meaning, Medicine and the 'Placebo Effect'* (Cambridge University Press, 2002).

The 1954 bleeding-ulcers study was reported in Daniel Moerman's book, cited earlier.

For the study involving hidden arm pain, see F. Benedetti, "The opposite effects of the opiate antagonist naloxone and the cholecystokinin antagonist proglumide on placebo analgesia," *Pain,* 1996, 64(3), 535–43.

For the dental injections given with an "oversell" or "undersell" message, see S. L. Gryll and M. Katahn, "Situational factors contributing to the placebo effect," *Psychopharmacology,* 1978, 57(3), 253–61.

For the study on the effect of positive and negative consultations, see K. B. Thomas, "General practice consultations: is there any point in being positive?" *British Medical Journal,* 1987, 294, 1200–02.

For the studies of optimists and pessimists and how they respond in the placebo effect, see the following:

— For the pessimists study, see A. L. Geers, S. G. Helfer, K. Kosbab, P. E. Weiland, and S. J. Landry, "Reconsidering the role of personality in placebo effects: dispositional optimism, situational expectations, and the placebo response," *Journal of Psychosomatic Research,* 2005, 58(2), 212–17.

— For the optimists study, see A. L. Geers, K. Kosbab, S. G. Helfer, P. E. Weiland, and J. A. Wellman, "Further evidence for individual differences in placebo responding: an interactionist perspective," *Journal of Psychosomatic Research,* 2007, 62(5), 563–70.

For the conditioned immunosuppression using cyclosporin A, see M. U. Goebel, et al., "Behavioral conditioning of immunosuppression is possible in humans," *FASEB Journal,* 2002, 16, 1869–73.

For Benedetti's conditioning of immune and growth hormone levels, see F. Benedetti, A. Pollo, L. Lopiano, M. Lanotte, S. Vighetti, and I. Rainero, "Conscious expectation and unconscious conditioning in analgesic, motor, and hormonal placebo/nocebo responses," *Journal of Neuroscience,* 2002, 23, 4315–23.

Chapter 3

For the 2008 antidepressants analysis that found over 80 percent placebo effect, see I. Kirsch, B. J. Deacon, T. B. Huedo-Medina, A. Scoboria, T. J. Moore, and B. T. Johnson, "Initial severity and antidepressant benefits: a meta-analysis of data submitted to the food and drug administration," *PLoS Medicine,* February 2008, 5(2), e45, 0260–68.

A number of the studies reported in this chapter were also cited in Daniel Moerman's excellent book, cited earlier. I thoroughly recommend it to anyone seeking a fuller understanding of the placebo effect and its implications.

For the quote from C. G. Helman, see his chapter entitled "Placebos and Nocebos: The Cultural Construction of Belief" in *Understanding the Placebo Effect in Complementary Medicine: Theory, Practice and Research,* ed. D. Peters (Churchill Livingstone, 2001).

For the study of blue and pink sedatives and stimulants, see B. Blackwell, S. S. Bloomfield, and C. R. Buncher, "Demonstration to medical students of placebo responses and non-drug factors," *Lancet,* 1972, 1(7763), 1279–82.

For the study of injections versus tablets in the U.S.A. and Europe, see A. J. de Craen, J. G. Tijssen, J. de Gans, and J. Kleijnen, "Placebo effect in the acute treatment of migraine: subcutaneous placebos are better than oral placebos," *Journal of Neurology*, 2000, 247(3), 183–88.

For the study of Tagamet performed in France, see R. Lambert, et al., "Treatment of duodenal and gastric ulcer with cimetidine. A multicenter double-blind trial," *Gastroenterologie Clinique et Biologique*, 1977, 1(11), 855–60. For the study in Brazil, see J. A. Salgado; C. A. de Oliveira; G. F. Lima, Jr.; and L. de Paula Castro, "Endoscopic findings after antacid, cimetidine and placebo for peptic ulcer—importance of staging the lesions," *Arquivos De Gastroenterologia*, 1981, 18(2), 51–3. Both studies are reported in Daniel Moerman's book, cited earlier.

The reduction in effectiveness of Tagamet once Zantac was available is described in Daniel Moerman's book. It is also mentioned in Herbert Benson, M.D.'s, *Timeless Healing* (Scribner, 1995).

For the University of Keele aspirin study, see A. Branthwaite and P. Cooper, "Analgesic effects of branding in treatment of headaches," *British Medical Journal*, 1981, 282, 1576–78.

For the suggestion that Viagra is enhanced by its name, see A. K. Vallance, "Something out of nothing: the placebo effect," *Advances in Psychiatric Treatment*, 2006, 12, 287–96.

For the study of four placebos being better than two in antiulcer trials, see A. J. de Craen, D. E. Moerman, S. H. Heisterkamp, G. N. Tytgat, J. G. Tijssen, and J. Kleijnen, "Placebo effect in the treatment of duodenal ulcer," *British Journal of Clinical Pharmacology*, 1999, 48(6), 853–60.

For adherence in the clofibrate trial, see Coronary Drug Project Research Group, "Influence of adherence to treatment and response of cholesterol on mortality in the coronary drug project," *New England Journal of Medicine*, 1980, 303(18), 1038–41.

For adherence in the propranolol trial, see E. J. Gallagher, C. M. Viscoli, and R. I. Horwitz, "The relationship of treatment adherence to the risk of death after myocardial infarction in women," *Journal of the American Medical Association*, 1993, 270(6), 742–44.

For adherence in the antibiotic trial, see P. A. Pizzo, K. J. Robichaud, B. K. Edwards, C. Schumaker, B. S. Kramer, and A. Johnson, "Oral antibiotic prophylaxis in patients with cancer: a double-blind randomized placebo-controlled trial," *Journal of Pediatrics*, 1983, 102(1), 125–33.

For the real versus sham mammary-ligation studies, see:

— E. G. Dimond, C. F. Kittle, and J. E. Crockett, "Comparison of internal mammary artery ligation and sham operation for angina pectoris," *American Journal of Cardiology*, 1960, 5, 483–86.

— L. A. Cobb, G. I. Thomas, D. H. Dillard, K. A. Merendino, and R. A. Bruce, "An evaluation of internal-mammary-artery ligation by a double-blind technique," *New England Journal of Medicine*, 1959, 260(22), 1115–18.

For the naproxen study where patients either knew or didn't know that they were receiving it, see J. F. Bergmann, O. Chassany, J. Gandiol, P. Deblois, J. A. Kanis, J. M. Segrestaa, C. Caulin, and R. Dahan, "A randomized clinical trial of the effect of informed consent on the analgesic activity of placebo and naproxen in cancer pain," *Clinical Trials Meta-Analysis*, 1994, 29(1), 41–7.

The Benedetti quote, "The existence of the placebo effect suggests that we must broaden our conception of the limits of human capability," can be found in F. Benedetti, H. S. Mayberg, T. D. Wager, C. S. Stohler, and J.-K. Zubieta, "Neurobiological mechanisms of the placebo effect," *Journal of Neuroscience*, 2005, 25(45), 10390–402.

Chapter 4

For the study of brain changes in symphony musicians, see V. Sluming, T. Barrick, M. Howard, E. Cezayirli, A. Mayes, and N. Roberts, "Voxel-based morphometry reveals increased gray matter density in Broca's area in male symphony orchestra musicians," *NeuroImage*, 2002, 17(3), 1613–22.

The reference to brain-map changes as blind people learn braille can be found in Norman Doidge, M.D., *The Brain That Changes Itself* (Penguin, 2007).

For the study of brain changes while students were studying for exams, see B. Draganski, C. Gaser, G. Kempermann, H. G. Kuhn, J. Winkler, C. Büchel, and A. May, "Temporal and spatial dynamics of brain structure changes during extensive learning," *Journal of Neuroscience*, 2006, 26(23), 6314–17.

For the London taxi-drivers study, see E. A. Maguire, K. Woollett, and H. J. Spiers, "London taxi drivers and bus drivers: a structural MRI and neuropsychological analysis," *Hippocampus*, 2006, 16, 1091–101.

For the study showing brain changes in mathematicians, see K. Aydin, A. Ucar, K. K. Oguz, O. O. Okur, A. Agayev, Z. Unal, S. Yilmaz, and C. Ozturk, "Increased gray matter density in the parietal cortex of mathematicians: a voxel-based morphometry study," *American Journal of Neuroradiology*, 2007, 28(10), 1859–64.

For the study of the effects of meditation on the brain, see S. W. Lazar, C. E. Kerr, R. H. Wasserman, J. R. Gray, D. N. Greve, M. T. Treadway, M. McGarvery, B. T. Quinn, J. A. Dusek, H. Benson, S. L. Rauch, C. I. Moore, and B. Fischl, "Meditation experience is associated with increased cortical thickness," *Neuroreport*, 2005, 16(17), 1893–97.

The Eric Kandel quote, as well as a discussion of brain changes due to psychotherapy, can be found in Norman Doidge's book, cited earlier.

For the study showing 15 percent increase in hippocampal volume due to environmental enrichment, see G. Kemperman, D. Gast, and F. H. Gage, "Neuroplasticity in old age: sustained fivefold induction of hippocampal neurogenesis by long-term environmental enrichment," *Annals of Neurology*, 2002, 52, 135–143. See also L. Lu, G. Bao, H. Chen, P. Xia, X. Fan, J. Zhang, G. Pei, and L. Ma, "Modification of hippocampal neurogenesis and neuroplasticity by social environments," *Experimental Neurology*, 2003, 183(2), 600–09.

For discovery of neurogenesis in the hippocampus, see P. S. Eriksson, E. Perfilieva, T. Björk-Eriksson, A.-M. Alborn, C. Nordborg, D. A. Peterson, and F. H. Gage, "Neurogenesis in the adult human hippocampus," *Nature Medicine*, 1998, 4(11), 1313–17.

The identification of neurogenesis right up to our final days can be found in the paper cited immediately above, on the discovery of neurogenesis in adults. The scientists received permission from terminally ill patients to inject them with a biological marker, bromodeoxyuridine (BrdU). When the patients died, neurogenesis was discovered.

For a good review of neurogenesis, see P. Taupin and F. H. Gage, "Adult neurogenesis and neural stem cells of the central nervous system in mammals," *Journal of Neuroscience Research*, 2002, 69, 745–49.

Chapter 5

For a good description of the brain and how it changes with our thoughts and emotions, see Joe Dispenza, *Evolve Your Brain* (Health Communications Inc., 2007).

For the research showing that hostility slows the rate of wound healing, see J. K. Kiecolt-Glaser, T. J. Loving, J. R. Stowell, W. B. Malarkey, S. Lemeshow, S. L. Dickinson, and R. Glaser, "Hostile marital interactions, proinflammatory cytokine production, and wound healing," *Archives of General Psychiatry,* 2005, 62(12), 1377–84.

For the effects of stress on growth hormone levels and on the "upregulation" and "downregulation" of genes at wound sites, see S. Roy, S. Khanna, P.-E. Yeh, C. Rink, W. B. Malarkey, J. Kiecolt-Glaser, B. Laskowski, R. Glaser, and C. K. Sen, "Wound site neutrophil transcriptome in response to psychological stress in young men," *Gene Expression,* 2005, 12(4–6), 273–87.

For social support speeding up wound healing, see C. E. Detillion, T. K. S. Craft, E. R. Glaser, B. J. Prendergast, and A. C. DeVries, "Social facilitation of wound healing," *Psychoneuroendocrinology,* 2004, 29(8), 1004–11.

Trumping our genes refers to the science of epigenetics. To learn more about epigenetics, see Bruce Lipton, *The Biology of Belief* (Hay House, 2008). See also Dawson Church, *The Genie in Your Genes* (Elite Books, 2007).

For information on neurogenesis and the suggestion that the mind interacts with DNA in stem cells, see Ernest L. Rossi, *The Psychobiology of Gene Expression* (Norton, 2002).

Chapter 6

For the study where experimental pain was induced in fingers, see G. Montgomery and I. Kirsch, "Mechanisms of placebo pain reduction: an empirical investigation," *Psychological Science,* 1996, 7(3), 174–76.

For the study involving capsaicin, see F. Benedetti, C. Arduino, and M. Amanzio, "Somatotopic activation of opioid systems by target-directed expectations of analgesia," *The Journal of Neuroscience,* 1999, 19(9), 3639–48.

In an e-mail communication, I asked Fabrizio Benedetti whether a person with two different ailments would get better from one of them if he or she was given a placebo for that specific ailment (believing it to be a real drug) but not the other. Would a person with Parkinson's, say, who also had a headache, and who received an anti-Parkinson's drug (which was really a placebo) find the tremors reducing but not the headache, and vice versa? Professor Benedetti agreed that this would most likely be the case.

For the Karolinska Institute research showing that imagined movements of fingers, toes, and tongue activated brain regions that governed them, see H. H. Ehrsson, S. Geyer, and E. Naito, "Imagery of voluntary movement of fingers, toes, and tongue activates corresponding body-part-specific motor representations," *Journal of Neurophysiology,* 2003, 90(5), 3304–16.

For the piano study, see A. Pascual-Leone, D. Nguyet, L. G. Cohen, J. P. Brasil-Neto, A. Cammarota, and M. Hallet, "Modulation of muscle responses evoked by transcranial magnetic stimulation during the acquisition of new fine motor skills," *Journal of Neurophysiology,* 1995, 74(3), 1037–45.

For the study where volunteers' fingers got 35 percent stronger through imagined training, see V. K. Ranganathan, V. Siemionow, J. Z. Liu, V. Sahgal, and G. H. Yue, "From mental power to muscle power—gaining strength by using the mind," *Neuropsychologia,* 2004, 42(7), 944–56. See also G. Yue and K. J. Cole, "Strength increases from the motor program: comparison of training with maximal voluntary and imagined muscle contractions," *Journal of Neurophysiology,* 1992, 67(5), 1114–23.

For the study showing the differences in muscle activation depending upon the imagined weight, see A. Guillot, F. Lebon, D. Rouffet, S. Champely, J. Doyon, and C. Collet, "Muscular responses during motor imagery as a function of muscle contraction types," *International Journal of Psychophysiology,* 2007, 66(1), 18–27.

For the study where the tetraplegic person opened an e-mail with his mind, see L. R. Hochberg, M. D. Serruya, G. M Friehs, J. A. Mukand, M. Saleh, A. H. Caplan, A. Branner, D. Chen, R. D. Penn, and J. P. Donoghue, "Neuronal ensemble control of prosthetic devices by a human with tetraplegia," *Nature,* 2006, 442, 164–71.

For research into mental walking in virtual-reality simulators, see G. Pfurtscheller, R. Leeb, C. Keinrath, D. Friedman, C. Neuper, C. Guger, and M. Slater, "Walking from thought," *Brain Research,* 2006, 1071(1), 145–52.

For mirror-neuron research where volunteers watched hands, mouth, or foot movements, see G. Buccino, F. Binkovski, G. R. Fink, L. Fadiga, L. Fogassi, V. Gallese, R. J. Seitz, K. Zilles, G. Rizzolatti, and H.-J. Freund, "Action observation activates premotor and parietal areas in a somatotopic manner: an fMRI study," *European Journal of Neuroscience,* 2001, 13(2), 400–04.

For the *Bend it like Beckham* paper, see P. Bach and S. P Tipper, "Bend it like Beckham: embodying the motor skills of famous athletes," *Quarterly Journal of Experimental Psychology,* 2006, 59(12), 2033–39.

For the study where volunteers increased finger strength through watching training, see C. A. Porro, P. Facchin, S. Fusi, G. Dri, and L. Fadiga, "Enhancement of force after action observation: behavioural and neurophysiological studies," *Neuropsychologia,* 2007, 45(13), 3114–21.

For improvements gained by stroke patients through watching people perform routine actions, see D. Ertelt, S. Small, A. Solodkin, C. Dettmers, A. McNamara, F. Binkofski, and G. Buccino, "Action observation has a positive impact on rehabilitation of motor deficits after stroke," *NeuroImage,* 2007, 36, Supplement 2, T164–73.

For activation of mirror neurons while watching someone playing a guitar, see G. Buccino, S. Vogt, A. Ritzl, G. R. Fink, K. Zilles, H.-J. Freund, and G. Rizzolatti, "Neural circuits underlying imitation learning of hand actions: an event-related fMRI study," *Neuron*, 2004, 42, 323–34.

For activation of the brain by listening to sentences describing motion, see G. Buccino, L. Riggio, G. Melli, F. Binkofski, V. Gallese, and G. Rizzolati, "Listening to action-related sentences modulates the activity of the motor system: a combined TMS and behavioral study," *Cognitive Brain Research*, 2005, 24(3), 355–63. See also M. Tettamanti, G. Buccino, M. C. Saccuman, V. Gallese, M. Danna, P. Scifo, F. Fazio, G. Rizzolatti, S. F. Cappa, and D. Perani, "Listening to action-related sentences activates frontoparietal motor circuits," *Journal of Cognitive Neuroscience*, 2005, 17(2), 273–81.

For activation of tongue muscles by listening to speech, see L. Fadiga, L. Craighero, G. Buccino, and G. Rizzolati, "Speech listening specifically modulates the excitability of tongue muscles: a TMS study," *European Journal of Neuroscience*, 2002, 15(2), 399–402.

A good review of mirror-neuron research is G. Buccino, A. Solodkin, and S. L. Small, "Functions of the mirror neuron system: implications for neurorehabilitation," *Cognitive and Behavioural Neurology*, 2006, 19(1), 55–63.

For information on increasing the sensitivity of your own body part by looking at someone else's, see P. Bach, N. A. Peatfield, and S. P. Tipper, "Focusing on body sites: the role of spatial attention in action perception," *Experimental Brain Research*, 2007, 178(4), 509–17.

For use of guided imagery for treatment of chronic obstructive pulmonary disease (COPD), see S. W.-S. Louie, "The effects of guided imagery relaxation in people with COPD," *Occupational Therapy International*, 2004, 11(3), 145–59.

For the use of guided imagery for treatment of osteoarthritis in older women, see C. L. Baird and L. P. Sands, "Effect of guided imagery with relaxation on health-related quality of life in older women with osteoarthritis," *Research in Nursing & Health*, 2006, 29(5), 442–51.

For the use of guided imagery for treatment of interstitial cystitis, see D. J. Carrico, K. M. Peters, and A. C. Diokno, "Guided imagery for women with interstitial cystitis: results of a prospective, randomized controlled pilot study," *Journal of Alternative and Complementary Medicine*, 2008, 14(1), 53–60.

For the effect of guided imagery on the reoccurrence of breast cancer, see L. Freeman, L. Cohen, M. Stewart, R. White, J. Link, J. L. Palmer, and D. Welton, "Imagery intervention for recovering breast cancer patients: clinical trial of safety and efficacy," *Journal of the Society of Integrative Oncology,* 2008, 6(2), 67–75.

For the use of guided imagery in wound healing after gallbladder-removal surgery (cholecystectomy), see C. Holden-Lund, "Effects of relaxation with guided imagery on surgical stress and wound healing," *Research in Nursing & Health,* 2007, 11(4), 235–44.

For the use of guided imagery for treatment of fibromyalgia pain, see E. A. Fors, H. Sexton, and K. G. Götestam, "The effect of guided imagery and amitriptyline on daily fibromyalgia pain: a prospective, randomized, controlled trial," *Journal of Psychiatric Research,* 2002, 36(3), 179–87.

For the effect of visualization ability, see:

— E. Watanabe, S. Fukuda, H. Hara, Y. Maeda, H. Ohira, and T. Shirakawa, "Differences in relaxation by means of guided imagery in a healthy community sample," *Alternative Therapies in Health and Medicine,* 2006, 12(2), 60–66.

— E. Watanabe, S. Fukuda, and T. Shirakawa, "Effects among healthy subjects of the duration of regularly practicing a guided imagery program," *BMC Complementary and Alternative Medicine,* 2005, 5, 21.

— K. Kwekkeboom, K. Huseby-Moore, and S. Ward, "Imaging ability and effective use of guided imagery," *Research in Nursing and Health,* 1998, 21(3), 189–98.

For use of mental imagery in stroke rehabilitation, see:

— S. J. Page, P. Levine, and A. C. Leonard, "Mental practice in chronic stroke: results of a randomized, placebo-controlled trial," *Stroke,* 2007, 38(4), 1293–97.

— S. J. Page, P. Levine, and A. C. Leonard, "Effects of mental practice on affected limb use and function in chronic stroke," *Archives of Physical Medicine and Rehabilitation,* 2005, 86(3), 399–402.

For use of mental imagery in rehabilitation after spinal-cord injury, see S. C. Cramer, E. L. Orr, M. J. Cohen, and M. G. Lacourse, "Effects of imagery training after chronic, complete spinal cord injury," *Experimental Brain Research,* 2007, 177(2), 233–42.

For use of mental imagery by Parkinson's patients, see R. Tamir, R. Dickstein, and M. Huberman, "Integration of motor imagery and physical practice in group treatment applied to subjects with Parkinson's disease," *Neurorehabilitation and Neural Repair,* 2007, 21(1), 68–75.

For a summary of mental-imagery research, see R. Dickstein and J. E. Deutsch, "Motor imagery in physical therapist practice," *Physical Therapy,* 2007, 87(7), 942–53.

For use of visualization in asthma treatment, see L. W. Freeman and D. Welton, "Effects of imagery, critical thinking, and asthma education on symptoms and mood state in adult asthma patients: a pilot study," *The Journal of Alternative and Complementary Medicine,* 2005, 11(1), 57–68.

Chapter 7

The reference for the 2004 meta-analysis linking stress with the immune system is S. Segerstrom and G. E. Miller, "Psychological stress and the human immune system: a meta-analytic study of 30 years of inquiry," *Psychological Bulletin,* 2004, 130(4), 601–30.

For the effects of stress on composition of wound fluid, see E. Broadbent, K. J. Petrie, P. G. Alley, and R. J. Booth, "Psychological stress impairs early wound repair following surgery," *Psychosomatic Medicine,* 2003, 65, 865–69.

For the effects of stress on HIV and how it increases viral replication, see S.W. Cole, B. D. Naliboff, M. E. Kemeny, M. P. Griswold, J. L. Fahey, and J. A. Zack, "Impaired response to HAART in HIV-infected individuals with high autonomic nervous system activity," *Proceedings of the National Academy of Sciences, USA,* 2001, 98(22), 12695–700.

For the 18-month study linking shyness with rate of viral replication, see S. W. Cole, M. E. Kemeny, J. L. Fahey, J. A. Zack, and B. D. Naliboff, "Psychological risk factors for HIV pathogenesis: mediation by the autonomic nervous system," *Biological Psychiatry*, 2003, 54(12), 1444–56.

For the study where students wrote about traumatic experiences on four consecutive days, see J. W. Pennebaker and S. K. Beall, "Confronting a traumatic event: toward an understanding of inhibition and disease," *Journal of Abnormal Psychology*, 1986, 95(3), 274–81.

For the effect of writing about traumatic experiences and the hepatitis B vaccination, see K. J. Petrie, R. J. Booth, J. W. Pennebaker, K. P. Davison, and M. G. Thomas, "Disclosure of trauma and immune response to hepatitis B vaccination program," *Journal of Consulting and Clinical Psychology*, 1995, 63(5), 787–92.

For the effect of writing on viral load and CD4 cell counts of HIV patients, see K. J. Petrie, I. Fontanilla, M. G. Thomas, R. J. Booth, and J. W. Pennebaker, "Effect of written emotional expression on immune function in patients with Human Immunodeficiency Virus infection: a randomized trial," *Psychosomatic Medicine*, 2004, 66, 272–5.

For effects of emotional support on the health of breast-cancer patients, see B. L. Andersen, W. B. Farrar, D. Golden-Kreutz, C. F. Emery, R. Glaser, T. Crespin, and W. E. Carson, "Distress reduction from a psychological intervention contributes to improved health for cancer patients," *Brain, Behavior, and Immunity*, 2007, 21(7), 953–61.

For the effect of mindfulness-based stress reduction (MBSR) on the health of breast- and prostate-cancer patients, see:

— L. E. Carlson, M. Speca, P. Faris, and K. D. Patel, "One-year pre-post intervention follow-up of psychological, immune, endocrine and blood pressure outcomes of mindfulness-based stress reduction (MBSR) in breast and prostate cancer patients," *Brain, Behavior, and Immunity*, 2007, 21(8), 1038–49.

— L. E. Carlson, M. Speca, K. D. Patel, and E. Goodey, "Mindfulnessbased stress reduction in relation to quality of life, mood, symptoms of stress and levels of cortisol, dehydroepiandrosterone sulfate (DHEAS) and melatonin in breast and prostate cancer outpatients," *Psychoneuroendocrinology,* 2004, 29(4), 448–74.

— M. Speca, L. E. Carlson, E. Goodey, and M. Angen, "A randomized, wait-list controlled clinical trial: the effect of a mindfulness meditation-based stress reduction program on mood and symptoms of stress in cancer outpatients," *Psychosomatic Medicine,* 2000, 62(5), 613–22.

For use of MBSR in control of glucose levels in type 2 diabetes patients, see S. Rosenzweig, D. K. Reibel, J. M. Greeson, J. S. Edman, S. A. Jasser, K. D. McMearty, and B. J. Goldstein, "Mindfulness-based stress reduction is associated with improved glycemic control in type 2 diabetes mellitus: a pilot study," *Alternative Therapies in Health and Medicine,* 2007, 13(5), 36–8.

For improvement in mood, and for reduced stress and anxiety in healthy adults using meditation, see J. D. Lane, J. E. Seskevich, and C. F. Pieper, "Brief meditation training can improve perceived stress and negative mood," *Alternative Therapies in Health and Medicine,* 2007, 13(1), 38–44.

For the effect of meditation at the genetic level, see J. A. Dusek, H. H. Otu, A. L. Wohlhueter, M. Bhasin, L. F. Zerbini, M. G. Joseph, H. Benson, and T. A. Liberman, "Genomic counter-stress changes induced by the relaxation response," *PloS ONE,* 2008, 3(7), e2576, 1–8.

๛๛๛๛

ACKNOWLEDGMENTS

First, I'd like to thank my partner Elizabeth Caproni for her constant love and encouragement. Through Elizabeth I've come to believe in myself, and only from this space have I been able to write and speak at the level that I do.

From my earliest memories, my mum and dad have encouraged me to do what I want to do and to believe that I can. To Mum and Dad: This is me doing it! Thank you.

I wish to say a huge thanks to all of the people who shared their personal stories in this book and to those who contributed but didn't make the final version. I believe that it's the telling of our stories that inspires other people. To those of you who shared your stories, whether they made the final version or not, by having the courage to do so, you've inspired many people to recognize that they also have the ability to heal themselves. Words cannot convey just how important of a gift this is.

I would like to thank Kevin Doherty for the great job of editing this book and Lizzie Hutchins for her expert guidance. And with this being my third book with Hay House, I'd like to thank all of the Hay House staff, past and present, for their warmth and for helping me to feel such a part of the Hay House family.

I'd also like to thank my friend Kevin Waite for reading the first draft of this book (twice), for making some important suggestions, and also for creating some really great visualizations, all of which helped to bring this book into its final state.

I'd also like to thank my friend Bryce Redford for encouragement, inspiration, and motivation.

I've sought clarification from experts in the field for some important points in this book. I'd like to say thank you in particular to Barbara Andersen, Fabrizio Benedetti, Lyn Freeman, and Stephanie Wai-Shan Louie for this and also for sending me important research information or pointing me toward relevant pieces that I wasn't aware of.

I spend a lot of my writing time in coffee shops and even refer to the ones that I frequent the most as my offices. So, last but not least, I would like to say thanks to the staff at Starbucks and Caffè Nero in Windsor, UK, for creating the perfect atmosphere for me to write.

ശശശശ

ABOUT THE AUTHOR

David R. Hamilton acquired an honors degree in biological and medicinal chemistry, and a Ph.D. in organic chemistry before working as a scientist in the pharmaceutical industry for several years. His research into the mind-body connection ultimately led him to leave that profession and become a motivational speaker. He went on to co-found an international relief charity, and he appears regularly in the media. He spends most of his time writing, giving talks, and leading workshops.

Website: **www.drdavidhamilton.com**

෴෴

Free e-newsletters from Hay House, the Ultimate Resource for Inspiration

Be the first to know about Hay House's dollar deals, free downloads, special offers, affirmation cards, giveaways, contests, and more!

 Get exclusive excerpts from our latest releases and videos from *Hay House Present Moments*.

 Enjoy uplifting personal stories, how-to articles, and healing advice, along with videos and empowering quotes, within *Heal Your Life*.

 Have an inspirational story to tell and a passion for writing? Sharpen your writing skills with insider tips from *Your Writing Life*.

Sign Up Now!

Get inspired, educate yourself, get a complimentary gift, and share the wisdom!

http://www.hayhouse.com/newsletters.php

Visit www.hayhouse.com to sign up today!

 HAY HOUSE

 HAYHOUSE RADIO
radio for your soul

HealYourLife.com